STUDIES IN JAINA SANSKRIT LITERATURE

STUDIES IN JAINA SANSKRIT LITERATURE

SATYA VRAT
M.A., Ph.D.,
Head, Department of P.G. Studies in Sanskrit,
Government College,
Sriganganagar (Raj.)

EASTERN BOOK LINKERS
DELHI : : (INDIA)

Published by :
EASTERN BOOK LINKERS,
5825, New Candrawal, Jawahar Nagar,
DELHI-110007.

First Edition : 1994

Price : Rs. 450/-

ISBN : 81 - 85133 - 60 - 3

Printed at :
Orient Offset,
Shahdara, DELHI-110032

Laser Typeset by :
Compu-Media-The D.T.P. People,
43, Bunglow Road, Kamla Nagar, DELHI-110007
Phone : 2911869

PREFACE

The volume represents a collection of some of my articles on Jaina Sanskrit literature, published, over the years, in leading journals of the country besides many a reputed Felicitation volume. Thanks are due to their editors for kindly according me permission to include the respective papers in the present volume. The usefulness of bringing out the papers, scattered in various journals, in a book-form can hardly be over-emphasised. The studies deal with some of the unknown or little-known texts and knotty problems of the Sanskrit literature of the Jainas. The studies on Maṇḍana, Padmasundara and Samayasundara, which, taken together, form the bulk of the volume, deserve special attention. They are marked by such a rich wealth of material that they may well form the basis of full-fledged disserations on the respective authors.

If the book serves, in its own humble way, to arouse interest in the Jaina Sanskrit Literature, I would deem myself to have been amply rewarded.

7/34, Purani Abadi,
Sriganganagar (Raj.)

SATYA VRAT

CONTENTS

PRIME MINISTER MAṆḌANA AND HIS WORKS

Maṇḍana, the poet-prime minister of Māṇḍū, forms an important link in the long chain of litterateurs, who wielded pen and sword with equal effect. By all accounts, Maṇḍana was endowed with the most pleasing and colourful personality. A bundle of contradictions, he represented a unique amalgam of a scholar, administrator, diplomat and a devout *śrāvaka* - all rolled into one to result in a multi-focal entity that spurred Maheśvara to recount his varied attainments in the poem *Kāvyamanohara*,[1] which, in essentials, seeks to detail, with poetic trappings, the saga of the Śrīmāla lineage, in seven cantos. The Śrīmāla dynasty was admittedly adorned with a series of colossui who made, down the years, substantial contribution to the enrichment of the social and political life of Mālava. Maṇḍana was an heir to the chequered tradition of ministerial skill and religious fervour. All his predecessors from Ābhu to Jhañjhaṇa had held ministerial office with various rulers, and had undertaken pilgrimage at the head of a multitude of devotees, that earned them the proud epithet of *saṁghapati*.[2] Maṇḍana sought to diversify his innate administrative competence by fruitful forays into the hitherto unexplored domain of music and literature. Maheśvara is warmly liberal in his pronouncements on Maṇḍana's multiple literary equipment. We have it on his authority that besides being endowed with keen intellect, Maṇḍana was well-versed in grammar, poetics, dramaturgy, music, *Belles letters* and a host of other śāstras. He thus imbibed, in equal measure, an admixture of what, in the jargon of poeticians, is known as *śakti* and *vyutpatti*. While his frequent visits to the centres of pilgrimage elevated him to the status of *saṁghapati*, much in the manmner of his predecessors; the profusion of his liberality brought him the sobriquet of *Kalpataru*.[3]

Of the six great sons *(ṣaṭ tanayā mahāntaḥ)* of Jhañjhaṇa, who all were ministers *(sacivāḥ samastāḥ)* celebrated for their riches *(sampannavittāḥ)*,[4] Dehaḍa was especially known for his compassion and munificence. During his stewardship as a minister, he had been instrumental in securing the release of Keśirāja,

Harirāja and Amaradāsa from the fetters they had been condemned to.[5] Maṇḍana, the crest-jewel of the Śrīmāla dynasty, was the second and the youngest son of Bāhaḍa.[6] With personable mien and sweet tongue, he was an extremely cultured minister.[7] From the fact that his achievements in literature and music are repeatedly stressed in the *Kāvyamanohara* (*KM*), it would be reasonable to hold that he was rated fairly high both as a poet and a musician. His writings bear it out in abundant measure.

In view of the catholicity of vision that breathes through the *Kāvyamaṇḍana (Kāv.m.)*, one may plausibly entertain a modicum of doubt about Maṇḍana's precise religious predilections. From the sincerity of devotion with which Lord Śankara and Viṣṇu and some of the religious places and sacred rivers of the Hindus are extolled therein, in puranic style, he may well be inferred to have been a follower of the *Bhāgavata* or *Saivite* faith. Though liberal to a fault, Maṇḍana has unequivocally expressed his devotion to Jina, in almost all his works. while he tenders homage to Jina in the concluding verse of each canto of *Kāvyamaṇḍana (Jinendranirbharanateḥ)*, in the *Alaṅkāramaṇḍana* (*AM*) he proudly evaluates himself as *Jinabhakta* (v.75) and Maheśvara hails him as a great devotee of Jineśvara (*Jineśvara-mahābhakta*, *KM*.I.9). Not unlike his predecessors, he has been frequently alluded to as *saṁghādhipa* or *saṁghapati* by the author of the *KM* (II.22). By the *Dhāma* and *Pareśa* eulogised in the benediction to the *Kāv.m.*, he like Nayacandra, seems to imply *Paramajina*.[8] The strong revulsion to violence and persecution expressed in the *Kāv.m.*, also appears to emanate from his puritan jainistic belief. Maṇḍana should not be thus confused with the author of *Kāmasamūha* (1457 A.D.) who though named Maṇḍana, was, unlike our author, Brāhmaṇa by caste. He was a scion of Bhāmalla family and his grandfather was Nārāyaṇa.

Besides the six works issued in *Śrīhemacandrācārya-granthāvalī*, Maṇḍana is credited with the authorship of *Upasargamaṇḍana* and *Saṅgītamaṇḍana* as well. His *Kavikalpadruma* is noticed in the Catalogus Catalogorum, but seems to be otherwise lost, perhaps irretrievably. The manuscript that forms the basis of the current edition of *the Kāv.m.*, was copied in V.S. 1504 (1447 A.D.).[9] The MSS of *Kādambarīdarpaṇa* (*KD*), *Campūmaṇḍana* (*CM*), *AM* and *Śṛṅgāramaṇḍana* (*SM*) are also dated in the same year. In the penultimate verse (107) of *SM*, Maṇḍana has used for himself the epithet *sārasvatakāvyamaṇḍanakaviḥ*, which seems to reveal that he had composed a work *Sārasvatamaṇḍana* by name.

Of the two manuscripts of the *Sārasvatamaṇḍana* preserved in the Bhandarkar Oriental Research Institute, Poona, one (New No.36) is dated in the year 1575 A.D. (V.S. 1632). The beginning and concluding parts of the manuscript confirm it beyond cavil that the author of *the Sārasvatamaṇḍana* was identical with Prime minister Maṇḍana. Thus the date of transcription of six of Maṇḍana's works is now known to us. All the aforesaid works sans the *Sārasvatamaṇḍana* must therefore be referred to the years anterior to 1447 A.D. On its own admission, the *Kāv.m.* was written at a time when Alamashah was ruling over Māṇḍū. The *Śṛṅgāramaṇḍana* (*SM*) also had its genesis in the regime of Alamshah.[10] And Maheśvara joins Maṇḍana in upholding the fact that Bāhaḍa and his brothers owed their elevation to this ruler.[11] Alamshah was a powerful ruler, a veritable scourge to the enemy.[12]

P.K. Gode is convinced that in view of the sequence of the Muslim rulers of Mālava, Alap Khan alias Hoshang Ghori (1405-1432 A.D.) is the only ruler who can be justifiably identified with Maṇḍana's patron Alamshah. Alap Khan had ascended the throne of Mālava after poisoning his father Dilawar Khan to death. He invaded the neighbouring Gujrat twice, in 1411 and 1418 A.D. Though Maṇḍana seems to credit him with victory over the Gujrat rulers that allegedly resulted in their flight from the homeland[13]; Ahmedshah, the contemporary of Alap Khan, is known for certain to have administered resounding rebuff to his evil designs. Alap Khan was reduced to such dire straits that after his defeat at the hands of Ahmedshah in 1419 A.D., he had to fall back to the safe sanctuary of Maṇḍapadurga[14]. If Alamshah's identification with Alap Khan alias Hoshang Ghori is correct, *Kāvyamaṇḍana*, *Śṛṅgāramaṇḍana* and *Campūmaṇḍana* can be dated, with certainity, between 1419 and 1432 A.D. And it would be hardly off the mark to assign Maṇḍana's entire literary output to the first half of the fifteenth century, beyond which he could have hardly prosecuted his writings.

MAṆḌANA'S WORKS

By all standards, Maṇḍana was a gifted writer. His versatility is reflected in the variety of works he is credited to have authored. Maṇḍana's sound grounding in various disciplines had suitably equipped him to make considerable contribution to such diverse branches as poetry, grammar, music and poetics. It would be worth-while to undertake a succinct evaluation of his works to drive home his achievements as a poet.

KĀVYAMAṆḌANA

By its sheer bulk and poetic worth, the *Kāvya-maṇḍana* (*Kāv.m*) occupies the highest rung in the galaxy of Maṇḍana's works, and, as such, it may justifiably be rated as his *magnum opus*. A Mahākāvya in thirteen cantos, it purports to describe, with established mannerisms, a brief episode from the *Mahābhārata*, beginning with the Pāṇḍavas' miraculous escape from the lac-house to their return to Hastināpura, following their arduous wanderings coupled with Arjuna's feat in winning Draupadī's hand in the *svayaṁvara*-ceremony, conducted with royal fanfare. The *Ādiparva* forms the main source of Maṇḍana's theme. The episode of Kirmmīra that has come to be accorded high importance in the poem is narrated in the *Vanaparva* (III.11), being somewhat distinct from the main narrative, though closely related to Bhīma's exploits. Maṇḍana has subjected the epic narrative to drastic trimming to make it square with the limitations of the Mahākāvya, though, in the process, he has skipped over some of the momentous details. While it was essential to convince the Kauravas of the success of their fiery operation, contrary to its source (*MB*,I.147.4), the burning of Purocana and six substitutes is not even remotely hinted in the *Kāv.m*. It is, however, a distinct matter, if they are still confident of the sizzling end of their adversaries (*Kāv.m.*,XII.35). The strenuous itinerary of the Pāṇḍavas and the sequential description of the various places of pilgrimage and holy rivers are not so conspicuous in the *Mahābhārata*. The *Ādiparva* contains no more than a skeletal account of Arjuna's pilgrimage, intended to serve as a backdrop to his various marital alliances, not preculding abductions (*MB*,I.212-216). The Pāṇḍavas, as described in the *Kāv.m*, stay at Ekacakrā with an indigent Brāhmaṇa and their mother Kuntī offers to save his only son from the menace of the Baka demon even at the cost of one of her own sons. In the *MB*, the offer is made to the Brāhmaṇa while the *Kāv.m.* directs it to his wife, tormented with the supposedly imminent end of her son (*MB*,I.160-3; *Kāv.m.*,IX.8). By substituting one arrow for the five in the *Mahābhārata*, Maṇḍana has evidently sought to simplify the imperative of the *svayaṁvara* (*Kāv.m.*,XII.18 ; *MB*,I.184.35). Kuntī's imprudent direction to her sons to share equally their newly acquired possession (Draupadī) is smugly admitted in the *Kāv.m.* as well (*MB*,I.192.2; *Kāv.m.*,XII.19). Incensed at the assassination of his brother Baka and friend Hiḍimba and at the abduction of the latter's sister, Kirmmīra, according to the epic, assails Bhīma but is killed in the combat ; in *Kāv.m* Bhīma is credited to have slain him to obtain the release of his brothers and mother, forcibly kidnapped by him (*MB*,III.11.30-32 ; *Kāv.m.*,VII.37). By effecting change in the epic version, Maṇḍana has evidently shifted the onus of the duel to the demon. The episode seems to have been transplanted in the poem to underline the ferocity and insurmoutability of Bhīma.

The form of the *Kāv.m.* is obviously out of tune with its contents. Maṇḍana has raised a mighty edifice on the slender base of the epic story, which, in itself could well have been disposed of in a tiny poem. However, as executed in the *Kāv.m.*, it often seems to sink into oblivion. The fact that five (II,V-VIII) of the thirteen cantos have been dissipated on digressions, basically alien to the theme, is a telling commentary on Maṇḍana's sense of proportion.

Being primarily concerned with the exploits of the Pāṇḍavas, particularly Bhīma and Arjuna, the *Kāv.m.*is dominated by the heroic sentiment which may be admitted as its principal *rasa*. The poem is enlivened throughout by Bhīma's awe-inspiring prowess and ferocity. With him unquestionably rests the credit for conducting out his kin from the death-trap, the *lākṣā-gṛha,* for subsequently securing their release from the iron-clutches of Kirmmīra and ending the menace of the Baka-demon. All his combats occasion powerful expression of the *Vīra-rasa*, which is addedly reinforced by Arjuna's valour. Bhīma's solioquy in Canto Four, on escaping unscathed from the lac-house, though chiefly intended to scoff at Yudhiṣṭhira's commitment to peace, is pervaded with extreme hauteur and brusqueness, fully worthy of a *kṣatriya* warrior. He is determined to reduce the Kauravas to ashes like so many moths, provided the cloud of Yudhiṣṭhira's compassion does not crop up to quench the fire of his anger.[15] However, the most effective delineation of *Vīra-rasa* stems from his terrific battle with Kirmmīra.[16]

Of the ancillary sentiments, the *Bhayānaka-rasa* tends to match the principal sentiment in intensity and depth. In a bid to overpower the Pāṇḍavas, Kirmmīra resorts to the gimmick of the *mahābhicāra* sacrifice. Crowded with witches and vampires and resounding with frightful sounds of bisons, rams, drums and demons, his sacrifice-grove, the cemetry, strikes terror down to one's spine.[17] Besides the two major sentiments, *Karuṇa, Raudra, Śānta, Śṛngāra*, and *Adbhuta* also considerably contribute to the aesthetic pleasure of the poem and thereby invest it with added charm.

While in deference to the rhetorical precepts Maṇḍana sticks, by the large, to the traditional style in depicting nature in its various forms, it is the ornate description that engages attention in the *Kāv.m.* It bears testimony to his fertile imagination coupled with an expertise in exploiting it to the maximum effect. His skill in personifying the natural phenomena has greatly enlivened the description in the poem. The banal description of the sun-set has been elevated to great heights by investing the dusk with the function of a skilful goldsmith. The goldsmith of dusk, who had heated the mass of gold, (the sun), in the crucible of sky, has now consigned it to the depth of the western ocean so that he may subsequently fashion, at will, the attractive oranments of moon and stars (*Kāv.m.*,V.53). However, Maṇḍana is at his best while depicting nature in its undiluted pure form, with the figure of speech *Svabhāvokti* (III.36).

Maṇḍana's equipment in various disciplines had enabled him to gain enviable command on Sanskrit language. As it is employed in the *Kāv.m.*, it represents a combine of the natural and the flamboyant. While on the one hand, it is characterised by diaphanous perspicuity, on the other it is larded with a wealth of compounds, that, occasionally, tend to turn it into an exercise in artificiality. The deftness in striking balance between the two enables Maṇḍana to cope with an array of situations in their variety and entirety. Be it the aflame lac-house or the *mahābhicāra* sacrifice, Kuntī's wailings or terrific combats, Śaṅkara's boisterous dance or the holy current of the Ganges, all these have come to vibrate with realism at the touch of Maṇḍana's pen.

The phraseology that marks Yudhiṣṭhira's arguments to reassure his brothers, accords with his philosophy of peace (*Kav.m*,IV.31). The arguments with which Bhīma seeks to counter his weak-kneed policy, on the other hand, are couched in a language that emits arrogance and furiousness. He is unequivocal in denouncing Yudhiṣṭhira for reposing trust in the wily Kauravas, who, like the beasts of prey could never be expected to abandon their wickedness (*Kāv.m.*,IV.33,37).

Maṇḍana has not been miserly in interspersing his language with inverted constructions and sesquipedalian compounds. The language used in eulogising the sacred rivers and the presiding deities of the various Tīrthas is decidedly laboured. *Yamaka* and the *Sragdharā* metre combine to turn it into a far-fetched affair.

The language that is intended to extol *Aṣṭamūrti* Śaṅkara must have posed serious challenge to the mighty god (VIII.61). It is however to Maṇḍana's credit that though artificial at places, his language is never shorn of diginity and poise.

But for his favourite *Yamaka*, with which the *kāv.m.* is deliberately stuffed, Maṇḍana is not much enamoured of *alaṅkāras*. The ode to Śaṅkara (VIII.63-67) should suffice to illustrate the complexity of his *Yamaka*. Of the *arthālaṅkāras Upamā, Utprekṣā, Vyatireka, Rūpaka, Svabhāvokti* and *Arthāntaranyāsa*, besides others, have been approvingly admitted in the poem. Maṇḍana is the master of simile. The *Kāv.m.* abounds in charming similes. Maṇḍana uses both abstract and concrete *upamānas* to ensure the clarity of the subject. While he compares in XIII.44 Yājñasenī with abstract *Kuṇḍalinī* power, the five organs of perception (*Jñānendriyas*) form the standard of comparison for the Pāṇḍavas. It is however *Svabhāvokti* that projects Maṇḍana in true colours. The pen-picture of the farmer, perched on the improvised *machan*, guarding his crop from the deperadations of the birds with sling and shrill cries, is extremely happy (III.14).

Maṇḍana seems to have wilfully flouted the rhetorical injunction in respect of metre. The precept that prescribes the preponderance of a solitary metre in the canto has not met his approval. Consequently eight out of the thirteen cantos of the *Kāv.m.* are dominated by plurality of metres. In all twenty three metres have been exploited in the poem that serve to illustrate his thorough grounding in metrics.

The *Kāv.m.* forms an eloquent dissertation on Maṇḍana poetic talents. He has executed a non-Jaina theme in its original setting. Although he had zealously imbibed the contemporary *Mahākāvya*-tradition, he has been at pains to keep it within the bounds of moderation. He has doubltless made frequent forays into artificiality of style, but, all in all, the *Kāv.m.* is not unreasonably laboured.[18]

MAṆḌANAKĀDAMBARĪDARPAṆA

Of over a dozen compendiums and adaptations of uneven worth, both in prose and verse, that emerged, down the years,[19] to bring Bāṇa's *Kādambarī*[20] within the reach of lay readership, the *Maṇḍanakādambarīdarpaṇa*[20a] or *Kādambarīdarpaṇa* (*KD*) of Maṇḍana, deserves notice by reason of its lucid style and close pursuance of the original, besides its being the solitary abridgement of Bāṇa's *magnum opus*, ever undertaken by a Jaina author.

Written in deference to the wishes of the author's patron (I.15-18), the *Kādambarīdarpaṇa* embarks upon the frustrating task of pruning the *Kādambarī* down to a size that may reflect its *summum bonum* without in any way infringing upon the grace and essentials of the story and requirements of an epitome. A gifted writer as he was, Maṇḍana has acquitted himself with admirable credit. It is a measure of his poetic equipment that he has summed up the whole of *Kādambarī* within the body of mere 574 verses, imaginatively arranged in four rounded sections (*adhyāyas*).

Not unlike Bāṇa, Maṇḍana has prefaced his epitome with an account of his lineage. While Bāṇa's family was known for its literary attainments, Maṇḍana's represented an admixture of riches and letters (I.9) and was essentially a veritable repository of eminent ministers (I.3), he himself being a peer of Bṛhaspati (I.13). Maṇḍana has wisely dispensed with the series of descriptions that characterise *Kādambarī* in its inception. He has relegated them, in a severly truncated form, towards the close of his narrative and are there to form a link with the earlier segment of the story. Such of the descriptions as being inextricable ingredients of the main story and therefore essential to its flow and proper understanding he has chosen to incorporate in the epitome are, reduced to the barest minimum with practically no possibility to slash them further. The account of the Acchoda lake (I.94-103), the shifting phenomena at dusk (II.64-70) and the *nakhaśikha* description of Kādambarī's physical beauty (III.1-18) are cases in point. It may be noted in respect of the last that while it does not share many of the ideas of the original, it has the merit of not ignoring any of its salient features and represents a worthy compendium of its parallel in Bāṇa.[21] Maṇḍana's description of the shifting phenomena at the onset of night *vis-a-vis* Mahāśvetā's emotional stresses, effectively brings out her anguish born of separation from Puṇḍarīka (II.64-70). For the other descriptions that menacingly beset Bāṇa's narrative Maṇḍana has effectively resisted the temptation that could have well deflected a lesser poet from his goal, exposing him, in the process, to ridiculous situations, irrelevant to an abridgement.

Maṇḍana seems to have launched upon his task with the zeal of a missionary and equipment of a well-versed author. He had not only a thorough grasp and transparent understanding of Bāṇa's text but had also mastered all the nuances of his language and various situations of the narrative. And, if the unending similarity in phraseology is any pointer, he seems to have committed to heart the whole of *Kādambarī*, almost verbatim. Otherwise it would be difficult to account for the deep sprinkling of Bāṇa's ideas and phrases that the *KD* has received in profusion.

That the *Kādambarī-darpaṇa* forms an excellent epitome of *Kādambarī* is to restate the obvious. The divergences are too insignificiant to admit of serious consideration. Of the four sections, the first summarizes, preliminaries apart, the story from Tārāpīḍa to Mahāśvetā's account upto the advent of her youth, related to Candrāpīḍa in her first encounter with him. The second section carries the narrative to Candrāpīḍa's visit to Kādambarī on Hemakūṭa, preceded by the touching account of Mahāśvetā's meeting with Puṇḍarīka and the latter's succumbing to his emotional upsurge. Candrāpīḍa's meeting with Kādambarī followed by the lovely description of their love, the prince's return to his capital and his journey back to Kailāsa, apparently in search of his friend Vaiśampāyana, form the contents of the thrid section. Section Four deals with the rest of the narrative. The *KD* is faithful to its prototype not only in theme which is the basic requirement of a compendium, but in the matter of language as well. This two-fold adherence to the original had enabled Maṇḍana to capture the depth of feelings and emotional and physical torments of his characters in pithy verses in a manner that he compares creditably well with the master.[22]

Maṇḍana's indebtedness to Bāṇa is evident at every step. There is hardly any verse in the *KD* that does not pulsate with Bāṇa's phraseology. While it is neither feasible nor advisable to detail all such similarities, some of the more glaring may be reproduced to drive home the quantum of debt Maṇḍana owes to the author of the *Kādambarī*.

In describing Candrāpīḍa's pursuit of the Kinnara-couple and his consequent arrival at Kailāsa, Bāṇa remarks :

> *Atra gṛhyate'tra gṛhyate idam gṛhītamidam*
> *gṛhītamityatirabhasākṛṣṭacetasā mahājavatayā*
> *turaṅgamasya muhūrtamātreṇaiva.....*
> *pañcadaśayojanamātramadhvānam jagāma/*
> *tacccānubadhyamānam kinnaramithunamavalokya*
> *evāsya sammukhāpatitamacalatuṅgaśikharmāruroha.*[23]

With it may be compared the following verses from the *KD*:

> *mahatyā vāñchayāviṣṭo vājinā vāyuraṁhasā/*
> *atyavāhayadānītaḥ panthānam pañcayojanam. (I.82)*
> *idam gṛhatamityeva tasyānudravataḥ puraḥ/*

adreḥ śikharamatyuccamaśvo' gamyamavāpatat.(I.83).

Candrāpīḍa's subsequent vacillation at his venture is described by Bāṇa as follows :

kimanena gṛhītenāgrhitena vā kinnarayugalena prayojanam/[24]

Maṇḍana has adopted the sentence almost in toto :

gṛhītenāgṛhītena kim vānena prayojanam/(I.86)

Bāṇa has delineated the state of Puṇḍarīka's emotions with a pretty Sahokti.

karatalādaksamālām lajjayā saha galitāmapi nājñāsīt/
.....athāham tām kaṇṭhābharaṇatāmanayam/[25]

Maṇḍana's description of the situation is not much dissimilar:

na viveda tadā pāṇicyutām sphaṭikamālikām/
anayam hārapadavīmādāya tām drutam. (II.23).

All this should serve to highlight the fact that the *Kādambarī-darpaṇa* with its commitment to the prototype and lucid style, matched by pleasing ease, is one of the best epitomes of Kādambarī. It has the distinct merit of disseminating to the lay reader what was earlier the preserve of the well-equipped scholar alone.[26]

CAMPŪMAṆḌANA

The admixture of prose and poetry, alternating at measured intervals, though first encountered in ancient texts like the *Brāhmaṇas, Arthaśāstra* and *Pañcatantra* took pretty long to establish itself as a genre of poetry, popularly known as Campū, some time before Daṇḍin (7th century) who is the earliest of the poeticians to notice and define it[27] in a manner which, minor variations apart, continued to hold ground, down the years. Though otherwise commendably rich, the Jaina literature suffers from a disgusting paucity of Campūs. It is therefore all the more surprising that despite its merits the *Campūmaṇḍana*[28] continues to suffer undeserved neglect.[29] It commands attention because of its colourful author and the ennobling story of Nemi and Rājīmatī that it seeks to detail with poetic trappings.

The seven chapters (*paṭalas*) that the *Campūmaṇḍana* (*CM*) is made of, are evidently disproportionate to the quantum of details set forth therein. Besides preliminaries,the first chapter opens with the description of Samudravijaya's metropolis *Vijayavardhana*, followed by an account of his equipment as a powerful ruler and the beauties of his noble wife Śivādevī. With no organic nexus with the theme, Chapter Two amounts to a glaring digression. The couple's water-sports in Chapter Three are followed by emergence in the dream of a *dvija* to offer three jewels, the peers of *Kaustubha*, to Śivā who promptly apprises her husband of the amazing occurrence. An *Ācārya*, in the fourth chapter, assures Samudravijaya that the sight of jewels heralds the attainment of a jewel-like son. The child is appropriately named Nemi. He embodied the munificience of *kalpataru*, depth of ocean, charm of cupid and compassion of sage. Chapter Five sees Nemi in Dvārikā, the metropolis of Kṛṣṇa, at the latter's inviation. His marriage is fixed with Rājīmatī, the comely daughter of Ugrasena, the ruler of Mathurā. Ugrasena gears the town to the extravaganza of the royal marriage. At the opportune moment reaches Nemi at the head of the marriage-party. Chapter Seven represents both the climax and anticlimax of the theme. Overwhelmed with revulsion at the proposed mass butchering of the cattle for the marriage-feast, Nemi leaves marriage in the midst of its execution and flees to Raivataka to escape the mundane frivolities. Rājīmatī is left aghast. However, she follows her 'lord' to his resort and attains supreme bliss even before him.

Maṇḍana has been rigorous in shearing the details so that the theme is reduced to a bare frame to sustain the rather heavy portrayal that *Campūmaṇḍana* turns out to be. Occasionally the thread of the story tends to snap under the weight of descriptions that beset the Campū. Maṇḍana has indeed been brusque in dealing with the story. As a form of a poetry the Campū had caught the fancy of Maṇḍana to the extent that he likened it to a lovely damsel who imparted pleasure with her tenderness, imaginative embellishment and innate sentiments.[30] Doubtless, by its very nature the Campū opens up wider avenues for the muse of the author to unfold itself in both prose and poetry. Maṇḍana embarked upon the Campū with the decided objective to project himself as a prose-writer of some order. While his equipment as a poet is evidenced by his poetic works especially the *Kāvyamaṇḍana*, the *Campūmaṇḍana* with an overabundance of prose in preference to poetry, serves to establish him as a prose-author of no mean merit. Maṇḍana had a clear vision of the type of prose that he wanted to foster. It is to his credit that he did not mean to overawe the reader with sesquipedelian prose tranished by inverted construction, with compounds heaped upon compounds and replete with *śāstric* allusions, to emerge, like Somadeva, Haricandra or Arhaddāsa, as a rival to Bāṇa. His modest aim was to describe the story in simple and lucid prose marked with such literary devices as had established themselves as inseparable ingredients of the literary prose.

In ultimate analysis, the *Campūmaṇḍana* adds up to a mass of prose-pieces, spun out to draw sketches that form the warp and woof of the poem. The innate characteristic of Maṇḍana's description is to focus on the totality of the object to draw an integrated picture. This he has been able to achieve through his keen power of observation coupled with an equipment that reveals itself in an apt and lucid phraseology, which, even if occasionally infested with longer compounds, is never divested of effect and precision. The description of spring bears it out in ample measure (p.5-6). Even pithy sentences are used here to the maximum effect. Maṇḍana is equally at home in drawing the wide spectrum of descriptions. Whether it is the trite sunrise or Śivā's pregnancy or Dvārikā's grandeur, all have come to be invested with pleasing aptness and freshness. The skill in mustering appropriate *upamānas* lends added effect to his prose that results in enlivening the various descriptions. While the description of *Grīṣma* based on a string of similes, brings into relief the rigours of the Indian summer with burning sky and breathless people (p.10) ; the pen-sketch of the *Ācārya*, invited to interpret Śivā's dream, highlights, at one stroke, his manifold equipment in the science (p.13). And poetry has been liberal in contributing to bringing the stateliness of Dvārikā to life.

Maāḍana's grounding in poetics and metrics is beyond question. While an undercurrent of alliteration runs throughout his prose and poetry in the *Campūmaṇḍana*, other figures of speech lend strength to the expression. He is at home in handling the short *Anuṣṭup* and the longer metres like *Pṛthvī* and *Śārdulavikrīḍita*. *Upajāti* and *Mālinī* are, however, his *forte*.

With his multiple equipment Maṇḍana has thus contributed to the neglected branch of Campūs a work that, on all counts, deserves a treatment kinder,than what it has so far received.

CANDRAVIJAYA-PRABANDHA

Though Maṇḍana's love for nature and his skill in describing it in various facets is amply evident from his poetic works, the *Candravijaya-prabandha*[31] (*CVP*) is sought to be an index to the minister's adroitness in depicting *Candrodaya* - the moon-rise - in its various manifestations that had settled down as a sort of digressive mannerism, right from Kālidāsa's era.

Divided into two parts, the first Paṭala, on the poet's own admission, forms prologue to the '*Prabandha*' proper. The prelude conerns itself with describing successively the myriad situations from moon-rise to its setting. Though mainly stereotyped in nature, Maṇḍana's fertile imagination and judicious use of the *arthāntaranyāsa* coupled with his penchant for personifying the phenomena have invested the description with a measure of charm and freshness.

The tiny crescent that bore resemblance with the nail-mark and cupid's tender bow (7-8), soon develops into full orb, the peer of ear-ornament of the orient quarter and roving mirror of the world (15). Reflected in the ocean alongwith the stars, it invited comparison with Viṣṇu's conch laced with pearls emanating from its own belly (17). The intermingling of its beams with darkness is happily conceived as the torrent of the heavenly Ganges descending upon Śiva's matted locks (20). In describing its retreat from the sky, the poet tends to personify the phenomenon. The angler of the moon had cast the net of his sheen far and wide in the sky. While withdrawing, he carries a rich haul of fish in the form of stars (33). An happy idea to describe the *Candrāsta* ! The strand of personification is stretched further with fruitful results. The voluptuous moon dared into the harem of the sun in his absence. On seeing him return, the poor fellow fled in panic to the western-quarter. However, harsher treatment awaited him there. The seasoned harlot of the western quarter, having robbed the youthful dandy of his riches (*vasu*), unceremoniously bundled him out of her campus (32).

Pained at the fall of the mild-mannered moon, the poet decides to detail his triumph that forms the contents of the second part of the *prabandha*.

Though born of the same parents, the sun incurs the wrath of the father (ocean), while he lavishes care and affection on the moon for his solicitude for the masses (11-17). That serves to stir the envy of the sun which was further inflamed by the proposed marriage of the moon with the lovely damsel of the night (25). He promptly decides to fight it out. Soon the two are pitted against each other on the battle-ground. The volley of arrows discharged with measured frequency by the moon lacerated the repository of valour (*tejonidhi*) to the extent that the ground was soaked with the torrent of his blood (37-39). The haughty creature had to beat a hasty retreat. In the true spirit of the Rajput women the herd of his spouses perished in *jauhar* (45). The moon emerged victorious. He ruled the empire of the sky with abandon and enjoyed himself with his new spouse (87).

Besides being an eloquent testimony to Maṇḍana's expertise in depicting nature in a variety of styles, the *CVP* forms a slim thesaurus of charming *sūktis*, some of which may be reproduced here.

1. *Patiṣytām pāparatā hi vṛttiḥ/ II.9*
2. *Vairasya mūlam vanitā hi puṁsām/ II.25*
3. *Yūnoḥ sandeśavārttā khalu saṅgakalpā/ II.28*
4. *Parābhibhūtermaraṇam hi mānyam/ II.43*
5. *Sarve ca kāle prabalāh svakīye/ II.53*

ŚṚṄGĀRAMAṆḌANA

Though not rated as a *śataka*, the *Śṛṅgāramaṇḍana*[33] *(SM)* of Maṇḍana adds up, in essentials, to a century of erotic verses[34]. Written in a bid to further the tradition enriched by Bhartṛhari and Amaru, it describes the myriad situations that the young lovers undergo in union and separation, without sharing the depth, suggestiveness and refinement of the earlier stalwarts. The defective text, tarnished by many a lacuna, robs the poem of much of its charm. However, Maṇḍana's delineation of the joys and sorrows of love, with its varied nuances, is marked by warmth and insight. In his reckoning the young comely damsel forms the quintessence of life, and in comparison to her all else sinks into sterility. It is she who imparts immaculate non-dualistic pleasure to the aspirant by entering into *yoga* with him (*viśadānandādvyam*).[35] To him the release of man from inverted copulation constitutes the real *mokṣa*. No bliss is greater than the exulation emanating from the warm embrace. Only the unwise wear themselves down through a variety of penances for attaining *Brahman* in preference to woman - the fountain-head of all bliss (99). While Maṇḍana is occasionally uninhibited in expression, some of the situations are happily drawn. "The callous hearts of the lovers are locked in embrace only after they, like two pieces of iron, have undergone sufficiently harsh heating in the fire (of separation), fanned by the series of breath" (75).

ALAṄKĀRAMAṆḌANA

Primarily intended as a manual to set forth, in brief, the main precepts of Sanskrit poetics, the *Alaṅkāra-maṇḍana* (*AM*)[36] serves to establish Maṇḍana as a poetician of some worth. Maṇḍana had a long, varied and rich tradition, extending over fifteen centuries, to draw upon. He has doubtless utilised Mammaṭa's *magnum opus* with fruitful results. However, despite this well-entrenched tradition, the way he has chosen to skip over some of the momentous issues perforce leads one to conclude that he has presented in the volume what he, according to his lights, deemed to constitute the essence of poetics. Maṇḍana has not only dispensed with the *Śabda-śaktis*, his treatment of the classification of poetry is also perfunctory to the extreme, which in Mammaṭa forms the most authentic and exhaustive dissertation on the subject. His handling of *Rasa* likewise lacks depth and penetration. On his own admission, the work is intended to be a guide to the new poets.[37]

The praise of poetry that characterises the beginning of the *AM* sets the tone for the rigorous adherence to rhetorical injunctions that Maṇḍana demands of a poet. To the author of the *AM*, poetry serves twofold purpose. It brings fame to the poet which is essentially instrumental in raising him to the divine status (I.4). It is however the aesthetic pleasure (*pramoda*) that is the life-breath of poetry (I.7). It represents a doctored version of Bhāmaha's view on the issue who accords equal status to *kīrti* and *prīti*.[38] While Bhāmaha and following him Maṇḍana represent the *kāvya-prayojana* in essence, Mammaṭa [39] seems to have assimilated all that was handed down to him by his predecessors.

Mammaṭa's definition of poetry,[40] through bitterly denounced by Viśvanātha,[41] established itself as a reasonably complete and pragmatic definition. Maṇḍana deemed it best to repeat it, albeit in a disguised form, perhaps in the belief that it was futile to improve upon what the master had bequeathed to the posterity. Like Mammaṭa, to him also poetry consists of both 'word' and 'sense' which echoes the considered view transmitted to him by celebrities like Bhāmaha,[42] Kuntaka[43] etc. and blessed with approval by poets like Kālidāsa[44] and Māgha.[45] It should additionally be endowed with poetic qualities (*guṇas*) and ought to be free from blemishes (*doṣas*), evidently as far as possible. While Mammaṭa wisely tones down the importance of figures of the speech (*alaṅkāras*) by making their use optional, Maṇḍana seems to accord them as elevated a status as to the *guṇas: sālaṅkāraguṇā sārthādoṣā vāk kāvyam ucyate* (*AM*,I.9). Maṇḍana has classified poetry into three well-known categories, the degree of excellence being dependent on the position of *dhvani* therein. He has however refrained from critical evaluation thereof which forms the heart of the *Kāvyaprakāśa* (*KP*) and has been mainly responsible for elevating it to exalted heights.[45a]

In the absence of *vṛtti* on the text, it is difficult to ascertain if Maṇḍana, like Hemacandra, drew distinction between the primary and ancillary causes of poetry. If the singular form *hetuḥ*[46] is any pointer, Maṇḍana does not seem to favour such arbitrary distinction. Not unlike Mammaṭa he is disposed to hold all the three as an integrated whole that forms the cause of poetry, jointly and not separately, as Mammaṭa wisely puts it.[47] Maṇḍana rather represents a bloated version[48] of Mammaṭa's text on the subject[49] *Pratibhā* in Maṇḍana is a counterpart of Mammaṭa's *Śakti*; *Vyutapatti*, as viewed by the author of the *KP*, is wide enough to embrace in its swoop *sarvaśāstrāvalokanam, devabhāṣāparijñānam* and *sadasallokacāturyam*. All else in Maṇḍana is included in *kāvyajñaśikṣābhyāsa* of Mammaṭa.

It is difficult to understand the rationale of dealing with *Rītis* in the first chapter, that are usually relegated to a lower rung. Maṇḍana's treatment of *Rīti* is very casual. He has neither defined it in general nor any of its varieties. However, he has illustrated them with appropriate examples.

In Maṇḍana's conception of the imperatives of poetry, blemishes (*doṣas*) are to be shunned with meticulous care. He therefore has detailed the various types of faults that are likely to plague the *kāvya*, in a chapter (ii) that outweighs in extent all others combined together, sans the fifth. Following in the footsteps of his predecessors, Maṇḍana has classified the poetic blemishes into four categories : those pertaining to *pada* (word), *vākya* (sentence), *artha* (sense) and *rasa* (sentiment). While unlike Mammaṭa, Hemacandra etc., he has transposed the *Rasadoṣas* to the chapter (IV) devoted to the treatment of sentiments, he has dealt with others at the appropriate place. Maṇḍana follows the great author of the *KP* (VII.50-51) in enumerating and illustrating the sixteen *pada-doṣas*, preceded by a succinct but lucid definition of each fault. But unlike in Mammaṭa the *vākya-doṣas* and *artha-doṣa*s in the *AM* are only illustrated, not defined. Maṇḍana has combined *vidhiyuktatā* and *anuvādayuktatā* to bring down the number of *arthadoṣas* to twenty-two.

Chapter Three, devoted to the treatment of the poetic qualities, is by far the slimest in the work. Maṇḍana has neither defined *Guṇa* in general, nor has he sought to draw distinction between *Guṇa* and *Alaṅkāra* that forms one of the complex problems in poetics. Unlike Mammaṭa and Hemacandra who have reduced with sound arguments the inflated number of *guṇas* to three,[50] Maṇḍana continues to cling to the older view[51] that favoured ten qualities. He has been rather hasty in disposing of the *kāvya-guṇas*, doubtless with appropriate definitions and illustrations.

Maṇḍana seems to accord to *Rasa* a place higher than the *Alaṅkāra* (*AM*, IV.1) which may be taken to reflect his adherence to the *Rasa*-school of poetry, though his treatment thereof is perfunctory, almost half-hearted. While he could not afford a full-fledged discussion on the nature, character, number and process of development of *Rasa (rasa-niṣpatti)* in a slim tract, he explicitly hints his preference for Bhaṭṭa-lollaṭa's doctrine of *utpatti vis-a-vis* the poetic sentiment (*AM*, IV.2). It runs counter to Hemacandra, who, in pursuance of the *KP*, is a champion of Abhinavagupta's *abhivyaktivāda*.[52] In admitting nine *Rasas* including the *Śānta*, Maṇḍana is indebted to Mammaṭa and Hemacandra, who likewise had argued in favour of nine poetic sentiments,[53] though the former, like Bharata and the authors of the *Daśarūpaka*,[54] dismisses as impossible its development in a visual art like drama.[55] *Bhāva, Bhāvābhasa* and *Rasābhāsa* are duly noticed. All the illustrations are remarkable for their precision and lucidity. The enumeration of *Sthāyibhāvas* and *Vyabhicaribhāvas* at the end of the chapter is enigmatic.

As usual, the figures of speech claim the last chapter . Maṇḍana has dealt with the *alaṅkāras* based on both *śabda* and *artha*, which, as enumerated by him (*AM*,V.2-10), number sixty-eight against Mammaṭa's sixty-six. Mammaṭa has rightly brought *Mālādīpaka* under the parent *alaṅkāra*.[56] Hemacandra has reduced them to thirty-one. Maṇḍana has defined and illustrated almost all the major *alaṁkāras*, but some of the definitions and illustrations are inapt, if not erroneous (e.g. *Prativastūpamā, Bhrāntimān*). The fact that he has detailed sixty-eight *alaṅkāras* in a tiny work may testify to the fancy he had taken to the outward embellishment of poetry.[57]

Maṇḍana was thus bountifully endowed with administrative skill and high literary attainments. In his own words, both the goddesses of learning and riches resided in his campus in perfect harmony.[58]

REFERENCES

1. *Śrīhemacandrācāryagranthāvalī*, No. 7, Śrīhemacandrācārya-sabhā, Patan, 1918 A.D.
2. *Kāvyamanohara (KM)*, VII.3-17

3. Ibid.,I.9,12; II.22
4. Ibid., VII.34
5. Ibid., VII.28
6. *KM*, VII.24; *Kāv.m.*, XIII.55; *Campūmaṇḍana (CM)*, p.35 (verses 8-9) ; *Kādambarī - darpaṇa* (*KD*), I.4-8; *Śṛṅgāramaṇḍana* (*SM*), 105-107.
7. *Kāvyamanohara*, VII.43
8. In the benediction to the *Alaṅkāramaṇḍana* obeisance is paid to the lotus-like feet of Jinendra (*Jinendra-padābjarajaḥpavitram* - *AM*, I.1)
9. *Saṁvat* 1504 *varṣe śāke* 1369 *pravartamāne.....bhādra-śudi-pañcamyām tithau budhadine pustkamalekhi.* Scribe's insertion at the close of *Kāv.m.*
10. *SM*, 103
11. *KM*, I.5; *CM*, p.35 (verse 8).
12. *Kāv.m.*, XIII.53; *SM*, 103.
13. *vijahati hetibhirjarjarā gūrjarāḥ*/ *SM*, 104.
14. Jain Antiquary, XI.2, p.25-26, F.N. 1.
15. *Matkrodhavahnāvayakāradīpte , pāpāḥ patiṣyanti pataṅgavatte/na cettavoddāmadayāmbudāli tacchāntikartrī bhavitāntarāyaḥ* // *Kāv.m.*, IV.39
16. *Ibid.*, VII.38
17. *Ibid.*, VI.26-28
18. For an exhaustive critique on *Kāv.m.* see my book *Jaina Saṁskṛta Mahākāvya*, p.48-74
19. The new Catalogus Catalogorum, Madras University, Vol.III, p.388.
20. M.R. Kale (ed.), *Kādambarī* with auto-commentary *Bālabodhinī*, Delhi, 1968.

20a. *Śrīhemacandrācāryagranthāvalī*, No.18, Patan, 1918.

21. *Kādambarī*, pp.282-88
22. Compare *KD*, II.34, III.49
23. *Kādambarī*, op.cit., p.193
24. *Ibid.*, p.194
25. *Ibid.*, p.232
26. For a fuller discussion on the subject see my paper 'A Versified Jaina Epitome of Kādambarī', Jain Journal, Vol.XX, No.1, p.24-27.
27. *Gadyapadyamayī kāciccampūrityapi vidyate*/ *Kāvyādarśa, I.31.*
28. *Śrīhemacandrācārya-granthāvalī*, No.9, Patan, 1918 A.D.

29. Kapura chand Jain, who details the Jaina Campūs including some modern attempts in his study, is not even remotely aware of its existence. See *Purudeva-campū kā ālocanātmaka pariśīlana*, Delhi, 1985, p.51-76.
30. *Campūmaṇḍana*, p.2, verse 2.
31. *Śrīhemacandrācāryagranthāvalī*, No.10, Patan, 1918 A.D.
32. *Jaivātṛko jālikavatsamantāt vikṣipya vistāritam aṁśujālam/ saṅgṛhya tārāśafarānaśeṣān punryayau puṣkarataḥ parastāt//* CVP, I.33

    vikarttane kvāpi gate vilāsī tasyāvarodhe viharannabho'nte/ samīkṣya śaṅke tamupetamindurbhayādagat paścimavartmanaiva// Ibid., I.35
33. *Śrīhemacandrācāryagranthāvalī*, No.11, Patan, 1918 A.D.
34. *Śṛṅgārabhaṅgyā śataślokī/ SM*, 108
35. *SM*, 101.
36. *Śrīhemacandrācāryagranthāvalī*, No.11, Patan, 1918 A.D.
37. *AM*, I.8.
38. *Prītim karoti kīrtim ca sādhukāvyanibandhanam/ Kāvyālaṅkāra (KA)*, Patna, I.2.
39. *Kāvyaprakāśa* (*KP*), Vārāṇasī, 1960, I.2.
40. *tadoṣau śabdārthau saguṇāvanalaṅkṛtī punaḥ kvāpi/ Ibid.*, I.4.
41. Jīvānanda (ed.), *Sāhityadarpaṇa*, Calcutta, 1934, I. p. 9-20
42. *śabdārthau sahitau kāvyam/ KA*, op.cit., I.16
43. *Vakroktijīvita*, I.7
44. *vāgarthāviva sampṛktau.../ Raghuvaṁśa*, I.1.
45. *śabdārthau satkaviriva dvayam vidvānapekṣate/ Śiśupālavadha*, II.86.

45a *KP*, op,cit., Chapters 4-5

46. *kāvyasya hetuḥ pratibhā.../ AM*, I.10.
47. *trayaḥ samuditāḥ na tu vyastāḥ tasya nirmāṇe..... heturna hetavaḥ/ Vṛtti* on KP, I.3, p.17
48. *AM*, I.10-12
49. *KP*, op.cit., I.2
50. *trayaste na punardaśa/ KP*, op.cit., VIII.68
51. *....gunā daśa/ AM*, III.2.
52. R.C. Parikh (ed.), *Kāvyānusāsana* (*KAS*), Bombay, 1964, *Vṛtti* and *viveka* on II.1, p.88-103.
53. *śānto'pi navamo rasaḥ/ KP*, IV.35; *KAS*, op.cit.,II.2.
54. *śamamapi kecitprāhuḥ puṣṭirnāṭyeṣu naitasya/ Daśarūpaka*, Nirṇaya-sagara Press, Bombay, 1928, IV.35.

55. ....*aṣṭau nāṭye rasāḥ smṛtāḥ*/ *KP*, op.cit., IV.29.
56. *KP*, op.cit., Chapters IX-X.
57. For an exhaustive critique on *Alaṅkāramaṇḍana* see my paper, Alaṅkāramaṇḍana : Maṇḍana's Tract on Poetics, *Tulasī-prajñā*, Vol.XII, No.3, Ladnun (Raj.)
58. *KD*, I.10.

ŚUBHATILAKA

A JAINA COMMENTATOR ON GĀYATRĪMANTRA (Rv.III.62.10)

In the introduction to his edition of the *Gāyatrīmantravivaraṇa,*[1] a unique commentary on the famous *Gāyatrīmantra* of *Ṛgveda* (III.62.10), which purports to explain the aforesaid *ṛc* in accordance with the canons of all major schools of Indian philosophy viz. *Sāṁkhya, Nyāya, Mīmāṁsā*, Vaiṣṇavism, Jainism and Buddhism, N.M. Kansara has sought to spotlight its importance *vis-a-vis* the literary activities in contemporary Gujrat, besides bringing into focus the life account of its author. While no umbrage can possibly be taken against his brief evaluation of the commentary, the biographic sketch of the author, as drawn by him, can scarcely stand a searching scrutiny.

As vouchsafed by the colophon, the author of the *Gāyatrīmantravivaraṇa* is one Śubhatilaka, a Jaina monk of the rank of *Upādhyāya*[2]. However, a line appended to the *Vivaraṇa*, closely following the accredited colophon, in some of the MSS including Kansara's text, enigmatically assigns its authorship to Jinaprabha Sūri[3], an *Ācārya* so well known as a writer of sacred and profane Jaina literature and frequetly eulogised in the pontific lists. Its attribution to Jinaprabha Sūri is meaningfully upheld by one of the transcripts of the commentary[4], preserved in the Abhaya Jaina Granthālaya, Bikaner. There is overwhelming evidence to believe that the latter attribution could not have been made anterior to V.S. 1341. The key to the identity of the author lies in the correct understanding of the relationship that might have subsisted between the two claimants, Śubhatilaka and Jinaprabha. Kansara seems to treat them as not only two distinct individuals, but is at pains to make Śubhatilaka one of the disciples of Somatilaka Sūri whom he avers to have been a disciple of Jinaprabha Sūri[5]. Contrary to his assertion, the name-ending 'tilaka' was not the prerogative of Jinaprabha Sūri's disciples alone. As a matter of fact, in view of the absence of his name in the pontific lists of Jinaprabha's successors, Somatilaka *cannot strictly* be said to have been his disciple. He was not even an adherent of the *Kharataragaccha* which Jinaprabha pontificated with glory. But there is positive evidence to suggest that his literary passions combined with catholic outlook, led Jinaprabha Sūri to teach, ordain into monkhood and elevate to higher religious ranks, the prospective incumbents of other *gacchas* as well, an astounding phenomenon indeed in the face of sectarian rivalries. Some of the followers of other pontific groups are known, on their own statements, to have owed their literary and religious achievements to his benign generosity and wide erudition. Thus, Rājaśekhara Sūri of the *Harṣapuragaccha* had not only studied Śrīdhara's *Nyāyakandalī* from Jinaprabha Sūri but the latter was also the driving force that led him to write a brief commentary, *Pañjikā* , on it[6]. Saṅghatilaka expressly acknowledges him as his *vidyāguru*[7]. The quantum of help that Jinaprabha rendered to Malliṣeṇa Sūri in his composing the exhaustive commentary, popularly known as *Syādavādamañjarī*, on Hemacandra's *Anyayogavyavaccheda-dvātriṁśikā* may justifiably entitle him to claim its co-authorship[8]. And Somatilaka Sūri alias Vidyātilaka Sūri, whom Kansara presumes Śubhatilaka to quote, was awarded the status of *Ācārya* by Jinaprabha.[9] While these are some of the adherents of the other gacchas who owe to Jinaprabha their multifarious activities, his *de jure* disciples and successors in the group include, besides others, Jinadeva Sūri, Jinameru Sūri, Jinahita Sūri, Jinacandra Sūri, Jinasamudra Sūri and the polymoth Cāritravardhana, author of a large number of commentaries on celebrated works.

Somatilaka is thus admittedly indebted to Jinaprabha Sūri for his elevation to the status of *Gaṇabhṛt* and may broadly be called his disciple but he cannot, by any stretch of imagination, be taken to have been a teacher of Śubhatilaka for the simple reason that Jinaprabha and Śubhatilaka are one and the same person. In keeping with a well-entrenched practice prevalent to date, Subhaṭapāla, son of Ratnapāla, a resident of Mohilavāḍī, when ordained into monastic life by Jinasiṁha Sūri in V.S. 1326, was given the happy name of Śubhatilaka[10]. This name he continued to bear till V.S. 1341, when, on his assuming the stewardship of the *gaccha*, Śubhatilaka was rechristened as Jinaprabha Sūri. The identification of Jinaprabha with Śubhatilaka can be established on good grounds. In one of the verses of *Ādijinastotra*, impregnated with eight languages, Jinaprabha has ingeniously, though covertly, incorporated his earlier name, Śubhatilaka.[11] The *Avacūri* on the *stotra* written in V.S. 1583, is still more illuminating. The author of the *Avacūri* significantly remarks : शुभतिलक इति प्राक्तनं नाम । श्रीजिनप्रभसूरिरचितभाषाष्टकसंयुतस्तवावचूरिः। It leaves little doubt that Śubhatilaka is but another name of Jinaprabha, given at the time of his being initiated into monastic life. The alternative attribution of the *Gāyatrīmantravivaraṇa* to Jinaprabha thus ceases to be an enigma. The line (इति श्रीजिनप्रभसूरिविरचितं गायत्रीविवरणं समाप्तम्), however, could have been added only after V.S. 1341, the year when Śubhatilaka came to acquire the rank of Sūri and was given the new name.

The dates (1278-1331 V.S.) assigned to Jinaprabha by Kansara[12], on the authority of M. D. Desai's outdated *Jaina Sāhitya no Saṁkṣipta Itihāsa*, pp.416-418, are hypothetic, to say the least. As remarked earlier, Subhaṭapāla was ordained into monkhood in V.S. 1326, at the tender age of eight.[13] That would put his birth around 1318 V.S. Thus he had not even born in V.S. 1278, the earliest date given to Jinaprabha. And he was in his childhood in V.S. 1331 when he has been presumed to have died. Some of the dated works of Jinaprabha also convincingly bring out the untenability of the dates suggested for him. His *Kātantravibhramaṭīkā* was written in V.S. 1352[14] and the *Śreṇikacarita* was completed in 1356 V.S.[15]. The various *Kalpas* incorporated in the *Vividhatīrthakalpa* span an era, stretching from V.S. 1364 to 1389 V.S.[16] The *Gajapurastotra*, written in 1390 V.S. wherein he alludes to his pilgrimage to Hastināpura, appears to be his last dated work.[17] Thus Jinaprabha, on his own statement, was alive till at least 1390 V.S. As is well known, Jinaprabha was a spiritual friend of Sultan Muhammad Bin Tuglak of Delhi, whom he had successfully persuaded to undertake some benevolent measures for the welfare of the Jaina community. His regime extending from 1325 to 1351 A.D. also melts against the dates proposed by M.D. Desai.

Jinaprabha Sūri was a versatile scholar and a prolific writer. He was well-versed, besides Jaina canon, in numerous branches of learning and many a language, to wit Sanskrit, Prakrits, Apabhraṁśa, Paiśācī etc. His writings bring out, in bold relief, his scholarship in grammar, lexicography, poetics, prosody, *Belles Letters* and canonical literature. He was also a scholiast of high order, having elucidated *Kātantra*, *Anekārthakośa* of Hemacandra, *Śeṣasaṅgraha, Vidagdhamukhamaṇḍana, Gāyatrīmantra of Rv.* and a plethora of minor Jaina religious works. His *Śreṇikacarita*, in close adherence to the tradition blazed by Bhaṭṭi, seeks to illustrate the rules of grammar (*Kātantra*) and simultaneously details the well-known story of the devout king *Śreṇika*, a contemporary of Mahāvīra. The *Vividhatīrthakalpa*, his *magnum opus* in Prākrit, gives an account of the various places of pilgrimage, famous in his days, which invests the work with both religious and historical significance. Jinaprabha is a master of *stotras*. He is credited to have composed seven hundred hymns in praise of different *Tīrthaṅkaras*, but only seventy nine of them have so far been retrieved. These hymns demonstrate beyond cavil his unique skill in many a language including Persian and serve to establish him as an expert in *Citrakāvya* and Jaina theology. In the face of this massive literary output, Śubhatilaka (Jinaprabha) cannot be claimed to have been "resuscitated through this solitary work"[18] (*Gāyatrīmantravivaraṇa*), nor is he untraceable in the pontific lists. If anything, the *Vivaraṇa*, though it represents an extraordinary feat in extorting multiple meanings out of a single verse, is a mere drop in the ocean of his literary creation.

REFERENCES

1. The Gāyatrīmantravivaraṇa of Subhatilakopādhyāya, Indological Studies, Journal of the Department of Sanskrit, University of Delhi, Vol.III,1974, p.72-91
2. चक्रे श्रीशुभतिलकोपाध्यायैः स्वमतिशिल्पकल्पनया।
   व्याख्यानं गायत्र्याः क्रीडामात्रोपयोगमिदम् ।।
3. इति श्रीजिनप्रभसूरिविरचितं गायत्रीविवरणं समाप्तम् ।
4. Vinayasāgara : *Śāsanaprabhāvaka Ācārya Jinaprabha aura unakā Sāhitya*, Bikaner, 1975, p.35.
5. Indological Studies, op.cit., p.73.
6. श्री मज्जिनप्रभविभोरधिगत्य न्यायकन्दलीं किञ्चित् ।
   तस्या विवृतिलवमहं करवै स्वपरोपकाराय ।।३।।
7. प्राकाश्यं गमिता निजेन यशसा साकं च सर्वागम-
   ग्रन्थज्ञो जयतात् जिनप्रभगुरुर्विद्यागुरुर्नो मुदा ।।
   Samyaktvasaptativṛttipraśasti, 8
8. श्रीजिनप्रभसूरीणां साहाय्योद्भिन्नसौरभ !
   श्रुतावुत्तंसतु सतां वृत्तिः स्याद्वादमञ्जरी ।। *Tīkāpraśasti, 3*
9. शकक्षितिपबोधकृत् प्रभुर्जिनप्रभानुग्रहा-
   न्ववाप्तगणभृत्पदप्रमुखतत्त्वविद्यागमः।। *Śīlopadeśamālā-vṛtti, 9*
10. *Śāsanaprabhāvaka Ācārya Jinaprabha*, op.cit., p.35

11. नन्दाप्तोरुविशु[१]द्धयोगरभसोन्मी[४]लत् प्रतोषान्वितं
    शस्तं सौष्ठवभ[२]ग्नमोहरचनं त्वं कं[५]जहस्तच्छविः ।
    रुच्या भास्करति[३] ग्मसिद्धिरमणीसंक्लृप्तभावः परं
    रन्ता ज्ञानरमां शमास्तरुष मे तन्याः सुविद्यां चिरम् ।।४०।।
12. Indological Studies, op.cit., p.72
13. *Śāsanaprabhāvaka Ācārya Jinaprabha*, op.cit., p.33
14. *Ibid*., p.61.
15. स्कन्दास्येषुकृशानुशीतगुमिते संवत्सरे वैक्रमे ।
    बालेन्दुप्रतिपत्तिथौ विषगते सम्पूर्णमेतच्छनौ ।।
    Śreṇikacarita, Praśasti, 2
16. Jinavijaya's Write-up and *Vividhatīrthakalpa* (Hindi Tr.), Mevānagar Via Balotara (Raj.), 1978, p.4
17. इत्थं पृषत्कविषयार्कमिते शकाब्दे
    वैशाखमासि शितिपक्षगषष्ठतिथ्याम् ।।
    यात्रोत्सवोपनतः संघयुतो मुनीन्द्रः
    स्तोत्रं व्यधाद् गजपुरस्य जिनप्रभाख्यः ।।
18. Indological Studies, *op.cit*., p.72

ON SOME VARIANTS IN NEMINĀTHA MAHĀKĀVYA

None of the reviewers of my edition[1] of Kīrtirāja Upādhyāya's (1392-1468 A.D.)[2] *Nemināthа-mahākāvya* (*NNM*) deemed it fit to bestow thought on the comparative worth of the readings, adopted therein, out of a mass of tricky variants thrown up by the preceding editions and an old codex collated by us. The *NNM* was first issued in the Yaśovijaya Jaina Granthamālā (No.38). The edition[3] purports to be based on the oldest manuscript of the poem, copied at Delhi, in Saṁvat 1495 (1438 A.D.), which, by overwhelming consensus, is taken to be its first accredited transcript. The sources of the subsequent edition[4] of the poem are not known, but they could not have been widely divergent to represent an independent strand of text-tradition. The two editions, however, concur in not utilizing the excellent manuscript of the poem, copied in Saṁvat 1502 at Maṇḍapadurga, now deposited in the Mahimā Jñāna Bhaṇḍāra, Bikaner[5]. Not always defensible, the text of the *BM* is by far the most reliable. Not unoften, it preserves more faithful readings and thus serves to dispel the bewilderment inflicted on the reader by the hopelessly corrupt variants, incorporated in the hithertofore editions. To be sure, the text of the *NNM* is largely settled and does not lend itself to a massive revision. Still, there is a crop of patently questionable readings that call for a critical evaluation. This is precisely what is sought to be attempted here.

The graphic description of Sūryapura, 'the quintessence of beauty', which, preliminaries apart, forms the beginning of the poem, is characterised by an allusion to the courtesans of the metropolitan town. They are averred to inflame the passions of the gallant by the seemingly innocuous act of casting on them a mere glance. It hardly needs ingenuity to infer that the two acts could not but have been synchronistic. The reading दृष्ट्वैव घूर्णयन्ति (I.21), found in the *YE*, suggests an intermission, howsoever short, between the two acts and thereby exposes itself to question. The suffix *Ktvā* invariably denotes an earlier act to be followed by a subsequent one. The absurdity of the reading is significantly upheld by the *BM*, which, not unlike the *VE*, substitutes it by दृष्ट्यैव घूर्णयन्ति. दृष्ट्यैव accords with the instantaneous timing of the two acts and precludes any pause betweeen them. Mere glance of the courtesans was sufficient to arouse the passion of the gallant, *bhujangas*.

The affluence of Samudravijaya, the ruling sovereign of Sūryapura, has been sought to be spotlighted by the figure of speech, *Upamā*, in I.38. The riches are said to have flocked to him from their retreat as the young maidens repair to their husbands from their parental houses. In order to facilitate a better understanding of the context the verse merits reproduction.

यमन्यराजराजेभ्यः प्रतिजग्मुः श्रियोऽखिलाः।
प्रस्तावे पितृसद्मभ्यो भर्तारमिव कन्यकाः।। *(I.38)*

The reading यमन्यराजराजेभ्यः, adopted in the *VE* and the *YE*, though apparently blemishless, is shorn of precision and suffers as a subject of comparision, *upameya*. While the retreat of the damsels has been explicitly mentioned, the locale of the riches is at best implied in the aforesaid reading. The scribe of the *BM* was happily alive to the discrepancy. It is to his alertness that we owe the accurate reading. He has rightly rejected it in favour of यमन्यराजराज्येभ्यः. The kingdoms of the of the rival rulers were the original abodes of the riches as were the paternal houses of the maidens. This fine shade of distinction is possible to be drawn with the latter reading only.

I.46 enumerates certain characteristics which the poet has sought to apply, with the help of paranomasia (*Śleṣa*), to both Indra and Samudravijaya. गोप्तृत्वाच्च is one of the attributes that the *BM* concurs with the *VE* to retain in the text. The reading suffers from lack of aptness and effect. That Samudravijaya was a peer of the lord of the heaven because of his being a 'guard', leaves us cold. The particle च closely following गोप्तृत्वात् not only disturbs the rhythm of the verse but also appears to be redundant. It has been inducted in the verse to respect the scheme of the metre. गोगोप्तृत्वात्, the reading found in the *YE*, in place of गोप्तृत्वाच्च serves to pinpoint one of the distinctions that both Indra and Samudravijaya share. Samudravijaya was the guardian of the earth as Indra was the master of the heaven. गोगोप्तृत्वं along with other characteristics placed the two on equal footing. गोगोप्तृत्वात् has doubtless greater merit to commend itself.

Canto Two is distinguished by a charming description of the fourteen traditional dreams, the mother of a Śalākāpuruṣa supposedly sees as a prelude to her conceiving. The second verse of the canto describes the bull, which, in the pen-sketch, as drawn by the poet, is noted for its robustness and spotless whiteness. The adjective समुत्कीर्णमिवेन्दुमण्डलम् serves to focus attention on the latter characteristic. But the reading, as it stands in the *VE* and the *BM*, does not make a coherent sense. A carved out moon is a funny proposition. The dice is loaded in favour of समुत्कीर्णमिवेन्दुमण्डलात्, adopted in the *YE*. The bull, on account of its whiteness, appeared to be a mass, as it were, detached from the orb of the moon. An happy idea indeed.

फणीन्द्रचूडामणिमण्डितस्फुटैः (II.9) is obviously a mistake for स्फटैः. The verse in question describes the ceremonial jar which Śivādevī, the mother of Neminātha, sees in the dream. The jar, decked with green leaves, interspersed with flowers, has been compared with something connected with serpents and embellished with their crest-jewels. That something can naturally be their hoods. This is what स्फट means. The reservoir of nectar with the hoods of the serpents jutting out all around, forms an appropriate *upamāna* for the jar, as detailed in the verse.

समीष्यते, adopted in the *YE* and the *VE*, in II.27, which spells out the interpretation of the dreams by the astrologers, is decidedly inferior to समीक्ष्यते, encounttered in the *BM*. While the birth of high personages may be desired (समीष्यते) in any family, it is generally seen (समीक्ष्यते) in noble families alone. समीक्ष्यते seems to imply the birth of the Tīrthaṅkara with greater certitude than समीष्यते ।

विशकल्पवर्तं which occurs in II.47 is by far the most outrageous reading in the text of the poem. The reading was first admitted in the *YE* and has been reproduced in the subsequent edition, with incredible smugness. The commentator Harṣavijaya has compounded the absurdity with his breath-takingly naive gloss. नालदण्डसदृशवृत्तिम् is the interpretation that he expects the reader to swallow. Little did the uncanny commentator realise the import of his gloss. What precisely is the behaviour of the lotus-stalk and how, of all creatures, the swans ape it, passes comprehension. It should not have been difficult for a person of Harṣavijaya's equipment to detect the minor error in the phrase. But he has not only slavishly accepted the reading, as it was handed down to him, but has also made nonesense of the text by his interpretation which befittingly illustrates the dictum : अन्धेन नीयमाना यथान्धाः ! The simple fact is that the letter *pa* has been read erroneously in place of the original, which could not but have been *ya*. And विशकल्यवर्तं is actually what is preserved in the *BM*. With this reading the verse yields the intended sense. The swans, at day-break, enjoy themselves with the breakfast of lotus-stalks. आमोदवत्कोकनदव्रजानां कुर्वन्ति यस्मिन् विशकल्यवर्तम् (II.47). It is in keeping with the nature of the swans and the context in which the verse is placed.

The *BM* is again instrumental in dispelling the mist of confusion caused by a hopeless reading in III.8. The phrase तुषारभूषांशुकभूषितांगः that uniformly occurs in the earlier editions is meaningless, at worst, and is tarnished by tautology, at best. Harṣavijaya's interpretation तुषारवदुज्ज्वलानि भूषा चांशुकानि च यस्य सः stems from a lack of understanding of the text. The validity of the reading should hinge on the distinction whether the अंशुक is a part of the raiment or not. To be sure, अंशुक is not an inconsequential appendage to the royal attire, it itself being a complete robe. As a matter of fact, this distinction too is not intended to be stressed here. It is the spotlessness of Samudravijaya's silken attire (अंशुक) that is sought to be underscored. As such it needs an adjective which may render it comparable to the snow. The reading in the *BM* precisely does that. तुषारचोक्षांशुकभूषितांगः dispenses with avoidable repetition and performs the function it is intended to serve. Samudravijaya's silken dress, as he occupied the royal seat in the assembly-hall, was immaculate and glittering like a slab of snow.

The next verse of the canto describes the monarch attended upon by his ministers, in the royal assembly, with the figure of speech, *Mālopamā*. Samudravijaya shone forth with his ministers like the autumnal moon surrounded by stars and the heavenly tree encircled by the mango-grooves. The abstruseness of the third *upamāna* evidently emanates from an absurd reading. स्वयूथनाथैरिव यूथनाथः, adopted in the *YE* and the *VE*, baffles attempts at coherent interpretation. As indicated by the other two *upamānas*, the counterparts of the ministers (stars and mango-grooves) were inferior to the compeers of the king. It could not have been otherwise in the third. The reading स्वयूथनाथैरिव यूथनाथः, besides its patent meaninglessness puts both the monarch and his ministers on an equal footing and thus seeks to detract from the majesty of the king. It should therefore be replaced by स्वयूथनागैरिव यूथनाथः, found in the *BM*. It obviates the obvious anomaly and harmonises with the other two *upamānas* in the verse.

The reading कृतज्ञैः in the first hemistich of III.29 also presents difficulty. The verse purports to refer to the interprtation of the dreams, which Samudravijaya fondly communicates to his consort, Śivādevī. The adjective कृतज्ञैः used with reference to the astrologers is off the mark. While the astrologers might have had a plethora of reasons to feel beholden to the monarch, it is their knowledge of astrology rather than their gratefulness to the king that should be expected to be alluded to in the context. The belief is happily strengthened by the *BM* which has स्वप्नार्थमर्घ्यं कथितं च तज्ज्ञैः in place of कृतज्ञैः, found both in *YE* and *VE*.

Canto Five begins with an expression of Indra's wrath at the sudden shaking of his royal seat to reduce him to the miserable position of a lowly swan perched on an oscillating lotus. प्रस्फोटयामास करावितस्ततः (V.4) leaves much to be desired because of the inappropriateness of प्रस्फोटयामास in the context. As indicated by their conception as 'large leaves of the tree of wrath' (क्रोधद्रुमस्योल्बणपल्लवाविव), Indra violently agitated his hands in the fit of anger. He could not have used them to strike some one. प्रस्फोरयामास करावितस्ततः is the apt reading found in the *BM* and the *YE*. It is indeed interesting that while the commentator has given the correct rendering (चालयामास), he has retained the indefensible reading.

Verse 34 of the same canto, which means to initiate the description of the mount Meru, is susceptible to quite a sizable revision. The reading प्रभाकर in the first hemistich is ridiculous. How the sun can originate in precious stones defies comprehension (अनर्घ्यरत्नप्रकरप्रसर्पत्प्रभाकरध्वस्ततमःप्रतानः ,V.34) The commentator's rendering of the hemistich as अनर्घ्याण्यमूल्यानि च तानि रत्नानि तेषां प्रकरः समूहश्च, प्रसर्पंश्चासौ प्रभाकरः is muddled, to say the least. It is wholly indefensible to detach the present participle प्रसर्पत् from अनर्घ्य रत्नप्रकर. It seems to have been prompted by the commentator's desire to extort something, howsoever unworthy, from an absurd phrase. The *YE* shares this howler with the *VE*. The *BM* throws up the appropriate variant when it substitutes प्रभाकर with प्रभाभर 'Meru shattered the density of darkness with the mass of lustre, issuing from its exquisite gems.

It is again to the *BM* that we owe the correct substitute to जाम्बूनददृष्टकायः of the same verse. Harṣavijaya's gloss जाम्बूनद-वत्कार्त्तस्वरवद् दृष्टः कायः शरीरं यस्य सः is repugnant like the text. It does not need much cerebration to suggest that the verse herein has an illusion to the mythological belief that Meru is made of gold. This is what the reading जाम्बूनददृब्धकायः, preserved in the *BM*, means. सुवर्णखचितकायः, as the marginal note puts it.

The adjective कोविदनन्दनन्दनम्, (V.40), applied to the jungle on Meru, both in the *YE* and the *VE*, is intriguing. The absurdity evidently proceeds from the corrupt text. Meru, for once, may be credited with the fabulous forest *Nandana* but how it regales the connoisseurs, is not understandable. कोविद is obviously out of joint here. It is heartening to find the *BM* replace it by चन्दननन्दनन्दनम्. The *Nandana* forest maddened the people with the odour of its sandal-wood trees. The gloss in the margin - चन्दनैर्नन्दयतीति चन्दननन्दं तच्च तन्नन्दनं च वनम् is faultless.

सुधादीधितिमण्डलास्थाः in VI.7 could have been conveniently dismissed as a petty error but for the confusion occasioned by the commentator's rendering. सुधाया दीधितयस्तासां मण्डल आस्था स्थितिर्येषां ते कुम्भा : is how Harṣavijaya explains the phrase. Going by his comment, one cannot escape the conclusion that the jars, held by the deities in their hands (वृन्दारकाणां...करेषु कुम्भाः सुधादीधितिमण्डलास्थाः -VI.7), were set in the rays of the moon. A curious situation indeed? It is simply beyond reason, how the commentator came to believe that the jars could be held simultaneously by the gods and the rays of the heavenly luminary. And, is it at all a function of the rays to carry pitchers, howsoever sacred the occasion ? The *upamāna* (राजहंसाः) leaves little doubt that it is not the situation of the jars but their whiteness that is meant to be driven home, in the aforesaid phrase. The *BM* steps in to provide the reading, desired here: सुधादीधितिमण्डलाच्छाः

VIII.11 pointedly refers to the uniqueness of Nemi's tranquillity. He was endowed with all that tends to lead one astray but never for once did he swerve from the righteous path. Besides youth, riches and beauty, it is power that is traditionally believed to intoxicate a young man. प्रभुताद्भुता accords with the context. परमाद्भुता that the *BM* and *the VE* substitute for it, has no relevance and should be discarded without reservation.

Canto Eight is characterised by a brilliant description of the six Indian seasons. The spring undoubtedly prompts the young folk to gay abandon. ललनदोलनयोर्ग्रहजं सुखम् (VIII.28), found in the *VE*, suffers from the demerit of omitting the object of their enjoyment. The damsels enjoyed clasping in sports and on the swing, but what precisely did they clasp, is an enigma, so far as the present reading is concerned. The commentator too is not helpful is resolving the tangle. The credit of dispelling the ambiguity goes to the *BM* which has ललनदोलनदोर्ग्रहजं सुखम्. The maidens enjoyed the comforting touch of the arms of their lovers in the course of sports and swinging. The validity of the latter reading is meaningfully confirmed by the *YE*.

जलदात्यये, though apparently a mistake for जलदात्ययः, is found both in the *YE* and the *VE*. When it is remembered that the autumn and not the white clouds is intended to be alluded to here, one can hardly miss the error. The functions assigned to the autumnal clouds in the verse actually belong to the autumn itself. And that clinches the issue in favour of जलदात्ययः, incorporated in the *BM*. The autumn with its proverbial white clouds came to attend upon the Lord. सुखयितुं किल नाथमुपागतो धवलरुग्जलदो जलदात्ययः (VIII.40)

That the winter tames the turbulent rivers and impassioned peacocks alike is emphasised in VIII. 45 by an *Arthāntaranyāsa*. दर्पघनच्युतिः in the second hemistich (गतवतीष्टजने बलपुष्टिदे भवति कस्य न दर्पघनच्युतिः) is open to question. The commentator's attempt to reconcile the reading is also not convincing. So is the untenability of the printed editions in retaining it. Hauteur cannot, by any stretch of imagination, be compared with the cloud. Moreover loss of one's kinsman does not result in obliterating the cloud. It certainly causes dissipation of one's equipment not precluding many a human quality. The *BM* rightly compares *darpa* with *dhana* and thus provides the correct reading, दर्पधनच्युतिः.

The deities greet the Lord with an ode of eulogy, on his revulsion at the proposed massacre of the hapless animals for the table of the marriage-party and his consequent taking to the path of renunciation. As the description भास्करकायकान्तिप्रद्योतिताशेषहरिद्विभागैः (X.38) would imply, they used the sun to illuminate the quarters. It is difficult to understand how could they subject the heavenly luminary to their command and bid it dispel the darkness while it must have been engaged, on its own, in preforming the function. The absurdity of the situation proceeds from the reading भास्करकायकान्तिः which has no *locus standi* in the context. However, the difficulty is obviated by the *YE* when it replaces भास्कर by भास्वर. भास्वरकायकान्तिः is the only reading that suits the description. The deities, as they descended upon the earth, served to brighten the quarters with their refulgent persons.

The description of the lowly sugarcane *en route* to Ujjayant, the famed mount, apparently a banality, is intended to set forth the poet's views on the place of *alaṅkāras* in poetry. The editors of the *YE* and the *VE* demonstrate a miserable lack of perception in opting for अधरस्तथापि च तवाधरादसावपि भूषणाद् भवति नीरसो यतः (XII.10) as the second hemistich. As it stands, it means 'Despite its inherent virtues the sugarcane is no match to the sweetness of your lower lip because one suffers even by embellishment'. It is hardly convincing. The syllable *pi* is responsible for ruining what otherwise is a crisp dictum. When replaced by *ti*, the verse has its validity restored with telling effect. अतिभूषणाद् भवति नीरसो यतः is what is intended by the poet and is actually found in the *BM*. Excessive ornamentation melts against sentiment, the soul of poetry.

शंकिनूपुराः, used in त्रिजगद्गुरोः सदसि शंकिनूपुराः प्रविशन्ति पत्नि ! सुरनायिका अमूः (XII.15) as an adjective to सुरनायिकाः, should have not caused difficulty in straightening the anomaly, so perceptible in the reading. The commentator makes nonsense of the verse by interpreting the phrase as शंकिताः मंजीराः यासां ताः. He does not seem to realise that such gimmicks only expose him to ridicule. The alert scribe of the *BM* hit the mark when he replaced this monstrosity by संजिनूपुराः. The heavenly nymphs had their anklets tinkling as they entered the assembly of the Lord.

Mādhava is an embodiment of modesty and devotion while circumbulating Neminātha, as a token of his regard for him. Despite that, the editors have the temerity to retain here (XII.24) a phrase that abhors propriety and offends the context. विनयभ-क्तिमानदः implies Mādhava's majesty rather than his humility. One who is powerful enough to evoke reverence can only be a person of manifold attainments, whereas it is humility that Kṛṣṇa oozes in his deferential behaviour to the Lord. विनयभक्तिमानदः is thus a square peg in the round hole. And the *BM* actually replaces it by विनयभक्तिवामनः. Mādhava was humble with modesty and devotion as he lay at Nemi's feet.

There are certain readings, which though uniformly sanctioned by all the editions and manuscripts of the poem, scarcely satisfy the perceptive reader. The first of these वयःपावनयौवनं वयः (II.24) concerns itself with the likely virtues of the prospective son, to be born to Śivādevī. To be sure, the phrase forms part of the second hemistich, intended as an *upamāna* in the verse. Samudravijaya is convinced that the son will sanctify the Yadu race as youth adorns age. It hardly makes any sense. How, as it is implicit in the reading, a part of age can lend charm to the whole. We feel वयःपावनयौवनं वयः should be emended to वपुःपावनयौवनं वयः. The son will add grace to the Yadavas as youth embellishes the body.

गर्दभस्थगणोपमः (IX.15) is the adjective applied to the youthful Nemi, who resists all temptations, held out by Kṛṣṇa's wives to prompt him into marital life, which he detests as an obstacle in realising the Self. They are at pains to convince him that lovely damsels form the quintessence of life. He who despises them is an ass. It seems to be the sense intended here. The reading, however, is not liable to such an interpretation. गणोपमः, we think, is a mistake for गुणोपमः which somehow continued to evade the scribes and editors alike. 'He who hates the pretty maidens is comparable to the traits of an ass.' This is perfectly what is expected in the context.

ब्रह्मभिदाग्रचयष्टिभिः (XI.81) occurs in the description of the allegorical fight between the forces of Restraint and Delusion. The cohorts of Restraint ultimately overpower Delusion and break the heads (*brahmarandhras*) of his soldiers with strong sticks. Now, ब्रह्मभिदाग्रचयष्टिभिः is a compound, wherein retention of earlier members in their original cases, exceptions apart, is a taboo. ब्रह्मभिदा, the instrumental singular, is offensive in the compound. The requirements of grammar will be met if the instrumental case is restored to its uninflected base. ब्रह्मभिदग्रचयष्टिभिः satisfies the grammatical rules without infringing the metre.

REFERENCES

1. Bikaner, 1975.
2. For a detailed account of Kīrtirāja upādhyāya see my book '*Jaina Sanskrit Mahākāvya*, p.77-78.
3. Hereafter referred to as YE.
4. *Vijayadhanacandra Granthamālā* (No.1) with Harṣavijaya's Sanskrit Commentary, Siyāṇā (Marwar), Saṁvat 1992. Hereafter referred to as *VE*.
5. सम्वत् १५०२ वर्षे श्रीबृहत्खरतरगच्छे श्रीमालवदेशे श्रीमण्डपदुर्गे---गजपति-सुश्रावकेण बान्धवपारस-सहितेन श्रीनेमिजिनेन्द्रचरितं वा. लावण्यशीलगणि-निदेशेन हरशेखरगणिपठनाय स्वश्रेयोर्थं लेखितम् ।।
   Hereafter referred to as *BM*.

ON SOME CHARACTERISTICS OF JAINA SANSKRIT MAHĀKĀVYAS

The Jaina *Belles letters* is the appellation applied to the main current of the mighty river that gushed forth from the *Prathamānuyoga*. Taking cue from the skeletal sketches in the *Samavāyāṅgasūtra*, the subsequent Jaina poets and authors vied with each other to garner for their writings the biographic accounts of the holy personages, celebrated in the Jaina tradition, in order to invest them with sanctity and authority that could well evoke for them universal acceptance. The value of poetry as a medium for disseminating abstruse philosophical doctrines and ideals of conduct can hardly be exaggerated. As a matter of fact, the line that demarcates the Jaina *Belles letters* from the canon and Purāṇa has never been boldly perceptible. Even before the fifth century A.D., when the Jaina canon is overwhelmingly believed to have been streamlined and reduced to final redaction, the non-canonical literature had surfaced with a vengeance, with the result the two seem to intrude, not unoften, into each other's domain.

The Jaina Sanskrit Mahākāvya does not mark a substantial break from the classical tradition. It is an heir to the glorious tradition, that, originating with Aśvaghoṣa had firmly established itself, with all its virtues and vices, by the time of Śrīharṣa. And there is little doubt that, like worthy successors, the Jaina poets have put the legacy to profitable use that subsequently resulted not only in its perpetuation, but multiplication as well. The Jaina poeticians had, by and large, accepted the concept of Mahākāvya as it was transmitted to them[1]. However, Jinasena's dictum-*mahāpurāṇasambandhi mahānāyakagocaram*[2] - exercised so powerful an influence on the Jaina poets that what is now known as Jaina Mahākāvya emerged, in ultimate analysis, as a Purāṇa-oriented entity. Rather, the Jaina Purāṇas may justifiably be rated as the true precursors of the Mahākāvya. While the poetic worth of the Jaina Purāṇas is high and some of the segments therein smack of miniaturised Mahākāvyas; overdependance on the Purāṇas has turned the Jaina Mahākāvya into a handmaid of religious fervour. And most of the Jaina Mahākāvyas bristle with the objective to secure recognition for the Jaina doctrine based on the Three Jewels *(ratnatraya)*.[3] Exceptions apart, the Jaina authors tend to use the Mahākāvya as an omnibus to be loaded, besides the facade of theme, with the doctrine of Five vows, *Syādvāda*, seven *Tattvas* etc. to ensure liberation from human bondage. This combination of 'pleasure and profit' is admissible to the point it does not swamp or strain the soul of poetry. The non-Jaina poeticians also sanction a modest sprinkling of moral or religious instruction in poetry,[3a] but their true conception of *Śāstra* and *Kāvya* seems to be reflected in the following dictum of *Visṇudharmottara-purāṇa* :

Dharmārthakāmamokṣāṇām śāstram syādupadeśakam,
Tadeva kāvyamityuktam copadeśam vinā kṛtam. (15.1-2)

They are convinced that 'moral instruction' is what separates poetry from the Canon. A poem heavily infested with doctrinal jargon stands closer to the canon and should better be termed as 'poetic canon' rather than a *Kāvya*. In the backdrop of sectarian overtones of the Jaina poets, such fine distinctions do not have much relevance.

All the subsequent poetic activities in Jaina literature owe their genesis to the Purāṇas. The bestowal of the nomenclature Mahākāvya on such a stupendous work as *Triṣaṣṭiśalākāpuruṣacarita* (*TṢPc*) covertly underlines its tremendous potentialities as a perennial source of raw material and unfailing guide to the aspiring poets. The Jaina poets mean to prove and exemplify with their Mahākāvyas that religious or spiritual fervour serves to galvanise to fruitful activities not only the literature, but the society as a whole. To them the Purāṇas are the torchbearers of the ideals that spur the sensitive author to scale unprecedented heights. The Jaina poets have actually spun out a mass of Mahākāvyas on the warp and woof afforded by the sublime character of the holy personages (*śalākāpuruṣas*) and other colossuses, some of which do the wide range of poetic literature proud by the plethora of their excellences. The Jaina poets have not only been instrumental in perpetuating the Mahākāvya-tradition at a time it was believed to have gone dormant, they have also enriched it with some vigorous writings. The so-called dark age of the non-Jaina Mahākāvya is the golden era of its Jaina counterpart.

The Jaina Mahākāvya apparently represents an extension of the earlier tradition. However, the Jaina poets, who were overwhelmingly monks ordained into different orders, introduced, in accordance with their sectarian compulsions and objectives, certain notable innovations in the tradition that was sternly hedged by rigorous constraints. Their works are as such distinguished by certain novel characteristics which call for a dispassionate evaluation to facilitate proper appreciation of the Jaina Mahākāvya.

The Jainistic authors seem to subscribe to the rhetorical precepts with regard to such gross a characteristic as benediction.[4] The *maṅgalācaraṇa* to the Jaina Mahākāvyas is overwhelmingly salutatory or benedictive. Jayaśekhara, Puṇyakuśala and others of their ilk favour the third type, known as *vastunirdeśātmaka*. Besides the śāstric injunction, they were evidently actuated by stalwarts like Kālidāsa (*Kumārasambhava*), Bhāravi and Māgha who prefer to plunge headlong into the theme, without straying into preliminaries that after all add up to a prologue to the poem. What, however, distinguishes the Jaina benedictions is that they are not always confined to a solitary verse, nor do they invariably eulogize the poet's favoured deity. In some of the Mahākāvyas the Siddhas,[5] Gaṇadharas,[6] Vāgdevī and Three Jewels are glorified in the *maṅgalācaraṇa* that spills over a multeity of verses. In accordance with its general tenor, the benediction to the *Hammīra-mahākāvya* (*HM*) also defies the theory. Its lengthy benediction of seven verses boils down to a pretty ode to the 'supreme light' (*param jyoti*) and some of the Jaina Tīrthaṅkaras and Hindu deities, eulogized with winsome *Śleṣa*. This freedom from sectarian constraints bespeaks Nayacandra's catholocity of vision which is the hallmark of his poem.[8] With its formidable bulk, the benediction in the *Digvijaya-mahākāvya* transgresses all bounds of moderation. It embarks upon the prohibitive task of successively extolling, in twenty four long stanzas, all the pontiffs from Ṛṣabhadeva to Mahāvīra. Some of the Jaina Mahākāvyas tend to treat each canto as an independent unit, so far as the benediction is concerned. Rājamalla's *Jambusvāmicarita* is addedly unique as its twelve cantos, besides the *kathāmukha*, commence with the *maṅgalācaraṇa* that ultimately emerges as an eulogy of the twenty-four Tīrthaṅkaras. Such varied and exhaustive benediction in the non-Jaina Mahākāvyas is simply unimaginable. Thus while adhering, in essence, to the classical tradition, the Jaina poets have introduced conspicuous changes in the concept of *maṅgalācaraṇa* that tend to militate against Hemacandra's injunction as well. The *Neminātha-mahākāvya* (*NNM*) and the *Saptasandhāna* (*SS*) are two such poems that pay homage to none else than the hero himself.

In drawing upon the known sources for its theme, the Jaina Mahākāvya conforms to the theory. In the jargon of the poeticians, the theme, more often than not, is either *prakhyāta* (well-known) or *sadāśrita* (noble).[9] With the exception of the historical poems, the Purāṇas form the fountainhead of the Jaina Mahākāvyas. Therefore, whatever the type of the Mahākāvya, the Jaina poets deem it the realisation of their mission to detail and thereby extol, individually or collectively, the lives of the holy personages, revered in the Jaina tradition. This convergence on the Purāṇas sucks the Jaina Mahākāvya deep into its ambit, though the divergences between the two are tangibly formidable. The authors of the literary Mahākāvyas have doubtless prunned the puranic theme of the unpoetic details, but their sectarian propensities draw them to make frequent forays in the realm of the Purāṇas. The incessant involvement of the deities of various orders in the activities of the hero, his stout aversion to mundane pleasures, acclaim of the Jaina sect and biting denunciation of the rival faiths-such traits, encountered with frequency in the Jaina poems, accord more with the Purāṇa than the Mahākāvya. Motivated odes to the various deities, glued even to the literary poems, also betray the same tendency. Kālidāsa has also incorporated *stotras* in the body of his poems, but his odes are smoothly harmonised with the theme and form its inseparable ingredients. The eulogies in the Jaina Mahākāvyas, on the other hand, appear to be forced appendages; nor are they distinguished by high poetic or philosophic excellence. It is rather an unpleasant fact that the puranic contents defiantly prowl the Jaina Mahākāvya of all hues, threatening the reader into discomfiture. Even on shearing, as far as possible, these malignant accretions the Jaina poets have dealt with their themes with the poetic embellishments sanctioned by theory, which, not unoften, combine to turn the contents of the poem subservient to its form. Here their ideal is not Kālidāsa but those of the later poets who viewed the poetic trappings as the *summum bonum* of the Mahākāvya.

The puranic Mahākāvyas describe the theme, drawn from various Purāṇas, in the same backdrop and style. In order to demonstrate the inviolability of *karma*, these poems, doubtless under the influence of their sources, seek to describe, at length, the previous births of the hero, which often encompass half of the poem and thus deal a fatal blow to the theme, reducing it to a hapless non-entity. Furthermore these poems are beset, in an abundant measure, with the miraculous and the super-natural. The gods and demi-gods throng to convert the heroes into divine figures by bestowing upon them extra-terrestrial powers, curious charms and a plethora of miraculous objects and lores (*vidyās*) to be used, at will, to their advantage. The puranic Mahākāvyas have also not been frugal in admitting folk romanticism, with the result time-worn devices like change of form, abduction, journey to heaven or hell play no mean role in shaping and diversifying their themes. The actors on the stage of the puranic Mahākāvyas are mostly superhuman figures, endowed with unbounded prowess and inexhaustible resources. The world of these poems is indeed the incredible world of fantasy.

The Jaina puranic Mahākāvyas are basically religious works. They seek to instruct through the medium of poetry. Therefore moral and religious instruction prominently pervades their entire structure and Rasa - the soul of poetry sinks into oblivion. Ephemeral nature of the world, aversion to pleasures, right conduct, knowledge of the self and final emancipation etc., in essence, form the bastion on which is raised their edifice.

The historical Mahākāvyas of the Jaina authors may be divided into two broad categories. The *HM*, *Kumārapālacarita*, *Vastupālacarita* (*VC*) and others of their class concern themselves with the rulers or ministers celebrated in history for their various achievements, valour, diplomatic skill and liberal patronage to art and letters. While the historical data in the *HM* and the *VC* are, notwithstanding minor aberrations, correct and authentic, with Nayacandra emerging as a counterpart to a modern historian; the *Kumārapālacarita* is loaded with fiction to the extent that histriography therein is submerged in the spate of fantasy.

The second group of historical Mahākāvyas is formed by the poems that seek to depict, with poetic trappings, the pious and detached life of some of the outstanding Jaina monks. Because of their faithful presentation of the account of the pontiffs, these poems, besides being readable biographies, form worthy sources of religious history. Some of them are rated high for their poetic excellences also.

Bhaṭṭi left the trail of *Śāstra-kāvyas* ablaze in the Jaina literature as well. While the *Bhaṭṭi-kāvya* represents a *tour de force* in seeking to illustrate the rules of the Pāṇinian grammar besides momentous rhetorical precepts; Jinapati launches upon an equally strenous task of illustrating in his *Śreṇikacarita* the *Kātantra* grammar, as elucidated by the *Durgavṛtti*, in its entirety. By indulging in the popular device of *samasyā-pūrti*[10] and interweaving the lives of seven high personages,[11] Meghavijaya seems to divert the *Śāstra-kāvya* to an equally unhappy course. The *Śāstra-kāvya* has indeed been a favourite pastime with the Jaina poets.

Despite this four-fold division of the Jaina Mahākāvyas, the various forms are frequently seen to intermingle. Not unoften, it is the preponderance of the particular style that decides the form. As it analyses and illustrates the various metres, Māṇikayacandra's *Śrīdharacarita*, for instance, can be justly rated as a *Śāstra-kāvya*. Its smooth language and refined style, on the other hand, entitle it to be a literary poem. However, the spate of puranic contents in the last two cantos so overwhelms the poem that everything else is swept away and one is perforce driven to view it as a puranic Mahākāvya. On account of its being an authentic source of Hīravijaya's life and the saga of his friendship with the Mughal emperor Akbar, the *Hīrasaubhāgya* of Devavimala can be claimed to be a historical poem. But the way it contributes to perpetuate the *Naiṣadha*-tradition and the myriad poetic excellences that adorn it, couple to elevate it to the pinnacle of a literary Mahākāvya.

The rhetorical injunctions with respect to the hero (*nāyaka*) of the poem[12] have met the approbation of the authors of the Jaina Mahākāvyas, only partially. It is perfectly in keeping with the theory to accord to the divine figures or kings of the *kṣatriya* race the status of the hero. But in elevating the personages, not recommended by theory, howsoever great and noble they might have been, the Jaina poets make a conscious departure from the established norm. It is evidently an attempt to bring the Mahākāvya down to the earth from ethereal heights. The heroes of *Hīrasaubhāgya, Somasaubhāgya, Sumatisambhava* etc. are scions of the third varṇa.

Some of the Jaina Mahākāvyas are noted for the plurality of heroes, though they do not invariably belong to the same race (*Ekavaṁśabhavāḥ).* Bāhubali in Puṇyakuśala's *Bharatabāhubali-mahākāvya* (*BBM*), for example, so thoroughly permeates the warp and woof of the poem and meets such a sublime culmination that, by no stretch of imagination, can he be debunked from the highest pedestal. He is always more than a match to his elder brother Bharata, the acknowledged hero of the poem. It would be odious to treat him as a '*pratināyaka*'.[13] With his piety and towering personality, Hīravijaya Sūri, is the undisputed co-hero of the *Vijayapraśasti-mahākāvya* (*VPM*). The *Kāvya-maṇḍana* and *Saptasandhāna* are unique in having five and seven incumbents respectively.

A vast majority of heroes in the Jaina Mahākāvyas are endowed with the virtues, a *Dhīrodātta* type is required to imbibe.[14] However,such poems are also not wanting whose heroes, with their equanimity and detachment, belong to the *Dhīrapraśānta* class. The *Neminātha-mahākāvya*, *Somasaubhāgya*, *Dharmaśarmābhyudaya* are some of the poems sanctified by such noble characters. The incumbent in Ratnacandra's *Pradyumnacarita* bristles with the traits of a *Dhīroddhata nāyaka*. The hero of Padmanābha's *Yaśodharacarita*, on the other hand, is devoid of qualities like self-restraint, farsightedness, discernment and circumspection that are usually associated with a worthy hero.

To admit *Dhīrapraśānta* and *Dhīroddhata* hero in defiance of the norms, is another notable feature of the Jaina Mahākāvyas.

Quietism as principal sentiment in the Mahākāvya is recommended by theory,[15] but it did not somehow much fascinate the non-Jaina writers. The number of the non-Jaina Mahākāvyas, wherein the *Śānta-rasa* is accorded the dominant position, is indeed limited. The Jaina writers, on the other hand, have raised it to sublime heights by admitting it as the chief sentiment (*aṅgī rasa*) in their poems. According to an ancient tradition, recorded by the Kannada poet Raṇṇa, Jinendra is the sole upholder of quietism and 'knowledge of his true nature' (*tattvajñāna*) is its chief feeling (*sthāyibhāva*).[16] Hemacandra also seems to implicitly support the tradition.[17] To the Jaina poets quietism is the king of *rasas* (*rasādhirāja*) and a poem meets fulfilment only if it is thoroughly pervaded with the *Śānta-rasa*.[18] It was natural for the puranic poems to have been imbued with quietism, but interestingly, even the literary Mahākāvyas with heroic or erotic as the principal sentiment, frequently culminate into quietism. The *Srīdharacarita* and the *BBM* deserve special mention in this regard. It was indeed an achievement for the Jaina poets to establish quietism as *aṅgī rasa* in the Mahākāvya.

Contrary to the poeticians, the Jaina poets are equivocal, rather contradictory, in their views on the status the erotic sentiment is to be allowed in the Mahākāvya. To Ratnacandra, the *Śṛṅgārarasa* is abhorrent like the *kiṁpāka*.[19] Padmasundara, on the other hand, places it on the highest rung.[20] He is unambiguous in his belief that a poem without the *Śṛṅgārarasa* is worthless like a straw-man.[21] Though in the flush of emotion, Nayacandra is also disposed to catapult the '*ratirasa*' higher than the heavenly domain of '*paramātma-rasa*',[22] yet his considered view appears to be somewhat different. He is insistent that whatever be the dominant sentiment in the poem, an imaginative touch of *Śṛngāra* heightens it beyond measure.[23] There is obvious disparity between the *Śṛṅgārarasa* and the objectives the Jaina poets covertly espouse in the Mahākāvya. However, they have not only accorded the highest position to *Śṛngāra,* but have also delineated it, perhaps in imitation of Māgha, with such abandon that they emerge, not infrequently, as canny masters of the science of love. It is also a measure of Māgha's influence on them that they have fondly depicted the *Śṛṅgāra*rasa in its varied ramifications,with brutal frankness, even in poems that have *Vīra* as their chief sentiment, with the result the auxiliary *rasa* overpowers the dominant sentiment and these poems appear to be basically the thesaurus of *Śṛngāra*. However, such unbridled depiction of the erotic sentiment is not in tune with the monastic inhibitions of the Jaina poets. After all, woman to them is a crucible of filth -- excreta and urine.[24] They seem to have indulged in these gimmicks merely to honour the precepts of the poeticians.

Besides the historical Mahākāvyas, some of the literary poems also have *Vīra* as their principal sentiment. Nayacandra, who had earlier expressed himself in favour of *Śṛṅgāra,* has now no hesitation in putting the heroic sentiment (*samarasambhavarasa*) on a higher plane.[25] In the name of *Vīrarasa* the Jaina Mahākāvyas are more prone to focus on mannerisms like the twang of bows, trumpetings of elephants, dance of headless bodies (*kabandhas*), polemics and duels of the warring opponents, as a prelude to the final combat. The most absurd depiction of *the Vīra-rasa* is to be found in the *Śrīdharacarita*. Frequent intervention of the divine agencies, application of various lores and sudden eruption of the hero's compassion combine to convert the combat therein into a fictitious affair. But violence is basically abhorrent to the Jaina monks. The desire to conform to theory seems to have been the sole rationale behind its depiction in their poems. Otherwise battle in their ethos is synonymous with poison and what to speak of weapons, fighting even with flowers is despicable.[26] The statement in the *HM* -- *na puṣpairpi prahartvyavidhirvidheyaḥ* (12.83)--after prolonged description of the Rajputs' fight with the Khalji hordes, otherwise ridiculous, has to viewed in this light.

Bhavabhūti, who deems fulfilment of the *Karuṇarasa* in its capacity to move the stone to tears and to pierce the heart of the thunderbolt,[27] set the trend for the Jaina poets to follow in depicting the pathos. Like him, they are also disposed to treat wailings (*vilāpa*) as the potent substitute to pathos. The *Karuṇa-rasa*, as detailed in the Jaina Mahākāvyas, is, therefore, bereft of the incisive suggestiveness that characterises Kālidāsa's *Karuṇā*. It at times touches the depths of heart, but the Jaina poets are more enamoured of recounting the supposedly unmatched virtues of the deceased and cursing the fate to hasten his fall, rather than stirring the human heart to its moorings. And that, in their opinion, constitutes its success. It would be, therefore, an extravagant evaluation to rate this superficial depiction of pathos in the Jaina Mahākāvyas as 'a heart-moving torrent'.[28]

Other ancillary sentiments also contribute to heighten the pleasure, the Mahākāvya seeks to impart. Horror does not claim much of place in Sanskrit literature. The *Bībhatsarasa*, as it is delineated in the *Kāvyamaṇḍana* and *Kumarapālacarita*, serves to attenuate the deficiency.

Some of the gifted Jaina poets are precisely aware of the importance of *Rasa* in the Mahākāvya. The *YS, BBM, HM* and *SDC* are so criss-crossed by currents of various *Rasas* that they may justly be called the fountain-heads of the *prapānaka-rasa*. Reversely, some of the poems like the *Vastupālacarita* and the *Somasaubhāgya* are devoid of soul and one hardly encounters therein any drops of sentiments.

With a view to strengthen the theme and to lend it variety and charm, the Jaina Mahākāvyas, not unoften, break into poetic digressions. It is doubtless backed by rhetorical tenets.[29] The digressions are intended to serve two-fold purpose. On the one hand, they bring into relief the equipment of the poet in various arts and sciences besides his poetic talents, on the other they tend to reflect the contemporary society in its various facets. It is futile to expect all the poems to mirror, like Kālidāsa, the milieu in its entirety; but some of the Jaina Mahākāvyas present a faithful picture of the society and, as such, form a reliable source of social history.

For some of the motifs that distinguish these descriptions, the Jaina poets are obviously indebted to masters like Kālidāsa and Māgha. The description of dawn in the fifth canto (65-76) of the *Raghuvaṁśa*, for instance, has deeply influenced the Jaina Mahākāvyas. Jayaśekhara, Padmasundara and Kīrtirāja not only share with *Raghuvamśa* the locale in positioning their corresponding descriptions towards the close of the canto,[30] but have liberally borrowed some of its mannerisms also. The amorous descriptions of water-sports, boozing, copulation etc. in the heroic themes owe themselves to Māgha. Bhāravi and Māgha had exploited these amourettes to demonstrate their undisputed skill in the art of love (*kāmakalā*); but subsequently they established themselves as mannerisms that filtered down to many a Mahākāvya. It is surprising that the Jaina poets have no qualms in transplanting these frivolities in their poems where they run counter to their noble finale and avowed objective. The depiction of nature in the Jaina Mahākāvyas also follows, both in style and contents,the trend set by Māgha. In close imitation of Māgha, the Jaina poets vie with each other to work up the banal figure of speech *Yamaka* in detailing nature in its different hues. The device of *svayaṁvara* and the combat that invariably follows between the contending rivals thereafter, is first encountered in the *Raghuvaṁśa* (VI-VII). With unending prolixity and divine participation, Śrīharṣa, though himself indebted to Kālidāsa, has consigned it deep under the layers of improbabilities that combine to turn it into a fabulous affair. While the depiction of *svayaṁvara* in *the Kāvyamaṇḍana* and the *Śrīdharacarita* closely follows Kālidāsa in moderation and poetic beauties; the impact of *the Naiṣadha-carita* (*NC*) on Padmasundara is too deep to be belied. However, the description in the *Yadusundara* (IV-VI), notwithstanding the divine claimants who descend upon the Vidyādhara metropolis, is not wholly divorced from reality, though it could have been profitably compressed further.

The impatience of the womenfolk to have a glimpse of the hero is one such motif that has nothing in theory to buttress it up. Originating in Aśvaghoṣa, the device, howover, so captured the imagination of the successive generations of poets that it came to command unwritten sanction. The popularity it gained, over the years, can be gauged from the fact that almost all the classical poets contributed, in their own way, to establish it on firm footing. The motif filtered down to the Jaina Mahākāvyas as well and their authors readily exploited it to suit their purpose. While Jayaśekhara, Padmasundara and Kīrtirāja, obviously in imitation of the classical masters, have used the motif in the context of marriage;[31] the authors of the *HS*, *SS* and *Vijayapraśasti* have described the onrush to spotlight the eagerness of the city-damsels to see the *Kumāra*, proceeding to embrace asceticism. Kālidāsa had elevated the motif to its climax. Therefore, despite their unquestioned predilection for it, the subsequent poets including the Jaina writers only echo Kālidāsa's ideas.

The forays of the warring forces prefixed to the final combat of the main contenders have their genesis in the parallel descriptions of Bhāravi (XVII-XVIII) and Māgha (XVIII-XX), who have been chiefly instrumental in whipping them into a mannerism. These digressive descriptions are met with in almost all the Jaina Mahākāvyas that have *Vīra* as their principal sentiment, though they are not always uniform in worth.

Some of the Jaina Mahākāvyas are primarily intended to parallel the illustrious classical poems. In the conception and execution of its theme, arrangement of various situations, depiction of *Rasa* and close adherence to the tradition, the *BBM* is heavily indebted to Māgha.[32] Meghavijaya's *Devānanda-mahākāvya* not only follows the *Śiśupālavadha* in the scheme of its theme, it also serves to project the author's unquestioned learning by subjecting the first seven cantos of Māgha's poem to *samasyā-pūrti*. Māgha is indeed the undisputed master of the post-Kālidāsa era. Even a gifted historiographer of Nayacandra's stature has not been able to resist his pervasive impact. While these poems are partially inspired by Māgha, the *Jaina Kumārasambhava* is evidently intended to to be a counterpart to Kālidāsa's famed poem. The *Yadusundara,* on the other hand, represents an interesting adaptation of Śrīharṣa's *magnum opus*, the *Naiṣadhcarita*. Quite a few of the other Jaina Mahākāvyas are imbued, in a variety of ways, with the legacy of their predecessors.

It is indeed true that literature to the Jaina poets is not an exercise in artistry but a means to cultivate purity of conduct. However, the authors of the Jaina Mahākāvyas were convinced that language was a potent instrument to project one's equipment in various disciplines.[33] The Jaina Mahākāvyas are characterised by multiple tiers of language. They do not necessarily accord with the forms of the poems. A majority of the literary Mahākāvyas, besides some based on historical themes, are noted for their refined language, adorned with a variety of embellishments. Poems like the *JKS, HM, YS* and *HS* abound in learned gramatical forms that represent a conscious effort to mirror the author's equipment in grammar. The *Hīrasaubhāgya* is so heavily infested with learned usages, drawn from the *Naiṣadhacarita,* that they may well be catalogued into a sizable volume. The language of Meghavijaya's poems, whatever be their form, is consistently laboured and ponderous. The liberal use of *Ślesa* and *Yamaka* tends to make it a challenge even to the most mature scholarship. In poems like the *Naranārāyaṇānanda, NNM, SS, YS* and *Digvijaya-mahākāvya* one is confronted by fearsome *citrakāvya* of varied sorts. The author of the *Śrīdharacarita*, basically a puranic poem, has tried his hand at gimmicks like riddles and *Apabhraṁśabhāṣācitra* also. Vastupāla and Haricandra, obiviously following into the footsteps of Māgha, do not hesistate to lavish one whole canto on these literary gymnastics. Whatever their worth as an index to the poet's learning, they only serve to raise frustrating impediments that have to be negotiated with diabolic grit and determination. The *BBM*, on the other hand, represents the other pole by virtue of lucidity and simplicity of its language.

Since the puranic Mahākāvyas were primarily meant to disseminate the broad tenets of Jaina faith to the common folk, they could not simply afford abstruse or pedantic language. In their zeal to realize the objective, the authors of these poems have not been meticulous to ensure the chastity of the language. They are not only marked by a heavy sprinkling of the unpāṇinian forms and *Deśī* vocabulary, they also have no hesitation in admitting a plethora of *Prakṛta gāthās* and floating verses to underline various philosophic or religious doctrines. Both in style and subject-matter, these Mahākāvyas stand closer to the Purāṇas.

The Jaina poets did not embark on the course of poetry to parade their scholarship, though their equipment is beyond question. With the exception of Jinapati and Meghavijaya, the figures of speech to them are not an end in themselves, but serve as a means to lend clarity to the subject. They are doubtless conversant with the utility of the *alaṅkāras* as sure instruments of embellishment,[34] but justifiably caution modernation in their use.[35] Still, the authors of some of the poems seem to be at pains to establish their credentials as scholars well-versed in poetics, by various devices including the extravaganza of *Śleṣa* and *Yamaka*. Meghavijaya throws all norms to the winds in his obsesion with these figures of speech. Of the *arthālaṅkāras*, the Jaina poets have taken special fancy to *Upamā*. Some of their similes can be rated among the best in the literature. Not unlike the classical authors, they have culled their *upamānas* from a vast range of sources. Utprekṣā, Atiśayokti, Aprastuta-praśaṁsā, Arthāntaranyāsa, Samāsokti, Kāvyaliṅga, Prativastūpamā are some of the other *alaṅkāras* that have met their approbation.

In the use of metre the Jaina Mahākāvyas apparently conform to the norm. Preponderance of one metre in the canto, its variation towards the close and multiety of metres in one canto --these precepts, almost in their totality, have been accepted by the Jaina authors. However, their departure from theory varies from one metre in the entire poem to plurality of metres in cantos, more than one. While the first device, particularly the use of *Anuṣṭupa* serves to ensure uniformity and simplicity; the other is intended to display the poet's skill in handling various metres with ease and frequency. The *Śrīdharacarita* is remarkable not only for its use of ninety six metres, but it also seeks to illustrate the whole host from the pithy *Śrī to* the cumbersome Daṇḍaka. Besides pressing into service some rare metres like Vadanaka, Aḍillā, Ākhyānakī, Caṇḍakāla, Manikyacandra has dabbled with some *Prākṛta* and *Apabhraṁśa* metres as well. Cāritrasundaragaṇi seems to derive saddistic pleasure in confronting, in his *Kumārapālacarita*, the reader with an exuberance of metres in most of the cantos and *vargas*, the subdivisions of his *sargas*.

Thus the Jaina Sanskrit *mahākāvya*, though in essentials, a protrusion of the classical tradition, has an individuality of its own that engages attention because of its distinguishing traits.

REFERENCES

1. R.C. Parikh(ed.), *Kāvyānuśāsana*, Bombay, 1964, VIII.6 and vṛtti, p.449-462.
2. P.L. Jain(ed.), *Ādipurāṇa, Bhāratīya Jñanapītha*, Kāshī 1951, I.99.
3. *Padmapurāṇa* (Raviṣeṇa), I.1.

3a. *Kāntāsammitatayopadeśayuje / Kāvyaprakāśa* (KP), Vārāṇasī, 1960.I.2.

4. *Āśīrnamaskāravastunirdeśopakramatvam/ Kāvyānuśāsana* (*KAS*), VIII.7.
5. *Jambūsvāmicarita*, Māṇikaycanda Digambara Jaina Granthamālā, 35.
6. *Śrīdharacarita*, I.8-9; *Digvijaya-mahākāvya*, I.25.
7. *Devānanda-mahākāvya*, I.3-4; *Jambūsvāmicarita*, I.4; *Saptasandhāna*, I.4; *Somasaubhāgya*, I.6; *Candraprabhacarita*, I.6; *Śrīdharacarita*, I.7; *Hammīra-mahākāvya*, I.7.
8. Satya Vrat : Nayacandrasūri - A Literary Profile, Jaina Journal, Vol.XXI,No. I,p.10-14.
9. *Itihāsodbhavam vṛttamanyadvā sajjanāśrayam/ Sāhityadarpaṇa* (*SD*), Lucknow, V.S. 1978, VI.318
10. *Devānanda-mahākāvya*

11. *Saptasandhāna-mahākāvya*
12. *Sadvaṁśaḥ kṣatriyo vāpi dhīrodāttaguṇānvitaḥ/ Ekavaṁśabhavā bhūpāḥ kulajā bahavopi vā. // SD*, op. cit.,VI.316
13. The detailed depiction of the *pratināyaka* is denounced as a blemish. cf.*KP* op.cit.,p.362
14. *SD*, op.cit., VI.32
15. *Śṛṅgāravīraśāntānāmekopi rasa iṣyate/ SD*, op.cit., VI.317
16. Contribution of Jainism to Indian Culture : ED. R.C. Dvivedi, Delhi, p.43
17. *Tathāhi tattvajñānasvabhāvasya śamasya sthāyinaḥ.../ KAS*, op.cit., viveka, p.121.
18. *Rasādhirājam sevasva śāntam/ Pradyumnacarita (PC)*, XII.243; *Śāntai rasaiḥ pūritaḥ/ Hīrasaubhāgya*, XI.94.
19. *Kiṁpākasadṛśam muñca śṛṅgāram virasam puraḥ/ PC*,XII.243
20. *Anyarasātiśāyī śṛngāraḥ/ Yadusundara (YS)*, VI.53
21. *Akbarasāhiśṛṅgāradarpaṇa*, ED. K.Mādhavakṛṣṇa, Bikaner, V.S. 2000 (1943 A.D.)
22. *Ratirasam paramātmarasādhikam/ HM*, VII.104
23. *Raso'sti yaḥ kopi param saḥ kiñcinnāspṛṣṭaśṛṅgāraso rasāya/ HM*, XIV.36
24. *Purīṣamūtramūṣāsu yoṣāsu/ Śrīdharacarita*, IX.144; *Jambūsvāmicarita*, X.13; *HM*, VIII.44. Also compare *Puruṣārthopadeśa* (ED. K.V. Sarma), Hoshiarpur, 1969, Verse 28.
25. *Śṛṅgārataḥ samarasambhavo raso nūnam viseṣamadhuratvamañcati/ HM*, XII.13
26. *Saṅgaro gara ivākalanīyaḥ/ BBM*,XVI.21; *Vigraho na puṣpairapi kāryaḥ/* Ibid,XVI,24.
27. Uttararāmacarita (ED. M.R. Kale), Bombay, 1924, I.28.
28. *Rājasthān kā Jaina Sāhitya*, Jaipur, 1977, Introduction, p.17.
29. *SD*, op.cit., VI.322-323.
30. *Jaina Kumārasambhava*, X.70-84; *Yadusundara*, XII.59-88; *Neminātha-mahākāvya*, II.30-62
31. *Jaina Kumārasambhava*, V.37-45; *Yadusundara*, VII.73-87; *Neminātha-mahākāvya*, X.13-24
32. For a detailed discussion on the subject see my paper 'Sources of Puṇyakuśala's *Bharatabāhubali-mahākāvya*', Journal of Oriental Institute, Baroda, Vol.XXXII, Nos.3-4, p.280-86

33. *Ākṛtyaivāvabuddham ca pāṇḍityamiva bhāṣayā/ Pārśvanāthacarita*, III.161
34. *Sālaṁkāraḥ kaveḥ kāvyasandarbha iva vyabhāt/ Pārśvanātha-mahākāvya*, III.156
35. *Yathaucityamalaṅkārān sthāpayāmasa pārthivaḥ/ Pārśvanāthacarita*, IV.291.

CANDRAPRABHACARITA

A MINIATURISED JAINA MĀGHA-KĀVYA

Notwithstanding the difference in its sources and objectives and general tenor that combine to invest it with a distinct entity, the Jaina Sanskrit mahākāvya represents, by and large, an extension of the classical tradition. The better-equipped of the Jaina poets were fired with a burning zeal to produce counterpart to every classical work of worth. That evidently accounts for a number of Purāṇas that bear appellations identical with the Hindu Purāṇas. That also precisely underscores the rationale behind sustained efforts at preparing full-fledged adaptations or epitomes of such masterpieces as *Kumārasambhava, Raghuvaṁśa, Śiśupālavadha* and *Naiṣadhacarita*[1] and/or subject them to the popular literary feat, *samasyāpūrti*, thereby perpetuating the Mahākāvya-tradition at a time when it was supposed to have gone dormant.

The Jaina writers, like poets of other persuasions, had taken special fancy to the Mahākāvya-tradition as assiduously fostered by Māgha in a bid to outshine his predecessors. In view of the wide following he evoked among the successive generations of poets, that consequently resulted in the emergence of a powerful Māgha-school in Sanskrit poetry, by dint of his myriad characteristics that mark him out as the most colourful figure in the post-Kālidāsa era, it may not sound the least surprising. However, the devotion and tenacity with which they seek to perpetuate the broad frame-work of his poem along with the host of mannerisms whipped up therein, which otherwise are out of joint with their theme, aim and puritan proclivities, are a pointer to the extent to which the Jaina poets were imbued with Māgha's pervasive influence. While other Jaina poets imitated Māgha in parts only, as and when it suited their purpose,[2] Vīranandī (12th century A.D.) seems to have been deeply enamoured of his muse. However, the mainfold śāstric learning that distinguishes the ponderous style of the *Śiśupālavadha* and its bulk were frustrating to the Jaina monk. He therefore undertook the arduous task of attempting in his

Candraprabhacarita (CPC)[3], a biography, in eithteen cantos, of Tīrthaṅkara Candraprabha, a shorter version of Māgha's poem, shorn of such gimmicks as make it an unenviable tome. Looking to the wide divergence in his theme, with few channels of imitation, Vīranandī has acquitted himself with admirable credit. It is of note that Vīranandī's redaction of Māgha's poem concerns one of the earlier births of the pontiff and he has focussed on that part of *Śiśupālavadha* that harmonized with the theme, as executed by him on the canvas of his *Candraprabhacarita*. It has enabled him to reduce sixteen of Māgha's formidable cantos (II-XII. XVI-XX) to seven (*CPC* XII-XV,VIII-X), without doing violence to their spirit or effect.

The mission of Pṛthvīpāla's envoy to the court of Padmanābha that marks the beginning of the twelfth canto of the *CPC*, is evidently modelled on the corresponding exercise in Māgha's poem. In accordance with his undoubted penchant for elaboration, the description of the mission in Māgha spills over a sizable part of Canto Seventeen besides encompassing the Sixteenth, in its entirety. Vīranandī has compressed it, without damage to its purpose and impact, in the body of fifty-six verses. Shorn of accretions, the two poems concur in substance of the mission. The trend of arguments is not much dissimilar. Like the Cedi ruler's emissary, the envoy in the *CPC* asks Padmanābha to submit to his master (by releasing the prize tusker that had strayed into his kingdom), threatening consequences in case of defiance.[4] His impertinence evokes a sharp rebuff in both the poems. While in the *Śiśupālavadha* (*Śiśu*), Sātyaki stoutly repudiates his provocative message (XVI.17-37), in the *CPC* the function has been assigned to the heir-apparent, who does the job with aplomb and skill (XII.25-41). However, it only serves to provoke the envoy into another outburst, intended to strengthen the earlier strand of his arguments.

Śiśupāla's envoy is lost, for a considerable part, in the lybrinth of *doubie entendres*, thus inviting comparison for his speech with a leaf of the *mahāpātra* tree, which is hard and soft alike (*Śiśu*,XVI.18). Vīranandī has no love for such ambiguities. Whereas the message of the envoy in Māgha leads Kṛṣṇa's forces to take up arms to meet the enemy on the battle-field, in the *CPC* it results in a political conference, which, in the *Śiśu*, stems from the nagging conflict caused by Nārada's bidding and Yudhiṣṭhira's inviation to Kṛṣṇa to the Rājasūya sacrifice.

The deliberations in the later half of the canto (XII) seek to parallel the counsel that Kṛṣṇa takes of Uddhava and Balarāma in Canto Two of the *Śiśu*, in an identical manner. The parleys, as conducted in Māgha's poem, testify to his wide erudition in the science and art of statecraft besides other branches of learning and are characterised by a host of learned grammatical forms that combine to turn them into an exercise in artificiality. Vīranandī's account is happily more businesslike, bereft of incursions into abstruse theories of politics. However, he concurs with Māgha in the form and technique of discussions. In imitation of the *Śiśu*, the participants in the *CPC*[5] are formed in three groups to decide the line of action to be followed.

Padmanābha in Vīranandī's poem is a replica of Mādhava, the heir-apparent represents Balarāma, and the two ministers, Purubhūti and Bhavabhūti, combine to share the traits of the elderly Uddhava. Though the author of the *CPC* has no fascination for Māgha's pedantic diction, he follows the corresponding part of the *Śiśu* to the point that his account purports to be an epitome, sprinkled with verbal adoptions, of Māgha's canto. Some of his ideas are also traceable to the master.

Vīranandī is at one with the author of the *Śiśu* in likening the enemy to a disease, which unless curbed in the bud, spells disaster.[6] Padmanābha, not unlike Mādhava, advocates immediate operation, but seeks counsel of his ministers because an individual, howsoever equipped, is likely to err in judgement.[7] The heir-apparent follows Balarāma in lending powerful support to his father in his tough posture against the enemy. To both of them, humiliation is worse than death. A coward is a despicable creature, the cause of travail to his mother.[8] The *Yuvarāja* again emulates his prototype in his belief that conciliatory overtures to the enemy, who deserves to be humbled in war, serve to prompt him into reckless actions.[9]

The ministers, on the other hand, reflect Uddhava's mellowness in striking a flexible posture and opine patience and sobriety. They unanimously view polity and valour as inseparable components of a well-planned strategy. In unison they form the bedrock of success, in isolation they court failure.[10] Their advocacy of *sāman* as a stratagem for winning over the enemy has its genesis in Uddhava's espousal of the same policy.[11] In championing the imaginative use of *ṣāḍguṇya*, wait for appropriate time, deployment of spies and employment of forged documents, they are again indebted to Māgha, who on his part, owes them to ancient texts like the *Arthaśāstra* and *Kāmandakīya*.[12]

In describing Padmanābha's expedition in Canto Thirteen of the *CPC* Vīranandī has sought to match the third canto of the *Śiśu*, which likewise details the march of Kṛṣṇa's concourse preceded by his embellishments and enlivened by a brilliant sketch of Dvārakā (III.33-63). Vīranandī has nothing to parallel the description of the Yādava metropolis, but he follows Māgha in Padmanābha's adornments with such faithfuness that it truns out to be a free adaptation of the original, an impression one finds hard to shun about the canto as a whole, though it partakes some of the features of Māgha's fifth and twelfth cantos, that seek to describe the departure of the Yādava-forces, at different points of time.

How deeply was Vīranandī enthralled by the *Śiśu* can by gauged from the fact that he has emulated Māgha even in trivial details, some of which could have been conveniently dropped. Thus the army that followed Padmanābha has been described, like that of Kṛṣṇa, with a simile. Mādhava's forces followed him as do the fruits of actions, a prudent person (III.26). The feudatory chiefs who formed Padmanābḥa's concourse, on the other hand, invited comparison with the denizens of heaven, flocking to their lord (XIII.8). Following the author of the *Śiśu*, Vīranandī has pressed into service the figure Arthāntaranyāsa to highlight the charms of the personable hero. The palm, of course, lies with the master. As Māgha would have us believe, the whole populace of Dvārakā thronged to have a glimpse of Murāri, though a popular figure in the town. Indeed excessive love tends to turn a friend into a stranger (III.31). Vīranandī's description is rather bald. Though well-known, Padmanābha became the cynosure of the women folk. Beauty surely does not smother curiosity (XII.26).

Some of the interesting situations in the march of Padmanābha's army are also inspired by the corresponding parts of Māgha's poem. The poetic description of the slow advance of the cavalry in the crowded streets in the *CPC* emanates from the still happier piece in the third canto of the *Śiśu*. With their front legs raised high following stiff control on the reins, the horses are perceived by Vīranandī to have kicked up a mass of billows in the ocean of sky (XIII.10). It represents a partial modification of Māgha's idea wherein the horses are believed, in the similar situation, to be straining to march over the gigantic tuskers that had offended them in obstructing their course (III.29). The fun stirred by the camel, losing its nerve at the sight of an aggressive elephant, by its actions in casting off the wares and emitting loud brayings (XIII.28), has again been adapted from Māgha who has drawn a happy picture of the mutual fear struck by the two animals (V.5).

Some of the lively sketches of the simple folk-life also Vīranandī owes to the *Śiśu*. The attempts of the women-folk to steal view of the hero from over the fence (bent under the weight of gourds in the *CPC*) is zealouly described in both the poems.[13] He also shares with Māgha the charming depiction of the village-belles guarding their fields from the depredations of birds and animals.[14]

As a sequel to the departure of the royal concourse, the scene in the *CPC* shifts to the mount they coverage on. The description of Maṇikūṭa in the fourteenth canto, which presents a faithful redaction of the two subsequent cantos (IV-V) in the *Śiśu*, is, in its earlier half, an echo of Raivataka, described by Māgha with the jugglery of Yamaka. The mode of depiction in the two poems is identical. Apart from similar introduction, the general description of the hill[15] is followed, in both the poems, by an expatiation of its beauties,[16] by Dāruka in Māgha and Bhīmaratha, the army-general, in the *CPC*. Contrary to Māgha's eleborate description, stretching over fifty-one verses, Vīranandī has disposed of Maṇikūṭa in thirty-two stanzas. This part of Māgha's canto, as hinted earlier, is infested with fearsome Yamaka. The author of the *CPC* also has sought to give his description a sprinkling of the same *alaṅkāra*, but it is free, by and large, from the intricacies of Māgha. Rather, it is marked by a pleasing lucidity. The similarities between the two, however, do not extend beyond the casual. Interestingly, it bears a deeper imprint of the gorgeous description of the Himālayas in the opening canto of the *Kumārasambhava*[17] to which Māgha also seems to be indebted, in some measure.

The second segment (of Canto XIV), formed by the last thirty-one verses, attempts a counterpart to the fifth canto of the *Śiśu*, which contains an exhaustive account of the encampment of the Yādavas on Raivataka through an exceptionally brilliant picture of various limbs of the army, improvised market and courtesans, active in their trade in the bracing enviornments of the hill. Canto Five of the *Śiśu* occupies a unique place in Sanskrit poetry. It vouches, more then anything else, for Māgha's keen insight, unflagging commitment to details and high poetic powers, reinforced by profound *śāstric* learning. Vīranandī was so overwhelmed by the spell of Māgha's talents and exquisite charms of the canto, heightened by a plethora of Svabhāvoktis (V.51,52,59,64), that he could not do better than to reproduce it, in a truncated form, in the body of his poem, in a language not much different from the original. It is precisely because of that, that this part of Canto Fourteen gives an impression of being a tailored version of Māgha's description, replete with a fairly large number of verbal borrowings thereform. It is futile to undertake a comparative analysis, in the situation ; some of the similarities, however, merit notice.

Following Māgha, the author of the *CPC*, has fondly described the restiveness of the elephant with an Arthāntavanyāsa in almost indentical terms. When taken to a tree, scented with the ichor of a wild tusker, it refused to submit. Rather, it registered its indignation at the unflattering attitude of the *mahout*, by pulling it down, though it would have provided it relief from the oppressing heat. Misplaced anger surely results in one's loss (*CPC*.XIV.60). A powerful bull is descibed in Māgha (V.64) to have chased away a host of rivals, in the combat, to enjoy unchalleged, the pleasure of following the cows. Vīranandī has adopted the verse with a trifle modification and has substitued elephants for the bull. Having routed the aquatic elephants in a duel, the tuskers formed a proud procession, with their trunks placed on the hind parts of the female-elephants (XIV.59).

Canto Fifteen represents a stupendous feat on the part of Vīranandī. Herein he has accomplished the prohibitive task of reducing three of Māgha's formidable cantos (XVIII-XX), combined with a sizable part of the Seventeenth, to a readable form, in a wee more than 125 verses, with almost all their trappings unimpaired. Māgha, perhaps in obedience to the ancient texts, has detailed with verve and fanfare a series of battles leading to the final combat, with the preparations of the army in the beginning to be successively followed by the clash of rival forces, individual duels of the redoubtable combatants and culminating in the battle royal between Kṛṣṇa and Śiśupāla. The nineteenth canto of the *Śiśupālavadha*, itself tedious on account of a string of combats, has been rendered all the more frustrating by endless feats of verbal jugglery carried to ridiculous limits in an apparent bid to outsmart Bhāravi, who is guilty of introducing these gymnastics in the Mahākāvya. The author of the *CPC* has followed Māgha's scheme of description with such sagacity that his canto, though a replica of the relevant parts of the *Śiśu*, so far as its contents are concerned, is free from tedium and artificiality that are hallmark of Māgha's description. He has doubtless made occasional foryas into the domain of *citrakāvya* (XV.39,49,52) but they are intended to spotlight his equipment in the dubious art rather than innate predilection for it.

The motifs that characterise Māgha's description of war, and which may be said to have originated with him, struck so deep roots in the subsequent literature that they trickled down to the *Vīragāthā* period of Hindi poetry, almost in their original substance. They involve, besides other things, the soldiery's eagerness to measure swords, its mutual invective, the trumpetings of the elephants, dance of headless bodies (*kabandhas*), streams of blood and showers of flowers from the heavens. All these have been described fondly by Vīranandī, in obvious imitation of Māgha, as essential ingredients of the description of a combat.[18]

The final combat between Padmanābha and Pṛthvīpāla is, for all purposes, a doctored version of Canto Twenty of Māgha's poem. While in consonance with the divine status of Kṛṣṇa divine weapons are freely traded in his duel with the Cedi ruler,[19] the contestants in the *CPC* content themselves with conventional weapons only. The finale is reached in beheading the ememy, an act that has been described in almost indentical language in the two poems.[20]

The *Śiśupālavadha* ends at its natural denouement, in the *CPC* the war undegoes sublimation. Padmanābha, overwhelmed with the ravages and horrors wrought by war, seeks salvation in monkhood and is actually born as the eighth Tīrthaṅkara, Candraprabha, in the subsequent age.

The depth of Vīranandī's commitment to the Mahākāvya-tradition is obvious from the fact that he could not shake off fascination for the stereotyped digressions, which, though, sanctioned by poeticians, are, after all, not germane to the texture of the theme. He thought it unethical to impose them on Padmanābha, who was on the verge of attaining sublime heights of Tīrthaṅkara-hood in the succeeding birth. He has therefore relegated them to one of his earlier births. As described in the *CPC*, these banalities concern themselves with Ajitasena, the ruler of Kosala in east India. Strictly speaking, there too they do not glue properly and run counter to the spirit of the poem, as a whole. However, it is a measure of the powerful impact that the Māgha-tradition had on the subsequent poets that Vīranandī has described with gusto the sports in garden and water (*vanavihāra* and *jalakeli*) and sexual orgy besides a host of natural phenomena, to illustrate as much the precepts of the poeticians as his fondness for them.

The description of the impatience of the womenfolk to have

a glimpse of Ajitasena (VII.81-90), on his return from the victorious campaign, is doubtless inspired by the corresponding piece in the *Śiśu* (XIII.32-50) wherein the ladies of Indraprastha throng to see Mādhava, while he was entering the metropolis of the Pāṇḍavas. A reference to the loosening of the knot of their lower garment and other devices to highlight their eagerness is inherent in such descriptions. But more than the ideas, Vīranandī has adopted from Māgha the motif which had struck deep roots, as is evident from its espousal by the authors of the *Mahākāvyas*, down the ages. He seems to have borrowed some of the ideas from Kālidāsa as well, who has been chiefly instrumental in putting this motif on a firm footing. With collyrium applied to one eye, the other bereft of it, a lady is supposed by Vīranandī to have reminded the people of *Ardhanārīśvara* (VII.58). Kālidāsa's description of the lady in the situation, carrying additionally a collyrium-rod in her hand, serves to highlight her impatience more effectively.[21]

Contrary to all the six seasons that Māgha has dealt with in Canto Six, Vīranandī has chosen only the spring to project his love for the scenic beauties . However, it bespeaks his adherence to the tradition more than anything else. This is what accounts for his stretching the description of the solitary season to the size of a whole canto by resorting to the banal technique of stuffing it with the dubious activities of the messangers, followed by an intimate address to the queen, towards the close. Though inspired by Māgha, the similarities between the two are peripheral, the display of expertise in Yamaka with which the description in both the poems is infested notwithstanding.

The ninth canto of the *CPC*, devoted to the garden and water sports, is intended to match the corresponding description in the *Śiśu,* which therein spills over two independent cantos (VII,VIII). Magha has described the *vanavihāra* of the youthful Yādavas, with abandon, in the seventh canto of his poem. The entire description is extremely sensuous and volputuous. It is a measure of the moral degeneration in his milieu that he has described with brutal overtness the situations in love-making, one would have liked him to shun.[22] Vīranandī's account of the *vanavihāra* is general in nature. He has no liking for Māgha's eroticism, though he has borrowed at least one such motif which only serves to illustrate his submission to the author of the *Śiśu*.[23] As opposed to Māgha's one full canto, he has dismissed the *vanavihāra* in just eight verses (XI.19-26).

With it Vīranandī has clubbed the description of water-sports which in Māgha encompass the eighth canto, in its entirety. This he has been able to achieve by reducing the original to less than a half. Like the *vanavihāra*, Māgha's description of the *jalakrīḍā* also bears deep imprint of the ancient texts on erotics and is, as such, imbued with extreme sensuousness. The unmasked obscenities were an anathema to the Jaina monk. Nor has he been swept away by Māgha's mannerisms in the description. Yet he could not resist the temptation of incorporating in his account the quintessence of all the motifs, employed in the *Śiśu*, in the present context, though he has wisely toned them down with the result his portrayal, notwithstanding its stereotyped nature, exudes charm and retains effect of the original. Rather, the latter is further heightened by the lucidity of style and elegance of his language. Still there is much that he owes to his distinguished predecessor.[24]

Canto Ten of the *CPC*, composed of three well-demarcated segments, represents a *tour de force* on the part of Vīranandī. Herein he has sought to parallel three (IX-XI) of Māgha's eleborate cantos, which detail the hackneyed natural phenomena, prescribed by poeticians as essential trappings of the Mahākāvya. The first segment consisting of first forty verses, purports to correspond with Canto Nine of Māgha's poem. Māgha's description of sun-set and moon-rise, though poetic and keen, is loaded with unnecessary details, which, compounded with his laboured diction, tend to make it strained. And his minute account of the amorous activities of the youthful couples that he has detailed as a sequel to moon-rise,threatens to convert it into a thesaurus on erotics. Vīranandī has wisely skipped over such frivolities, being incompatible with his monastic puritanism. His description is throughout lucid and to the point. However, the influence of Māgha is evident and quite a few of his ideas have their genesis in the *Śiśupālavdha*.[25]

The sexual orgy in the tenth canto of the *Śiśu* is prefaced with a fairly detailed description (I-37) of the drinking bout which aptly sets the tone for what was to follow, soon thereafter. These mundane activities hardly accorded with the ascetic restraints of the Jaina monk. Vīranandī has dispensed with the *pānagoṣṭhī*, though his portrayal of the nocturnal sports, which form a sizable segment of Canto Ten, deals a deadly blow to his supposed inhibitions. Contrary to Māgha's fifty-four (38-91), he has devoted twenty-one verses to the description. Māgha's depiction is distinguished by a meticulous and methodical treatment of various situations leading to the final act and thereby serves to bring into relief his intimate knowledge of erotics. Though basically repugnant to his puritanism, Vīranandī is at pains to reflect Māgha's mannerisms in the affair and borrows or adapts some of his ideas in the context.[26]

The last segment of Canto Ten has for its prototype the gorgeous description of sun-rise in the eleventh canto of the *Śiśu.* which ranks high among similar pieces in Sanskrit poetry by reason of its ornate style and far-fetched fancies. Like most others, the description in Māgha is deeply tinged with his expertise in erotics. While Vīranandī owes the description to Māgha, the similarities between the two are meagre. Vīranandī is no match for Māgha's poetic talents, though his simplicity is not devoid of charm.

Thus Vīranandī has drawn upon the *Śiśupālavadha*, save the portions that were at odd with his theme, so heavily that his may be called a faithful reśume of Māgha's poem. Rather, the temptation to label it as a miniaturised Māgha-kāvya within the *CPC* cannot be lightly discarded.

REFERENCES

1. Refer to the following papers in the subsequent pages in the volume : "Jayaśekhara's Indebtedness to Kālidāsa", "A Versified Adaptation of *Abhijñānaśākuntalam* (I-IV)" ; "*Yadusundara*: An Interesting Adaptation of *Naiṣadhacarita*"; "Devavimala's Indebtedness to Śrīharsa".
2. Refer to "Sources of Puṇyakuśala's *Bharata-bāhubali-mahākāvya*", in the subsequent pages, and "*Meghavijaya ko prāpta Māgha kā dāya*", Sambodhi, Vol. X.pp.28-32.
3. Kāvyamālā, 30.
4. *CPC.*, XII.54 ; *Śiśu.*, XVI.85
5. *CPC.*, XII.42-56 ; *Śiśu.*, XVI.38-81
6. उत्तिष्ठमानस्तु परो नोपेक्ष्यः पथ्यमिच्छता । *Śiśu.*, II.10
   भजते गदवन्न विक्रियामुदयन्नेव रिपुश्चिकित्सतः । *CPC.*, XII.65
7. ज्ञातसारोऽपि खल्वेकः सन्दिग्धे कार्यवस्तुनि । *Śiśu.*, II.12
   मतयोऽसर्वविदो हि देहिनाम् । *CPC.*, XII.66
8. तस्याजनिरेवास्तु जननीक्लेशकारिणः। *Śiśu.*, II.45
   मृत एव विलीन एव वा वरमप्राप्तभवः पुरैव च । *CPC.*, XII.93
9. चतुर्थोपायसाध्ये तु रिपौ सान्त्वमपक्रिया । *Śiśu.*, II.54
   परवृद्धिनिबद्धमत्सरे विफलद्वेषिणि साम कीदृशम् । *CPC.*, XII.85
10. तौ हि मूलमुदेष्ययन्त्या जिगीषोरात्मसम्पदः । *Śiśu.*, II.76
    पुरुषेण जिगीषुणा सदाप्यवलम्ब्यौ नयविक्रमद्रुमौ । *CPC.*, XII.72

11. *Śiśu.*, II.88 ; *CPC.*, XII.77
12. *Śiśu.*, II.93,110, 111, 113 ; *CPC.*, XII.104-106 etc.
13. *Śiśu.*, XII.37 ; *CPC.*, XIII.43
14. *Śiśu.*, XII.42 ; *CPC.*, XIII.42
15. *Śiśu.*, IV.1-17 ; *CPC.*, XIV.1-18.
16. *Śiśu.*, IV. 18-68 ; *CPC.*, XIV. 19-40
17. *Kumārasambhava*,I.5,8,11,14 etc.,;CPC.,XIV. 18, 5, 12, 6, 26.
18. *Śiśu.*, XVII.37, *CPC.*, XV.38 ; *Śiśu.*, XVIII.2,53,12, *CPC.*, XV.40, 41, 48 etc.
19. *Śiśu.*, XX.32,41,52,59, 60, 65.
20. *Śiśu.*, XX.78 ; *CPC.*, XV.130
21. *Raghuvaṁśa*, VII.8
22. *Śiśu.*, VII.15, 16, 45, 49.
23. *CPC.*, IX.22; *Śiśu.*, VII.49
24. *CPC.*, IX.32, Śiśu., VIII.46 ; *CPC.*, IX.58, *Śiśu.*VIII.66 etc.
25. *CPC.*, X.18, *Śiśu.*, IX.26 ; *CPC.*, X.32, *Śiśu.*, IX.36; *CPC.*, X.37, *Śiśu.*, IX.39.
26. *CPC.*, X.47, *Śiśu.*, X.42 ; *CPC.*, X.53, *Śiśu.*, X.51; *CPC.*, X.44, *Śiśu.*, X.52.

PADMASUNDARA AND HIS NEWLY DISCOVERED YADUSUNDRAMAHĀKĀVYA

By virtue of his literary output and spiritual attainments, Padmasundara was decidedly the foremost in the galaxy of Jaina ascetics, who, notwithstanding the rigorous monastic inhibitions, had cordial ties with the Mughal emperor Akbar.[1] The overwhelming consensus is disposed to identify him with Paraminder, mentioned in the *Ain-e-Akbari* as one of the esteemed proteges at the royal court.[2] Ordained in the *Nāgapurīya Tapāgaccha*, an offshoot of the Śvetāmbara branch of the Jaina faith, Padmasundara, as testified by most of his works or colophons thereof, was privileged to have been the pupil of Padmameru, the mighty scholar *(paṇḍitottama)* of the day.[3] Akbar was so fascinated by his multi-dimensional personality that he came to entertain, over the years, intimate friendship with Padmasundara that virtually lasted till the latter's end.[4] At the conclusion of his very fruitful meeting with Hīravijayasūri, the emperor is said to have gifted him a sizable collection of books that originally belonged to Padmasundara, but had been retained with him ever since his death.[5] Devavimala, the author of the *Hīrasaubhāgya*, a poetic biography of Hīravijaya, not only vouches for the veracity of the details of the memorable event, but also enumerates by name, in his auto-commentary, the various works included in the collection, which comprised, besides others, the *Yadusundara-mahākāvya* (*Ys*) by Padmasundara himself,[6] that has hitherto suffered undeserved oblivion.[7] Hīravijaya is known to have visited Akbar's court at Fatehpur Sikri, in 1582 A.D. (V.S. 1639).[8] Obviously, Padmasundara had been dead for some time prior to 1582 A.D. Assuming *Pramāṇasundara*,[9] written in V.S. 1632, to be his last work, Nāthū Rām Premī was inclined to put Padmasundara's death some-where between V.S. 1632 and 1639 (1575-82 A.D.)[10] But the discovery of his *Yadusundara*, a Mahākāvya in twelve cantos, seems to contradict the conclusion. In view of its flamboyant style, laboured language and strong tendency to indulge in literary gimmicks like *citrakāvya*, all whipped up to prepare a full-fledged adaptation of Śrīharṣa's *Naiṣadhacarita*, it can justifiably be claimed to mark acme to Padmasundara's literary achievements.[11] The sentimental warmth with which Devavimala has depicted the emperor's anguish, leaves little doubt that to him (Akbar) Padmasundara's death was not a distant occurrence. He seemed to be undergoing, till the time, its unmitigated vehemence. Padmasundara might have died in proximity to the emperor's meeting with Hīravijayasūri, a year or so before, some time in V.S. 1637-38 (1580-81 A.D.). The discovery of the *Yadusundara* thus compels revision of the earlier view on the date of Padmasundara's death. If he may be, as he should be, taken to have been alive till 1581 A.D., then the *Yadusundara* can be confidently assigned to the interlude between 1575 and 1581 A.D. Padmasundara thus seems to have survived for at least six years after composing his supposedly last work, *Pramāṇasundara*, to crown his literary output with the *Yadusundara*, undoubtedly his *magnum opus*.

Some of his other works also serve to uphold Padmasundara's spiritual friendship with Akbar. His treatise on poetics the *Akbarsāhiśṛṅgāradarpaṇa* (*ASSD*),[12] as the title implies, was composed at the request of the emperor,[13] perhaps to acquaint him, in brief, with the theory of *Rasa* in Indian rhetorics. The *praśasti* to one of its codices is unambiguous in stating that as jayarāja and Anandarāya were patronised by Babur and Humayun respectively, so was Padmasundara the recipient of honour from Akbar, at whose court he had convincingly defeated a band of disputants in a debate.[14] Harṣakīrti's *Dhātutaraṅgiṇī* provides the additional information that Māladeva, the ruler of Jodhpur, was equally enamoured of Padmasundara's virtues and extended liberal patronge to him, and that Akbar had bestowed upon him a village, a blanket and a palanquin to commemorate his triumph in a disputation at his court.[15] Whether this debate is identical with the one alluded to in the *ASSD*, we are unable to determine. Sādhukīrti, a follower of the *Kharataragaccha*, had won a resounding victory in the discussion on *Pauṣadha*, at Akbar's court, in V.S. 1625 (1568 A.D.) The *Ja-itapadevali* confirms that Padmasundara then had his camp at Agra.[16]

Padmasundara seems to have been a prolific writer. He completed his *Bhaviṣyadattacarita* in V.S. 1614, on the fifth day of the bright half of Kārttika. *The Rāyamallābhyudaya* was completed on *Jyeṣtha śuklā pañcamī*, in V.S. 1615. The same year witnessed the completion of the *Pārśvanāthakāvya*.[17] In the short span of a wee more than one year, Padmasundara had spun out three sizable works, a mighty feat by any standards. The works themselves bear it out that the three were composed in deference to the wishes of Rāyamalla, a devout *śrāvaka* of Carasthavara (Carathavala in Muzzafarnagar district, U.P.).[18] Padmasundara's writings bespeak his equipment in various disciplines. It encompasses in its sweep such diverse fields as poetry, poetics, philosophy, grammar, medicine, music, lexicon and astrology. By all accounts, he, not unlike his mentor Padmameru, was a versatile scholar.

His *Yadusundara-mahākāvya* (*Ys*) purports to describe, in twelve cantos, the marriage of Vasudeva with the charming vidyādhara-princess Kanakā and their post-marital enjoyments, which combine to form the slender corner-stone on which is sought to be raised the mighty edifice of the poem. The first canto opens with the description of Mathurā, the metropolitan seat of the Yādavas, which is actuated by an eagerness to establish its superiority over the heaven itself. The sharp rebuke adiministered to Vasudeva by his elder brother, following persistent complaints against his outrageous behaviour with the womenfolk (*purāṅgānāśīlaparāsanoddhatastavānujaḥ samprati sāmpratam na tat*, I.45), eventually led him to flee to the vidyādhara-kingdom. In the second canto a swan descends upon the royal mansion and waxes eloquent on the virtues of Vasudeva. "You are a jewel of a maiden and Vasudeva is a lion among men. You would make an excellent couple," he confided into Kanakā. Vasudeva's portrait fires the princess's love beyond measure and she begins to pine for the vicinity of her prospective spouse. The swan flies back from the palace but not before assuring her of his good offices in realizing her dream. While the love-lorn Kanakā sights Vasudeva all around like *Brahman*, the latter is simply thrilled to hear of her steadfast devotion to him. The first thirty-three verses of Canto Three add up to a touching depiction of Kanakā's love-worn state. The goldsmith of cupid tested her so ruthlessly on the touch-stone of separation that she was reduced to a hazy figure. Vasudeva reaches the city-gate and breaks into a description of the nearby garden. Kubera's insitence that he should proceed on errand to Kanakā, on his behalf, throws Vasudeva into a tormenting dilemma. "He has the temerity to expect to win her through me, to whom she is deeply devoted. How would I conceal my surging emotions in her presence, whose mere thought suffices to send me into swoon," he mused restlessly. However, when invested with invisibility (*bhavatu tanuḥ parairalakṣyā*, III.72), he enters the harem, undaunted. There he reverts to the human form and asks Kanakā to accept the lord of riches as her husband, prefixing his pleadings with a touching description of his (Kubera's) *pūrvarāga* (*śrīdam patim nanu vṛṇuṣva*, III.147). She is piqued by his eqvivocation that had concealed more than what he had revealed. Kanakā's friend apprises the messanger of the deep fancy she had taken to Vasudeva in preference to all else, not precluding the divine personages (*eṣā nṛdeva vasudevapatim vinānyam nāśansate hi maghavantamapi pratīhi*, III.156). He, on his part, endeavours hard to win her over to Kubera and berates her severely for her imbecile resolve to marry a mortal in preference to the lord of wealth, but she is unbudged in her determination. Her firm devotion and helpless cries at the supposed frustration of her cravings so move the messenger that he perforce reveals his identity, throwing the sanctity of the mission to the winds. Kanakā is non-plussed to find herself confronted with her coveted consort. Vasudeva returns to post Kubera with the reality. The fourth canto finds the host of deities, lords of various islands and valorous rulers of the earth converge to the *svayaṁvara* to stake claim for her hand. The touch of Kubera's ring turns Vasudeva into his feint and the assembly was perplexed to find two Kuberas in its midst. The staff-bearer (*vetradhāriṇī*) first conducts the princess to the divine claimants but she brusquely repudiates them all. The remaining part of the canto combined with the next (Five), in its entirety, is devoted to the detailed description of ten of the participants which is distinguished by an account of their virtues and valour. The depiction of Kubera and his feint forms the contents of the sixth canto. The similarity of form throws Kanakā into utter confusion. However, as soon as Vasudeva regains his original form on discarding the ring, she garlands him, to the chagrin of the rival claimants, to signal her acceptance. The pre-marital adornments of the couple claim the next canto. Vasudeva leaves for the house of the bride, mounted on a horse. The women-folk surge forth to have a glimpse of the bridegroom which is described in nine verses (74-82), in the conventional style. The marriage ceremony, marital feast and the bride's departure combine to encompass the succeeding canto (viii). The description of the six Indian seasons in Canto Nine is extremely cumbersome, lost as it is in the labyrinth of *citrakāvya*. The tenth canto is devoted to the description of *svyaṁvara* of Rohiṇī, the princess of Ariṣṭapura. Rohiṇī's choice also falls on Vasudeva. The frustrated participants provoke Vasudeva to fight it out, but have to suffer the ignominy of defeat. The return of the newly wedded couple to Mathurā and their sexual sports are detailed in the next canto. The poem closes with the conventional descriptions of the natural phenomena, in Canto Twelve, that is intended to end the poem on a happy note.

In the conception and execution of his theme, Padmasundara is deeply indebted to Śrīharṣa's *Naiṣadhacarita*, which evidently forms its major source. He seems to have been deeply enamoured of the *Naiṣadhacarita* (*Nc*), but its complexities and bulk were deterrent to him. He, therefore, launched upon the prohibitive task of slashing it down, in his *Yadusundara*, to a handy size, pruned of Śrīharṣa's frequent incursions into marathon literary gymnastics. His manifold equipment has doubtless enabled him to spin out a worthy adaptation of Śrīharṣa's daunting tome,[19] but occasionally he tends to drift from his objective into overstepping the bounds of moderation. To him, the *svayaṁvara* seemed to have been the pivotal issue in the poem. That alone can be the rationale behind squandering away four of the twelve cantos on an event that, in essentials, forms a prologue to the culmination represented by marriage. It is surely the outcome of the impact of its model. The elaborate description of the *svayaṁvara* in five formidable cantos (x-xiv) in the *Nc* may not be at odd with its stupendous bulk; the disproportionate description in the *Ys*, however, speaks volumes of the poet's aversion to the deft handling of the theme. Even if the sterotyped descriptions of the natural phenomena (xii) are construed to have been intended as a backdrop to the love-sports of the newly married couple, the depiction of the six traditional seasons in Canto Nine has evidently been prompted by an anxiety to adhere to the rhetorical precepts.[20] The *svayaṁvara*, detailed in the tenth canto, is clearly out of joint with the poem. It has been conjured up to highlight Vasudeva's valour and skill in warfare that are held by the poeticians as essential traits of the hero of the Mahākāvya. These digressions do not stem from the context, but appear to have been forcibly thrust on the poem. They, in the process, have spilled over half of the Mahākāvya, leaving the remaining six cantos to form the canvas for the theme to unfold itself on.

In view of the pervasive influence of the *Nc*, it would be unfair to credit the *Yadusundara* with much of originality. The image of Padmasundara that emerges from the poem is that of an ornate poet, determined to exploit all the trappings that Sanskrit poetry admits to produce a worthy counterpart to the most intricate and burly Mahākāvya, the *Nc*. The impact of the *Nc* had indeed percolated down to its moorings. However, unlike his mentor, it was not Padmasundara's objective to stuff his poem with such complexities as would render it intractable to the reader, though the *Yadusundara* is not wholly absolved of the mannerisms and gimmicks, assiduously fostered by Śrīharṣa. Nor did he embark upon his poem after delving deep into the intricacies of the *Kāmaśāstra*. While it would be unkind to brand him as a master of the art of love (*kāmakalā*), the way he has gleefully detailed the vulgarities exchanged between the courtesans and Vasudeva's entourage in the marital feast and the sexual orgy of the new couple, bespeak his deep grasp of the science of erotics. The description of the marriage-feast rather tends to throw all ethical norms overboard. Quite a few of the actions of the participants therein are obscenely abhorrent.[21] These obscenities may or may not be indicative of Padmasundara's amorous proclivities but they undoubtedly make a mockery of his puritan professions.

Not unlike its prototype, the *Ys* is dominated by the erotic sentiment, which may be admitted as its *aṅgī rasa*. While Padmasundara unequivocally accepted the nine conventional sentiments,[22] he seems to have been especially enamoured of the *Rasarāja*, which, in his view, surpasses, in its sweep and sweetness, all other sentiments taken together.[23] In a bid to establish its pre-eminence, he has no qualms in pouring scorn on quietism, as a symbol of slothness.[24] Doubtless, the *Śṛṅgāra* has been exhaustively depicted in both its aspects - union and separation, but in keeping with the nature of the theme, it is the *vipralambha* that occupies the higher rung. The third canto is infested with the description of *pūrvarāga* of Kubera and Kanakā, followed by a string of touching expressions of the latter's agony. However, in emulation of the author of the *Nc*, Padmasundara has overlaid the description with such thick layers of ambiguities, inherent in his far-fetched imageries,that the anguish of the *vipralambha* seldom bares its sting through the overgrowth. Padmasundara seems to be impervious to the pangs of the princess. The hapless Kanakā appears to him to be engaged, while in the grip of agony, in churning out the *binducyutaka* variety of *citrakāvya* by turning *dānta* into *dāta* with her tears.[25] It is such gimmicks that have turned his description of *vipralambha* into an exercise in futility. In a bid to underscore Kanakā's agony, Padmasundara has grappled with a multiety of fancies, but most of them are too wild to convey her predicament even with a modicum of realism. This is how he seeks to highlight the physical decrepitude that separation has inflicted on Kanakā. "The metropolis of her body is under the command of a host of rulers. Cupid, Youth and Vasudeva are all ruling over her frame with equal vigour. They are also equally harsh in extorting revenue from her. The poor princess is driven to pay the toll of her charms (*aṅgalāvaṇya*) to meet the royal verdict. It has in the process ruthlessly sapped her of vitality. She is successively reduced to a physical wreck" (Ys.III.22). Some of the imageries are, however, attractive. Even if a petty and pliable hair pricks the body, it causes pain. One can only imagine the agony of Kanakā for not a meagerly hair but a mighty mountain (*bhūbhṛt*-king (Vasudeva)/mountain) has dented into her tender heart. It undoubtedly represents a doctored version of the corresponding verse in the *Nc* (IV.11). The whole beauty of the imagary stems from the pun. However, by appending the word *bhūbhṛt* to *yaduja* in the *Karmadhāraya* compound, Padmasundara has unwisely dissipated the poetic effect. Consequently, unlike its original, the verse fails to capture the poignancy of Kanakā's suffering.

तनुतनुरुहजव्यधतो व्यथा भवति तत्र विलासवतीहृदि ।
यदुजभूभृदसौ स्थितिमाश्रयद्यदुत बाधत एव किमद्भुतम् ।। *Ys*.III.12

Some of the verses, however, express the acuteness of her anguish with force and precision. In a bid to quench the surging flames of agony, Kanakā struggled to place on her breasts a succulent lotus but was frustrated in her attempt as the intense heat of her breath scorched it to ashes, midway. Climax of helplessness, expressed in a charming imagery ! Needless to say that this imagery has also been appropriated from the *Nc* (iv.29).

विरहदाहशमाय गृहाण निजकरेण सरोजमुरोजयोः।
द्रुतमपि श्वसितोष्मसमीरणादजनि मुर्म्मुर इत्यजहात्ततः।। *Ys*.III.21

Canto Eleven is characterised by a fascinating depiction of the love in union (*sambhoga śṛṅgāra*). Though inspired by the corresponding pieces in Kālidāsa (*Kumāra*, viii) and Śrīharṣa (*Nc*.xviii), nevertheless like them it purports to be an ode to the perceptive understanding of female psychology. How, with the passage of time the coy bride becomes responsive to the advances of her spouse is charmingly portrayed by the author of the *Ys*.

The depiction of *bhāvasandhi* gives powerful expression to the encounter in which *Kāma* is locked with *vrīḍā*. The spate of emotions caused by an eagerness to undergo the experience did not permit her to withdraw her gaze from the consort, the inherent modesty, on the other hand, desisted her from the venture. Her gaze was thus subjected to a torrid test.

स्थातुमेनमनिरीक्ष्य नाददात्सुभ्रुवो रतिपतिर्न च त्रपा ।
वीक्षितुं वरयितर्य्यनारतं तद्दृशौ विदधतुर्गतागतम् ।। *Ys*.XI.45

The verse, reproduced below, represents the other pole in the affair. At the sight of the mark she had planted on the lower lip of Vasudeva, Kanakā broke into laughter. When asked of the reason, she confronted him with the mirror to enable him to see for himself what now symbolised the nocturnal orgy.

तं च कोकनदचुम्बिषट्पदश्रीधरं तदधरं विलोक्य सा ।
सिस्मये, स्मितनिदानपृच्छकं प्रत्युवाच मुकुरार्पणात्करे ।। *Ys*.XI.75

Though accorded the ancillary status, the heroic sentiment, by virtue of its intensity, has claimed sufficient attention in the *Ys*. The *Vīra-rasa*, as it is detailed in the tenth canto, is worthless to the extreme. The chimera of *citrakāvya*, based on literary gimmicks like the monosyllabic verses and puzzling *bandhas*, as sought to be raised here, has relentlessly devoured all that passes for *Vīra-rasa*. Otherwise also, it means to project the time-worn mannerisms like respective combats of the soldiers, their war-cries, fearsome dances of the headless bodies, trumpetings of the elephants as substitues for the heroic sentiment. These motifs have doubless a tradition of their own that has filtered down to the Hindi poetry as well, but they grossly fail to reflect the valour of the combatants that forms the life-breath of the heroic sentiment. The description, in Cantos Four and Five, of the prowess of the various kings who had assembled to try luck with the princess, is replete with quite a few forceful sketches of heroism. Most of them owe themselves to Śrīharṣa. Like him, Padmasundara revels in depicting the *Vīra-rasa* in a typically courtly manner which is marked by Atiśayokti and an exuberance of well-chosen and neatly chisslled phraseology. The ruler of Sāketa has been described in this vein (*Ys*.IV.92). His preceding sketch is also an echo of the corresponding piece in the *Nc* (xii.12), but the poet's inability to work up appropriate imagery has landed him into an illogical situation and tends to mar the effect which the original exudes.

Herein the fame of the ruler of Sāketa is conceived as Gaṅgā, which, in view of the white colour attributed to fame, is most befitting. But the comparison of the sword with Yamunā is rather odd. Despite the similarity in colour, it fails to convey the intended sense. It would have been poetically more appropriate to liken the enemy's infamy with the Yamunā, as has been done in the original. On taking bath (dying) at this unique confluence, the enemies are deported to enjoy the heavenly nymphs in the same manner as an ablution at the *saṅgama* in Prayāga entitles the pious soul to the divine bliss. The heroic sentiment is here deeply tinged with the erotics inherent in the description of the sexual sports of the slain heroes with the nymphs of the heaven.

एतद्दोर्द्वयकीर्तिदेवसरिता धाराजलश्यामला-
कालिन्दीकरवालिका समगमद्वेणीत्रये तत्र च ।
दीनद्वेषिसरस्वतीमिलितया राजन्यवीरव्रजैः
स्नात्वाऽकारि सुराङ्गनासुरतक्रीडारसोद्वेलनम् ।। *Ys*.IV.91

In obedience to the theory, Padmasundara has apportioned two of his cantos for depicting nature in its varied contours. While the portrayal in the twelfth canto is so heavily indebted to Śrīharṣa that it may well be rated as an epitome of his corresponding cantos (xxii, xix), Canto Nine stands independent of the *Nc*, though it is deeply influenced by Māgha. The nature, as depicted by Padmasundara, serves to inflame human passions, both in union and separation. The description of the garden in Canto Three (35-44) goes far to fan Vasudeva's agony, stemming from his *pūrvarāga* for Kanakā. His tantalizing suffering leads him to view the *Campaka*-buds as a host of torches of Cupid's army (III.36). The sturdy mango tree seems to threaten him with its blossoms (III.39). The *Ketakī* appears no different from the saw, employed to harrow the hearts of the separated folk (III.41). And the *Palāśa* - flowers invite comparison with the crescent-shaped arrows of *Kāma*, which have been rendered red with the blood of the lovers undergoing the misery of separation (III.42).

The natural phenomena in Cantos Nine and Twelve, on the other hand, are intended to form appropriate setting to the sexual sports that were to follow, though the ninth canto is infested with fearsome *yamaka* and several varieties of *citrakāvya* that combine to make nonsense of the charming seasons that the author professes to describe with aplomb. But for certain flashes, the description is dreary to the extreme.

The depiction of the natural phenomena like evening, twilight and moon-rise in Canto Twelve is caught, not unlike its parallel in the *Nc*, in the vortex of baffling conceits and far-fatched fancies. While Padmasundara seems to be enamoured of the phenomena that mark the evening twilight, he is unable to shed the shackles that bind him to the *Nc*. Consequently, in describing the splendour of evening and the stars that emerge soon thereafter, he, like Śrīharṣa, has indulged in a series of frustrating imageries. The lioness of the evening (*sandhyā*), he is convinced, has rent asunder with her claws the tusker, that is day. The fountain of blood surging from his massive body has spread in the western horizon, in the form of the evening glow. And the pearls shedding from his harrowed forehead have assumed the form of the flickering stars (*Ys*,xii.6). In emulation of Śrīharṣa (*Nc*,xxii.13), Padmasundara loves to view the sun as a mighty ball of gold. The crafty trader of the western mount has appropriated from the sky the large ball of gold and has sold it, in return, the mass of cowries, masquerading as stars.[26] Padmasundara is again indebted to Śrīharṣa (*Nc*,xxii.31) for the strained Rūpaka that seeks to envisage the sky as an inverted earthen vase and the sun as a mighty lamp, in describing the pitch darkness that has crippled, with its density, the human vision. The vase was imaginatively placed over the lamp to gather soot, a basic ingredient of collyrium. However, despite its vastness and stoutness, it has given way under the weight of the mountain of soot, spilling darkness everywhere (*Ys*,xii.15). Equally strained is the imagery that conceives the red glow of the rising moon as emanating from the kisses, the heavenly nymphs had planted on his face.[27] The worst monstrosity is, however, committed in personifying the phenomena witnessed in the morning. Padmasundara has sought to represent the day-break as a fowler and the sun as a hawk. The fowler of the morning has released in the sky the hawk of the sun. Fearful of its deadly swoop, the moon has sought the sanctuary of the ocean for its protege, the hare (*śaśa*). The crows of darkness have fled away. The swarm of pigeons, that is stars, is resorting to acrobatic flights to escape the clutches of the hawk (*Ys*.xii.78). These strained fancies have turned Padmasundara's description of nature into an ethereal exercise, divorced from moderation.

The language of the *Ys* bears a deep imprint of the *Nc*. Such of its segments as purport to be independent adaptation of Śrīharṣa's *magnum opus*, are marked, not unlike his *Pārśvanāthakāvya*, by pleasing ease and lucidity; but whenever he was constrained to compress the corresponding parts of his prototype, laboured ornateness has crept into his language, though there too he has been at pains to shield it from abstruseness. The depiction of nature in the last canto and the elaborate exposition of the *svayaṁvara* ceremony are imbued with consciously cooked up phraseology. The latter description rather abounds in sesquipedalian compounds. It is however to the credit of Padmasundara that he, unlike Śrīharṣa, has not turned his poem into an arena to parade his manifold equipment. That explains why, despite the unhappy precedent to pursue, he has ably succeeded in containing his language within reasonable bounds of moderation, the exuberance of unwieldy compounds notwithstanding. (*Ys*.v.18). The language that clothes such of the ideas as have been borrowed from the *Nc*, in view of its perspicuity, invaribly contributes to their clarity in an ample measure. Kanakā's query about the messenger's antecedents and similar other episodes in the poem represent a pole apart from the cumbersome language, arrogantly fostered by Śrīharṣa.

By and large, *Yadusundara's* language is marked by lucidity, but there have been occasions when Padmasundara felt tempted to drift from his aim to make frustrating forays into the preserve of the *citrakāvya*. Here he has smugly fallen victim to Māgha's spell, unfolded in the plethora of mannerisms that he championed with unusual gusto. While the nineth canto itself is infested with disgusting varieties of Yamaka and *citrakāvya* including the intricate *bandhas*, in the tenth canto he zealously seeks to perpetuate the despicable tradition of detailing the series of combats in what represents the most ignoble form of *citrakāvya*, namely the monosyllabic verses[28] and *cyutaka* form of *Kāvya* pertaining to the instant (*mātrā*), syllable (*varṇa*) and anusvāra (*bindu*).[29] The ferocity of his Yamaka can well be gauged from the Mahāyamaka[30] that disfigures some of the verses in the description. The nadir in the *citrakāvya* is reached in the verses that are amenable to identical scanning from the beginning and the end, and thereby seek to establish the author as a wizard of sorts in torturing the language to suit his caprices.[31] Howsoever strongly these literary gymnastics may testify to the author's deep grasp of the nuances of language and his skill in exploiting it to serve his objectives, even if nefarious to the extreme, such atrocities pose challenge even to the most mature scholarship. It is simply impossible to resolve these complexities without the help of the commentary.

Though not wanting in fearsome compounds, Padmasundara's

style would be rated as of the *Vaidarbhī* variety, though it has received thick daubs of *Pāñcālī* and *Gauḍī*. Nothwithstanding its intricacies, Śrīharṣa's language is deservedly celebrated for the sweetness of its phraseology (*padalālitya*) to the extent that the dictum *Naiṣadhe padalālityam* has gained currency to project the excellences of his language. Padmasundara's language is also characterised by *padalālitya* which tends to add a new dimension to the poem. The *padalālitya* in the *Ys* emanates from the series of alliteration that pervades the better part of the poem. How it has heightened the sweetness of the language should be obvious from a number of verses.[32]

Like its model, the *Ys* is also dominated by *vakrokti* which, in the poem, stems from liberal doses of *utprekṣā, apahnuti, atiśayokti* and *samāsokti*, administered individually or severally. Padmasundara harbours special fancy for *sāpahnavotprekṣā* and *sāpahnavātiśayokti*. While in some of the verses *utprekṣā* and *apahnuti* join hands to bolster the *vakrokti* (III.25), the description of some of the participants in the *svayaṁvara* abounds in winsome *atiśayoktis*. Some other verses form illustrations of the most pleasing form of *atiśayokti* wherein the *prastuta* is fused into *aprastuta* (*Ys*,xi.57). *Aprastuta-praśaṁsā, arthāntaranyāsa, dṛṣṭānta, parayāyokti*, etc. are some of the other momentous *alaṅkāras* that padmasundara has fondly used to demonstrate his penchant for *vakrokti*. It is in the third canto that the popular figure of speech, *arthāntaranyāsa* is encountered most (*Ys*.III.84, 117, 136, 155, 156, 201). XI.30, that is intended to project Vasudeva's imperviousness to the sinful forays of the sensual pleasures, emerges as its best illustration.

तां रिरंसुरथ सोऽप्यहर्निशं पापमाप किमु तत्त्ववित् क्वचित् ।
ज्ञानिनां किल कलङ्कपङ्कता लिम्पते न विषयस्पृशामपि ।। *YS*.XI.30

It is the *arthāntaranyāsa* that combines with *dṛṣṭānta* to kick up the lovely *subhāṣitas* that are strewn in the body of the poem.[33]

The simile, as employed in the poem, attests to the poet's deftness in mustering appropriate *upamānas* that have been instrumental in purging the subject under description of the haze that might have otherwise stuck to it. He is equally at home in handling the whole gamut of diverse *upamānas*, not preculding the *śāstric*, philosophic and abstract standards of comparision. The description of the *svayaṁvara* is especially rich in the wealth of choice *upamānas*. The *upamāna* that represents an amalgam of the abstract and concrete merits attention. The palanquin-bearers conducted Kanakā from the lord of Mithilā to the duo of Kuberas as the rays of the sun bring cheer to the Cakravāka-couples.

तां निन्यिरे धनदयुग्ममिवावशिष्टं
प्रीतिं रथाङ्गमिथुनं हरिदश्वपादाः।। *Ys*.VI.1

Rūpaka, parisaṁkhyā, vyājokti, vyatireka, virodhābhāsa, sāra, ekāvalī, kāvyaliṅga, asaṅgati, anumāna, ullekha, udātta are the other favourite *alaṅkāras* that Padmasundara has used with some frequency. In a poem dominated by *vakrokti*, the *svabhāvokti* was bound to be scarce. Of the *svabhāvoktis* that are encountered in the *Ys*, the one that emerges at the top because of its faithfully detailing the apprehensions and actions of the messanger, merits reproduction.

दौवारिकस्य परविप्रतिषेधवाचा त्वं कोस्यरेऽपसर सोऽपि विशंकमानः।
ग्रीवां विभुज्य चकितः क्षणमित्यपास्तशंकः परामथ विवेश निशान्तकक्षम् ।।

Ys.III.79

The *Ys*. speaks volumes of the author's skill in prosody. He has used twenty seven metres in the poem, which are as follows: *anuṣṭup, indravajrā, kalahaṁsa, kālabhariṇī, jaladharamālā, toṭaka, drutavilaṁbita, puṣpitāgrā, pṛthvī, prabodhitā, pramitākṣarā, praharṣiṇī, mañjubhāṣiṇī, mattamayūra, mandākrāntā, mālinī, rathodhattā, rucirā, vasantatilakā, vaṁśastha, sārdūlavikrīḍita, śālinī, śikhariṇī, sāndrapada, sragadharā, svāgatā* and *hariṇī*. The list includes such metres as *kalahaṁsa, kālabhariṇī prabodhitā* and *sāndrapada* which are sparsely met in the literature. Cantos one, Two and Four are dominated by *vaṁśastha*. The fifth, sixth and nineth cantos, against the prescribed one, confront the reader with a plurality of metres. *Svāgatā* adds up as the major metre in Canto Ten, the first forty-one verses being couched in it. For the remaining thirty-one stanzas of the canto, Padmasundara has exploited the pithy *anuṣṭup* and the mighty *sārdūlavikrīḍita* and *sragdharā*.

The *Ys* is intended to be a counterpart of the *Nc*. But because of the poet's limitations in countering the powerful impact of Śrīharṣa that was bound to weigh on him in the situation, the *Ys* boils down to an adaptation at best and an abridgement at worst. Despite the constraints inherent in the process, it emerges as an important link in the *Naiṣadha*-school of poetry, which contrary to Kālidasa and Māgha, has not evoked much following.

NOTES AND REFERENCES

1. M.D.Desai (ed.), *Bhānucandracarita*, Singhī Jaina Granthamālā, No.15, Introduction, p.12 ; *Sūrīśvara ane samrāṭ* (Gujarati), p.120, quoted in *Jain Sāhitya aura itihāsa*, Bombay, 1956, p.396, F.N3
2. *Ain-e-Akbari* (English translation by Blochman), p.537-547
3. *Yadusundara*, Colophons; *Sundaraprakāśaśabdārṇava*, Colophons; *Pārśvanāthakāvya*, Colophons and VII.64 ; *Rāyamallābhyudaya, praśasti*, 100 etc.
4. पुराभवत्प्रीतिपदं वयस्यविशारदेन्दुर्मम पद्मसुन्दरः। *Hīrasaubhāgya, KM* 67, XIV.91.
5. Nathu Ram Premi, *Jaina Sāhitya aura itihāsa* (JSI), op.cit., p.396
6. *Hīrasaubhāgya*, op.cit, XIV.92,96 and Auto-commentary on XIV.99 :
   काव्यानि रघुवंश-मेघदूत-कुमारसम्भव-कादम्बरी-पद्मानन्द-यदुसुन्दराद्यानि ।
7. The *Yadunsundara* is known through its solitary MS (No.2858 Puṇya) preserved with the L.D. Institute of. Indology. Our study of the poem is based on its transcript. For an exhaustive critique on Yadusundara see our book *Jaina Saṁskrit Mahākāvya*, Jain Viśva Bhārati, Ladnun (Raj.), p.100-123. It has been recently edited by D.P. Rawal, L.D. Series, 105, Ahmedabad, 1987
8. *Bhānucandracarita*, op.cit., Introduction, p.5-8; *Unnatapurapraśasti,* Line 1
9. *Pramāṇasundara* (p.127-160) in Jaina Philosophical Tracts (ed. Nagin J.Shah), L.D. Institute of Indology, Ahmedabad, 1973, p.160
10. JSI, op.cit., p.396
11. Satya Vrat, *Jaina Saṁskṛta Mahākāvya*, op.cit., p.103
12. ED. K. Mādhavakṛṣṇa Sarmā, The Ganga Oriental Series, No.1, Bikaner, 1940
13. *ASSD*, op.cit., I.8
14. *ASSD*, op.cit., Introduction, p.xx
15. Quoted in *Anekānta*, Vol.IV, p.470; ASSD, Introduction, p.xxii and JSI, op.cit., p.395, F.N. 3
16. Agarchand Nahata, Aitihāsika Jaina Kāvyasaṅgrah, p.104
17. *Pārśvanāthakāvya* (MS, No.16, Amer Śāstra Bhandar, Jaipur), VII.44

18. Ibid., I.30 ; *Rāyamallābhyudaya* (MS), xx.24, quoted in JSI, p.397-398
19. For a detailed discussion on the quantum of debt that the *Yadusundara* owes to the *Naiṣadhacarita*, see *Yadusundara* : An Interesting Adaptation of Naiṣadhacarïta in the subsequent pages (76-95)
20. *Sāhityadarpaṇa*, Lucknow, V.S. 1979, VI.322.
21. अन्यः स्फुटस्फटिकचत्वरसंस्थितायास्तन्व्या वरांगमनुबिम्बितमीक्षमाणः । *Ys*.VIII.37. Also see VIII.52,54
22. नवरसनिलयैः को नु सौहित्यमेति । *Ys*.II.83
23. अन्यरसातिशायी शृङ्गारः । *Ys*.VI.53 Also :
    एतेन हीनमपि किं च कवेः कवित्वम् ।
    नैरस्यमेव तृणपूरुषवद् भजेत ।। *ASSD*, IV.20
24. शान्तरसैकमन्दधीः । *Ys*.IV.41
25. मां दान्तमेव किमु दातमलङ्करोषि । *Ys*.III.190
26. निकषमिषतां बिभ्रत्यस्ताचलस्तु शिलातले
    द्रुतकनकजं पिण्डं क्रीत्वा विकर्तनमण्डलनम् ।।
    जलनिधिरये दत्ते साक्षात्परीक्ष्य पितृप्रसू-
    हुतभुजि नभोहस्ते तारावराटकोटितम् ।। *Ys*.XII.8
27. किमु सुरवधूवृन्दैर्बिम्बं तदीयमचुम्बि तैः
    स्ववदनतुलारागाद्यावकद्रवारुणिताधरैः ।। *Ys*.XII.23
28. कुः काङ्कक‌ङ्कैकाकि काकिकाककुकैकिका ।
    काङ्काङ्कककाकाक ककाकुः कङ्ककाकका ।। *Ys*.X.44
29. बद्धमुष्टिं सदादाने कृपणं कोऽत्र नाश्रितः। *Ys*.X.41
30. सारङ्गता तरलतारतरङ्गसारा सारङ्गता तरलतारतरङ्गसारा ।
    सारङ्गता तरलतारतरङ्गसारा सारङ्गता तरलतारतरङ्गसारा ।। Ys.IX.29
31. सारसा रवसारा सा रुचा ता नवकारिका ।
    कारिकाऽवनता चारु सारा सा वरसारसा ।। *Ys*.IX.58
32. एतस्योद्धुरसिन्धुरैरपि मृधे क्रान्तां पुनर्जङ्गमै-
    र्जानानो धरणीधरैः स्म धरणीं धीरः पृथुः पार्थिवः।
    एतत्संगरसंगताऽमरसमज्यामध्यमध्यासितो
    भूयो भूधरभूरिभारहरणे मेधां विधत्तेतराम् ।। *Ys*.V.14
33. Some of the *subhāṣitas* are quoted here.
    (i) तृणाग्रनीरैः शममेति किं तृषा । *Ys*.I.34
    (ii) औचित्यं निकृतिपरेषु वक्रतैव । *Ys*.III.36
    (iii) प्रायो हि नामपदमेव मुखं क्रियासु । *Ys*.III.106
    (iv) दुःस्थे चेतस्यशेषमविषह्यम् । *Ys*.III.127
    (v) न मानमान्द्यं गणयन्त्यभीप्सवः। *Ys*.IV.6
    (vi) गरीयसितरा नियतेः समीहा । *Ys*.IV.72

YADUSUNDARA

AN INTERESTING ADAPTATION OF NAIṢADHACARITA

The *Naiṣadhacarita* (*Nc.*)[1] of Śrīharṣa is admittedly a daunting tome of misplaced pedantry. It symbolises the nadir which the Mahākāvya-tradition could touch in the hands of an erudite scholar, masquerading as a poet. Instead of making his manifold equipment subservient to poetry, Śrīharṣa has reduced poetry to the miserable status of a handmaid of his erudition, with the result the *Nc.* has assumed the form of a volume wherein lies enshrined, virtually at every step, his prolific learning. But Śrīharṣa is least perturbed at the situation. Rather, he boastfully bills his poem to be intractable for a self-styled scholar (*prājñmmanya*). He has cautioned such an ill-equipped novice not to burn his fingers with it because, in view of the intricacies he has stuffed it with, nothing worthwhile is going to accure to him.[2] This blissful seclusion, willingly imposed by Śrīharṣa, compounded with a host of blemishes that besmirch the poem, even if no credence is given to Mammaṭa's alleged wholesale denunciation thereof, has resulted in scaring away from it both the conniosseur and the layman alike. Not only its pedantic diction, its girth is equally fobidding. Thus, while Kālidāsa and Māgha, two of his illustrious predecessors, to whom he is indebted in a large measure,[3] have exercised powerful influence on the subsequent generations of poets, with Māgha emerging as the unquestioned master of the post-Kālidāsa Mahākāvya, Śrīharṣa has evoked little following among his successors. Only some of the late Jaina poets (17th century), with their unabating passion to produce counterpart to every classical work of worth, have pronounced predilection for Śrīharṣa's poem. Meghavijaya has subjected the first canto of the *Nc.* to *samasyāpūrti* in his *Śāntināthacarita*.[4] Devavimala, on the other hand, was inspired and influenced by Śrīharṣa to the extent that his *Hīrasaubhāgya*,[5] despite divergences in contents, may justifiably by rated as the *Nc.* of the Jaina literature.[6]

Padmasundara, one of Hīravijaya's predecessors in the *Tapāgaccha* and, like him, a spirtual friend of the Mughal emperor

Akbar, was deeply enamoured of the *Nc.* but its complexities and bulk seemed to have been a damper to him. He, therefore, launched upon the prohibitive task of pruning it, in his *Yadusundara* (*Ys.*)[7] which seeks to describe, in twelve cantos, the marriage and post-marital enjoyments of Vasudeva and the charming Vidyādhara-princess Kanakā, to a handy size, in lucid language, bereft of Śrīharṣa's frequent exercises in literary gymnastics. As vouched for by his literary output,[8] Padmasundara was well equal to the task. He has come out of the ordeal with admirable credit. However, there have been occasions when he felt constrained to reproduce the original, albeit in a truncated form, in a thinly garbed language. This accounts for the phenomenon why his *Ys.*, at places, purports to be a compendium rather than an adaptation of its model.

Nala is the prototype of Vasudeva in Padmasundara's redaction. Kanakā represents the Vidarbha-princess Damayantī. Padmasundara has reduced the feints of the hero, from four in the original, to one, who, in the *Ys.*, is Kubera, the lord of riches. The claimants to Kanakā's hand are almost identical with the personages who stake their claim for Damayantī in the *Nc.* Padmasundara has no fondness for divine personages like Nārada and Sarasvatī, who have a momentous role to play in the *Nc.* The *Vetradhariṇī*, charged with introducing to Kanakā, the various claimants, who flock in the *svayaṁvara*, measures well up to the function. These are the *Dramatis Personae* who combine to weave the drapery that is formed by the *Yadusundara*.

The *Ys.* opens with a graphic account of Mathurā, the principal seat of the Yādavas, sanctified by them with their might and celebrated the world over (I.2). The description obviously owes itself to the portrayal of Kuṇḍinapura in the second canto of the *Nc.* (74-105), which, as the birth-place of Damayantī, the heroine of the poem, holds an equally significant place. In keeping with his penchant for brevity, Padmasundara has disposed of the description within the space of seventeen verses (I.2-18) against Śrīharṣa's thirty-one. The author of the *Nc.* seems to be actuated by an eagerness to illustrate some of the objects prescribed by poeticians as inalienable characteristics of the description of the town. The systematic treatment therein of the garden, pleasure-tank, rampart, moat, mansions, market, etc., as ingredients of the description, seems to stem from the same commitment. While Śrīharṣa is keen to parade his misplaced love for far-fetched fancies, conceits and grammatical (II.95,98) and mythological

(II.101-102) subtlities even in such a innocuous context, Padmasundara aims at presenting a simple description, occasionally tinged with his religious fervour (*Ys*.I.112) and imbued with traditional devices like *Śleṣa* and *Parīsaṅkhyā* (*Nc*.,I.I,15-17), effectively exploited by him. Though this is one of the few pieces in the *Ys*. that have successfully broken the stranglehold of the *Nc*., some of the similarities cry notice. Padmasundara, for instance, has made pointed allusions to the sun and moon stones, so favourite with Śrīharṣa, though they are intended to serve different purposes in the two poems (*Nc*., II.94 ; *Ys*., I.13). Both, likewise, seek to detail, in obedience to theory, the rampart and moat that safeguard the town against alien assaults.[9] The two, however, differ in their style. To Śrīharṣa the moat appears to have rendered the town unassailable like the *phakkikās* of the *Mahābhāṣya* [10], in the *Ys*. it serves the purpose of *yogapaṭṭa* to the sun when it embarks upon severe penance (I.8). The role has been shifted to the rampart in the *Nc*.(II.78), while in the *Yadusundara* it is postulated to be engaged in a struggle to reach the heavenly Ganges, with its battlements (I.6). But these are marginal resemblances which are confronted in other poems as well.

Padmasundara has sought to parallel Nala's visit to the garden to seek diversion for his aching heart, tormented by his *pūrvarāga* for Damayantī, in the first canto of the *Nc*. (57-140), by Vasudeva's flight to the Vidyādhara - kingom following sharp rebuke by his elder brother, Samudravijaya, for his outrageous behaviour with the women-folk. The two, however, differ widely in their objective. While Vasudeva is rewarded with handsome guerdon including warm hospitality and pretty maidens, Nala's agony is further fired by the backdrop the garden serves to provide.[11]

Padmasundara's earnestness to adapt Śrīharṣa's *magnum opus* to manageable bounds is evident from the Second canto wherein he seeks to compress more than two cantos of the *Nc*. (III,VII), composed of about 250 verses. The description of the physical charms of Kanakā, in the earlier part of the second canto of the *Ys*., is an unmistakable echo of the corresponding depiction in the *Nc*. Śrīharṣa is so enamoured of female beauty that besides side-flashes elsewhere, he has described, in Canto Seven, Damayantī's person in the true *nakhaśikha* style. True to the moral degeneration that had sapped the social fabric in his feudal milieu, he had no qualms in gleefully describing even the female privy part of the princess.[12] Padmasundara has undeniably borrowed some of the ideas from Śrīharṣa, but, unlike Devavimala, he does not mean to attempt a parallel to the relevant description in the *Nc.* Within the narrow limits he has drawn for himself, his description of Kanakā is tarnished, at places, by lack of sequence and a nagging ambiguity. Śrīharṣa has so imbued the description with his overflowing *śāstric* skill that breathes through most of his *aprastutas*, that instead of contributing to its clarity they, not unoften, tend to blur the subject. Padmasundara has wisely toned down such atrocities, though the description bristles with verbal adoptions from Śrīharṣa. Some distinct trends are perceptible in Padmasundara's description. He has either borrowed Śrīharṣa's imagery as such or has replaced or strengthened it with his own. His unanimity on the conciet that the plantain tree would invoke comparison with the princess's well-rounded thighs if it were to undergo severe penance, with head turned down, in the desolate jungle ; and that the elephant rolls his trunk, eclipsed by them (thighs), out of disgust (*Nc.*, VII.94-95 ; *Ys.*, II.37-38), belong to the first category. The second segment is represented by quite a few verses. Her moon-like face had caused the lotus to wither. But the pair of Cakravākas in the form of her thick breasts surprisingly did not suffer separation thereby (*Nc.*VII.77). This exquisite Virodhābhāsa infused with Rūpaka has been ingeniously replaced by Padmansundara with an Arthāntaranyāsa, but, in the process, it has suffered loss in poetic effect. The third category is equally pronounced. At the time Cupid was burnt, his flowery bow had its filaments reduced to dark ashes. Śaṅkara, indignant at his outrageous venture, divided the bow-like dark filaments into two which the Creator seized upon to fashion her eye-brows (*Nc.*,VII.24). Padmasundara has transplanted the conceit in his description but has sought to strengthen it by contributing to it his own share of wildness. To him Kanakā's eye-brows appear to be two tender fingers of youth and Cupid, that they have joined to solemnize their friendship (*Ys.*,II.9).

The embassy of the swan in the *Ys.* is evidently modelled on the corresponding episode in the *Nc.* It encompasses one complete canto in the *Nc.*(III). Padmasundara has abridged the episode to form the later half of the second canto. Both the poems concur in assigning a momentous role to the swan to fire the heroine's passion for her lover which ultimately culminates in their marriage. The swan severely berates its captors in both the poems. He censures Nala to have failed in his primary duty of defending his subjects and thus put the earth to shame by his outrageous action in holding him in thraldom, in the *Ys.* he rates it as a flagrant violation of all canons of propriety and hospitality.[13] His pleadings result in his eventual release.[14]

Padmasundara's parallel description of the events, described in Canto Three of the *Nc.*, is distinguished by succintness and lucidity. The arguments that the swan advances to induce the princess, agree in essentials. Pruned of accretions, the suitability of the couple forms the quintessence of his pleadings. In emulation of Śrīharṣa, the hero has been described in the *Ys.* as a paragon of human excellences, valour and beauty included.[15] The swan reminds Damayantī of her being unmarried, Kanakā is made out to be the pinnacle of feminine charms.[16] And they are certain to form, the swan avers, on their marriage, an ideal couple like the moon and the night.[17] In both the poems, the princess beseeches the swan to bring about union with her prospective consort, which he fain condescends to do.[18] The portrait of the hero, which the swan claims to have drawn himself in the *Ys.*, is intended to match the replica of Damayantī in Śrīharṣa's poem.[19] The closing verses of Canto Two in the *Ys.* (II.77-80) wherein Vasudeva is described as a sure target of Cupid following the expression of love by Kanakā, have their genesis in the corresponding stanzas of the Nc. (III.126-128). As in the *Nc.*, the swan in the *Ys.* flies back to post his master with the success of his mission.[20]

Canto Three of the *Ys.* represents a *tour de force* on the part of its author. Here he embarks upon the arduous task of redacting no less than five formidable cantos of the *Nc.* (IV-VI, VIII-IX) in a solitary canto.

The successful mission of the swan results in fanning the flames of Kanakā's *pūrvarāga* that leaves her a physical decrepit and delivers a rude shock to her mental equipoise. The *pūrvarāga*, as detailed in the *Ys.*, is heavily indebted to the corresponding description of Damayantī's anguish in the *Nc.* Śrīharṣa's treatment of Damayantī's *pūrvarāga* (canto III), systematically highlighting the various stresses, physical and psychical, that one supposedly experiences in separation, touches a high watermark as it subsequently settled as one of the most powerful mannerisms that have filtered down to the later Hindi poets like Jāyasī, Bihārī and others of their ilk. Damayantī's anguish, which by reason of its intensity verges on pathos, climaxes in swoon, with her friends rushing medical aid. Kanakā too is made to undergo the same fate, though the culmination, in her case, sounds rather inane.[21] Padmasundara has sparingly chosen only forty-seven of Śrīharṣa's verses to redact. It is a measure of his abject submission to Śrīharṣa that twenty of his thirty verses, concerned with Kanakā's *pūrvarāga,* represent a helpless replica of the corresponding piece in the *Nc.* Some of the motifs Padmasundara has adopted from his predecessor merit attention. While underlying the acuteness of Damayantī's suffering, occasioned by her profound love for Nala, the king of Niṣadha, Śrīharṣa characteristically whips up the word *avanibhṛt,* which etymologically yields two meanings:king and mountain. The whole beauty of the description rests upon this pun. Even a petty blade of grass, when it pierces into flesh, causes unbearable pain. One can hopefully pray for Damayantī because not a meagerly blade but a mighty mountain/king has dented into her tender heart.[22] This *double entendre* has caught the fancy of Padmasundara but by appending the word *bhūbhṛt* to *yaduja* in a *Karmadhāraya* compound, he has unwisely dissipated the poignancy of her suffering.[23] In a bid to quench the surging flames of agony, Damayantī struggled to place on her breasts a succulent lotus but was foiled in her attempt as the intense heat of her breath scorched it to ashes, midway. Climax of helplessness, indeed, expressed in a charming imagery ! Padmasundara was so enthralled by the beauty of this imagery that he has smugly repeated it, in his phraseology.[24]

The touching description of human agony, caused by hitherto unconsummated love, is followed in the fifth canto of the *Nc.* by Nārada's embassy to Indra to apprise him of the ensuing *svayaṁvara* of Damayantī, a veritable missile of Cupid. Padmasundara has no use for Nārada or any other divine agency because Kubera himself descends upon the garden, close to the city-portal of the Vidyādhara metropolis (*Ys.*,III.46). Contrary to Indra's brief acclaim of Nala, in a solitary verse (*Nc.*,V.100) which seeks to bring into focus his suitability to execute the delicate mission, Kubera eloquently describes at length the plethora of Vasudeva's sterling virtues to mark him out as the most appropriate person to proceed on errand (*Ys.*,III.48-57).[25] His noble descent and solicitude for others constitute the *summum bonum* of Kubera's pleadings.

The apprehensions that afflict the prospective messengers are identical in the two poems. Nala views the attempt on the part of the deities as an exercise in swinding. Vasudeva brands the mission as a self-repoach (*Nc.*, V.107 ; *Ys.*,III.60). Nala brusquely tells the quarter-regents that in view of her firm devotion to him, his mission was bound to end in a fiasco, so far as they were concerned (*Nc.*,V.114). Vasudeva is not so blunt in his behaviour but the implication of his remark (*Ys.*, III.70) does not differ in substance. They unanimously view the proposed mission as a travesty of functions. It is rather the gods who are solicated to help the mortals out of impasse (*Nc.*,V.112 ; *Ys.*, III.62). But, when invested with invisibility, both are reconciled to the function.[26]

The scene in the sixth canto of the *Nc.* shifts to the royal palace of Vidarbha. The description of the mansion in the *Ys.* is a triffle longer. Its life-like sketch with fluttering banners, rut-shedding elephants, armed guards in attendance, porches, turrets of precious stones and pet birds, adept in many a repartee, perched on dove-cots, makes a happy reading.[27] Like Nala, Vasudeva enters the harem, undaunted, giving slip, with admirable strategy, to the vigilant guards on duty. The confrontation of the messenger with the immates of the seraglio, including the latter's actions and perceptions *vis-a-vis* them are described in a similar vein. With a reverence for *śāstric* injunctions, the messengers, in both the poems, withdraw their gaze from the naked women which, however, results in their ramming into others (*Nc.*, VI.13 ; *Ys.*, III.81). Despite all temptations, both of them emerge unscathed. While the messenger's equanimity has been highlighted with a Rūpaka in the *Nc.*(VI.19), Padmasundara has driven it home with an Arthāntaranyāsa (*Ys.*,III.84). Śrīharṣa has stuffed the canto with a long description of Damayantī's assembly-hall (*Nc.*,VI. 58-74) and the pleadings of the messenger to Damayantī to choose Indra as her husband, followed by an equally powerful rebuttal thereof by her (*Nc.*,VI.76-110) . Padmasundara has summed up the whole canto in mere twenty-four verses (*Ys.*,III.71-94) with equal effect and more clarity.

The segment of the third canto, formed by verses 95 to 142, is intended to be a counterpart to canto VIII of the *Nc.* Śrīharṣa has described, at great length, the feelings that overpower Damayantī on her confrontation with the messenger. The parallel description in the *Ys.*, though it follows Śrīharṣa closely enough to echo his ideas and phrases, is shorter but potent to drive home her astonishment at the exquisiteness of his mien and her resultant ecstasy (*Ys.*, III.94-101). Kanakā's address to Vasudeva (*Ys.*,III. 102-108), wherein she seeks to extend him welcome with courtly courtesies and inquires of him his antecedents including his name, which, after all, is a prelude to any fruitful relationship, does not differ from the corresponding portion of the *Nc.*, (VIII.20-31). Both the princesses are taken aback by the resourcefulness of the messenger in entering into the palace, watchfully guarded by a host of armed attendants. While Śrīharaṣa likens the act to crossing an ocean (*Nc*.VIII.26), to Padmasundara it is a plunge into the fire (*Ys*., III.107). The depiction of Kubera's *pūrvarāga* represents a doctored version of the torments that the quarter-regents are said to undergo (*Nc*., VIII 64-108). The piece in the *Ys*., however, is distinguished by a singularly lucid language which goes far to heighten the poignancy of Kubera's anguish.

The last sixty verses (*Ys*.III) purport to be an echo of the ninth canto of the *Nc*. They do not differ in contents, and have much in common in language and style. The trickery on the part of the messenger in cunningly flying into a narration that does not have much relevance to the princess, in a bid to withhold his identity, offends her to the extreme. She scolds him for equivocation (*Nc*.,IX.2-3; *Ys*.,III.143) which had given his speech resemblance with the river Sarasvatī, alternatively revealing and concealing its current (*Nc*.,IX.4 ; *Ys*., III.144). Kanakā, like Damayantī, insists on the antecedents of the messenger (*Nc*.,IX.5-6; *Ys*.,III.145). He, on his part, seeks shelter behind the safety of the *śāstric* injunctions to the contrary.[28] His audacious persistence with his pleadings, provkes the princess, in both the poems, to spotlight the absurdity of a divine personage craving for a mortal woman as his wife (*Nc*.,IX.27 ; *Ys*.,III.153). This plain-speaking on her part evokes sharp rebuke from the messenger, in both the *Nc*. and the *Ys*. The messengers unanimously question the wisdom of the princess in rejecting a deity in favour of a mere mortal and urge her to aspire for godhead as many an advantage flow from it (*Nc*.,IX.42; *Ys*.,III.169).

The princess, in both the poems, is driven to tears out of disgust and curses her lot for the predicament. Her wailings ultimately move the messenger to divulge his identity followed by repeated assertion of his love for her. Though conscious of the breach of trust, the messenger, in both the poems, is convinced of the truth of his cause (*Nc*.,IX.125 ; *Ys*.,III. 197-198). All this has been related with so close concurrence that but for Śrīharṣa's style, it is difficult to distinguish between the two. Padmasundara has tried to vie with the author of the *Nc*., in certain motifs as well. Damayantī, in a verse noted for *binducyutaka*, makes *sasāra* of *saṁsāra* by removing the *anusvāra* with her tears. Kanakā turns *dānta* into *dāta* with the same device.[29] In the *Nc*., Damayantī, overcome with utter despair, requests the *dakṣiṇa* (civil/southern) breeze to scatter her ahses, on death, in the direction tenanted by her coveted spouse. The southern breeze is doubtless her foe but animosity ends with death.[30] Taking cue from this exquisite imagery, Padmasundara has struggled to adapt the motif to suit his purpose but has failed to maintain the poetic effect. Kanakā, in his poem, implores her *prāṇavāvu* (breath) not to suffer misery in the wilderness of her body. It would rather do her a favour, were it to fly to the region, where lives her spouse.[31]

The *svayaṁvara* (*Nc*., X-XIV), as detailed by Śrīharṣa in hyperbolic terms, with gods, demons and other extra-terrestrial participants, besides the lesser mortals, staking claim for the princess, belongs to the realm of fiction.[32] In consonance with the semi-divine character of the assembly, Sarasvatī, the goddess of muse, described in detail (*Nc*.,X.74-89), has been deputed to introduce the youthful claimants. Śrīharṣa's description is doubtless based on the corresponding piece in the *Raghuvaṁśa*, but due to its prolixity and ponderous style it does not otherwise have much in common with Kālidāsa. Indumati's *svayaṁvara* forms an integral part of the theme and serves to contribute to the smoothness of its flow. Śrīharṣa's description, on the other hand, is an exercise in artificiality. The plethora of unweildy verses, in longer metres, that he has unimaginatively flung in the midst of the description, has made a mockery of the whole piece. The description of *svayaṁvara* in the *Ys*. (IV-VI), definite allusions to divine participation apart (*Ys*.,IV.5-25), is not wholly divorced from reality, though it would have been saner to abridge it further in the poem, which after all is no match to the bulk of the *Nc*.

The description in the two poems, however, begins on a similar note, the sequence of events described therin being almost idential. The claimants to the princess's hand have been unanimously described as paragons of virtues including valour, learning, riches and physical charms, putting to shame the puffed up Kāma (*Nc*.,X.1; *Ys*.,IV.2). Though unequivocally repudiated earlier through the messenger, the quarter-regents, Indra, Varuṇa, Yama and Agni had come to participate in Damayantī's *svayaṁvara* disguised as Nala, in the hope that she might choose them, mistaking for Nala. Vasudeva, in the *Ys*., was turned into a replica of Kubera on putting on the ring that the latter had craftily made over to him. Thus, as against Nala's four, there is only one feint of Vasudeva.[33]

The exuberance displayed in greeting the distinguished guests, the characteristics that tended to blur the distinction between the divine and mortal personages, the amorous actions preceding and succeeding the arrival of the princes in the *maṇḍapa* and the description of the young princes as so many Cupids to emerge, like phoenix, from his ashes, have all been detailed by both Śrīharṣa and Padmasundara, in almost similar phraseology.[34] The divine personages, in the two poems, have stolen thunder over the mortals in claiming attention first. While Śrīharṣa, in his zeal to do justice with the space he had apportioned to the description as a whole,has dilated upon them in the better part of Canto Eleven (8-85), Padmasundara had disposed of the divine claimants in four verses (*Ys.*,Iv.53-56). Both the princesses expressed their aversion to the divine beings with identical gestures (*Nc.*, XI. 11 ; *Ys.*, IV.56).

Hereafter, Padmasundara, evidently in imitation of his model, has set himself on describing the mortal claimants. Against Śrīharṣa's fourteen, he has dwelt upon, with minor exceptions, twelve rulers, with special emphasis on their individual prowess and skill in war. The ruler of Mathurā is not one of the participants in the *svayaṁvara*, as described in the *Ys.* But Vasudeva, as a scion of Yadu house, with its principal seat at Mathurā, may be taken to represernt Pṛthu of the *Nc.* A reference to Govardhana is inherent in any account of the ruler of Mathurā. While the hill, in the *Nc.*, is averred to abound in peacocks who have rendered a stroll in Vṛndāvana safe by driving away the snakes from the region (*Nc.*,XI.107), in the Ys., with its caves emitting sweet smell of the floral beds, tinged with the odour of wine, it proclaims the dalliance of the heavenly nymphs there (*Ys.*,VI.25). Apart from resemblance with the parallel description, Vasudeva shares some of the traits of other rulers, described in the *Nc.*[35]

Avanti, Gauḍa, Kāśī, Ayodhyā, Kaliṅga (Mahendragiri), Kāñcī, Nepal, Malaya, Mithilā and Kīkaṭa are the other countries/kingdoms whose rulers from the warp and woof of the drapery of the *svayaṁvara*. As described in the *Ys.*, they have much in common with the corresponding rulers in the *Nc.* Avantirāja is a replica of the parallel description in the *Nc.*[36] The mass of gems emanating from the heads of the lordly elephants of the enemy, when struck with sword by the lord of Gauḍa, has been fancied, by both the poets, as drops of sweat of the majesty of the rival kings.[37] Emphasis on religious and spiritual significance of Kāśī forms the bed-rock of the description of its ruler, which the two poets have sought to underscore with an allusion to its fame as a gateway to salvation.[38] Both speak of the holy Ganges in the context (*Nc.*, XI.120 ; *Ys.*, IV.78). Similarities in the description of the other rulers are equally pronounced.[39]

Padmasundara has successfully resisted the temptation to chase the chimera, masquerading as canto XIII of the *Nc.*, wherein Śrīharṣa has described with gusto, in an unabashed demonstration of his pedantry to carry Śleṣa to the extreme, Nala and his spurious plurals. Having thus wisely stepped over the thirteenth canto of the *Nc.*, the author of the *Ys.* has utilized the earlier part of the sixth canto (I-43), Which, on its part, forms an adaptation of canto XIV of the *Nc.* shorn of its beginning and unnecessary details elsewhere, to give a brief description of Kubera and Vasudeva in succession. while the description of Kubera bears an unmistakable imprint of the *Meghadūta*,[40] that of Vasudeva, as hinted earlier, is deeply influenced by the parallel account of Pṛthu, the ruler of Mathurā, in the *Nc.* The characteristics that led Kanakā to distinguish Vasudeva from Kubera are similar to those that came handy to Damayantī to distinguish between the actual Nala and his feints, with the exception that they are short by two in the *Ys.*[41]

The seventh canto of the *Ys.*, which seeks to describe with enviable flair, the pre-marital adornments of the young couple, with almost prefect communion with the parallel description in the *Nc.* in the matter of style, language and the sequence of events described therein, is no more than a tailored version of Śrīharṣa's fifteenth canto. Here Padmasundara has dispensed with even his characteristic brevity, the two descriptions being identical in size.

After the bridegroom, following his selection in the *svayaṁvara*, had retired to his camp, the royal palace was astir with a plethora of activities, as a prologue to the impending marriage (*Nc.*,XV.12; *Ys.*,VIII.11-14). Kanakā, like Damayantī is given ceremonial bath, seated on a squarish seat, by elderly ladies with golden jars, which, eclipsed in beauty by her breasts, were reduced to the miserable plight of the bearers of water.[42] While Damayantī, dressed in a spotless apparel, after the bath, invited comparison with delightful evenings of autumn and rainy seasons (*Nc.*,XV.21), Kanakā surpasses her in charms to be a counterpart of *śaratpūrṇimā* (*Ys.*,VII.25). The drops of water, dripping from the hair of Damayanti have been happily postulated as pearls of fame, acquired by their victory over black chowries, the allies of darkness (*Nc.*,XV.23). To Padmasundara they appear to be the torrents of tears of the mass of darkness, thoroughly routed by Kanakā's moon-like face (*Ys.*,VII.26). However, both converge on the use of Utprekṣā, as the medium of expression. With their forms rendered all the more pretty, consequent on wiping water therefrom, they shone forth like golden images, radiating splendour all around (*Nc.*,XV.24;*Ys.*,VII.27). These preliminaries are followed by a poetic description of the adornment of their respective persons, which, for all purposes, is identical in imagery and language. The total effect of their embellishment has been highlighted, in both the poems, by a telling Mālopamā.[43] As was natural, the two brides were so eager to see their decorated persons in the mirror. On seeing her reflection, Damayantī was baffled as to the precise difference, if any, between the moon and her face (*Nc.*,XV.50). Kanakā, on the other hand, found in her face, the graces of the goddess of water (*Ys.*,VII.56). As an apogee of female charms, both Damayantī and Kanakā, on the conclusion of their adornments, seemed to heighten the charms of the ornaments and not *vice-versa* (*Nc.*,XV.27 ; *Ys.*,VII.30).

The adornment of Vasudeva (*Ys.*,VII.59-71) also accords well with Nala's toilet in the *Nc.*, (XV.57-71). To be sure, their embellishment was carried out by attendants, well-versed in the art.[44] Studded with gold and gems and emitting pleasing rays, the diadem on their head appeared to be the fugitive heavenly tree.[45] The *vīrapaṭṭikā* on Nala's forehead bore resemblance with the nimbus of the moon (*Nc.*,XV.61), in case of Vasudeva it looked like a royal parasol, held aloft (*Ys.*,III.63). With his form reflected in the gems and oraments he had put on, Vasudeva, like Nala, had little use for the mirror.[46] Their exceptional beauty was thus a cynosure of not only the spectators, but of the impatient ornaments on their body, as well (*Nc.*,XV.71 ; *Ys.*,VII.71).

The description of the impatience of the city-damsels to have a view of Vasudeva, on his way to the bride's house (*Ys.*,VII.73-86), is evidently based on the parallel portion in the *Nc.* (XV.73-92). The norm that Kālidāsa had set in the description, finds echo, with or without modification, in subsequent poets including Śrīharṣa. But unlike his predecessors, Śrīharṣa has appended the description of the onrush of the womenfolk to an account of their mutual conversation which serves to highlight the remarkable suitability of the couple. Padmasundra has borrowed this pattern also. While Śrīharṣa chose to describe the parleys in a longer metre like Śārdūlavikrīḍita, the author of the *Ys.*, wisely exploits the current metre for this part of the canto also. Like the rest of the canto, this description is strewn with a good number of Śrīharṣa's ideas and phrases.

The description of the marriage and the post-marital feast, interspersed, not unoften, with loose/obscene talk between the courtesans and Vasudeva's retinue, in Canto Eight of the *Ys.*, purports to be a blind reproduction of the sixteenth canto of the *Nc.* The canto, in its beginning, is marked by remarkable unanimity (*Nc.*,XVI. 1-5) ; *Ys.*,VIII.1-4). The marriage in the *Ys.* is meticulously solemnized, in emulation of the *Nc.*, in strict accordance with the holy Vedic rites, which, apart from other formalities, include the *darśana* of the Arundhatī and Dhruva stars to ensure conjugal fidelity and longevity to the couple.[47] As the poets would have us believe, the couple was united in wedlock by way of punishment, as it were. The hand of the groom was guilty of subduing his foes, that of the bride had the dubious distinction of robbing the lotus of its beauty. In an ideal state they could not but suffer bondage with a nuptial thread.[48] Equally happy is the description of the ceremony of *añcala-bandha*. In the *Nc.*, the ceremony is said to have been observed to express distrust of Nala, who was to escape subsequently the marital lock (*Nc.*,XV.37). It was intended in the *Ys.* to foil Vasudeva's possible flight in the face of Cupid's shafts (*Ys.*,VIII.19). The conception of fried rice, in the *lājāhoma* ceremony, as teeth of the god of fire, is indeed poetic.[49] But to construe the bride's hand placed on that of the groom as indicative of inverted cohabitation (*viparīta-rati*), is abhorrent to good taste (*Nc.*,XVI.15 ; *Ys.*,VIII.14). The fugitive streak of smoke, issuing from the ceremonial fire, is conceived, in the two poems, to serve multiple functions. It created the illusion of musk-paint on the cheeks, of collyrium in the eyes, of *karṇapūra* on the ears and of tresses on the forehead (*Nc.*,XVI.41 ; *Ys.*,VIII.24). The onrush of emotions is averred to have led to the appearance of the *sāttvika-bhāvas* in the couples, which in the *Nc.* (XVI.43-44) included perspiration, horripilation, trembling and paralysis (*stambha*), reduced to mere two, *sveda* and *aśru*, in the *Ys.* (VIII.25). Kanakā's wedding gifts, with chariots, ornaments and betel-boxes of various types (*Ys.*,VIII.15-17), belong to the realm of reality from which Śrīharṣa's description seems to be divorced (*Nc.*,XVI.24-34). Spittoon, however, is a conspicuous item in both, which incidentally corroborates the wide prevalence of the habit of chewing betel in that feudal society.[50]

The bride's brother joins the fun that follows the marriage. He treats the concourse to a light-hearted talk and arranges a fabulous feast wherein the courtesans are employed to serve food (*Nc.*,XVI.84,*Ys.*,VII.29). His invitation to the guests, in both the poems, is patently vulgar (*Nc.*,XVI.49 ; *Ys.*,VIII.30). The description of the feast is longer and detailed in the *Nc.*(XVI.49-111).

Padmasundara has curtailed it to reasonable proportions (*Ys.*,VIII.31-63). The frolic stirred by the courtesans in their conversation with Nala's friends, promptly reciprocated by the latter with added vigour, is more impertinent and pronounced in the *Nc.* Padmasundara was so completely under Śrīharṣa's spell that he has incorporated this repartee, not precluding the obscenities,[51] in the body of his poem, in almost identical language, throwing all inhibitions to the winds. These vulgarities make a mockery of Śrīharṣa's devotion to Vedānta and deal a rude blow to the puritanism of the Jaina monk.

Cantos Nine and Ten which describe respectively the six Indian seasons and the armed combat, forced upon Vasudeva by the rival claimants, repudiated in the *svayaṁvara* by Rohiṇī, the princess of Ariṣṭapura, have been flung, rather unimaginatively, at a place where they threaten to retard the already interrupted flow of theme. These are the only two cantos in the *Ys.*, which stand independent of its model,with the *Nc.* having nothing parallel to inspire them.

Braving religious restraints, Padmasundara has described, in the eleventh canto of his poem, sexual sports of the newly wed couple, Vasudeva and Kanakā. The description is invested with historical significance, as contrary to the widely held belief, Padmasundara emerges as the last poet to have depicted these post-marital enjoyments. In keeping with his objective to spin out a shorter version of Śrīharṣa's burly poem, he has abridged to half the corresponding canto in the *Nc.* The description of sexual orgy in both the Mahākāvyas is preceded by an account of the lordly mansion, where a suitable bed had been laid for their enjoyments. Padmasundara has additionally prefixed the description with a happy depiction of Vasudeva's entry into Mathurā, his metropolis (*Ys.*,XI.1-11).

Blissfully oblivious of the orgy that was to follow, both the poets have been at pains to emphasise their spiritual equipment that supposedly rendered their heroes impervious to all contaminations that flow from sexual indulgence.[52] The description of the sexual sports, which closely follows the eighteenth canto of the *Nc.*, itself a replica of Kālidāsa's corresponding description in Canto Eight of the *Kumārasambhava*, is characterised by a deep understanding of female psychology. Initially the coy heroine, overwhelmed with emotions, is frigidly cool to the advances of her spouse. Her bashfulness makes her irresponsive to all the winning overtures[53] and leads her to sleep with her face turned aside[54] and resist the clever attempts of the hero to tamper with her girdle.[55] Kisses and caresses form the core of the concerted approaches made to win her over (*Nc.*,XVIII.41 ; *Ys.*,XI.38). However, with the passage of time which inevitably results in wearing out the coyness of the girl, the intensity of her resistance weakens. Her bashfulness is then inturded upon by a keen desire for the proximity of her husband. The situation is exquisitely described in the two poems. The spate of emotions caused by an eagerness to undergo the experience did not permit her to withdraw her gaze from her consort ; the inherent modesty, on the other hand, desisted her from the venture. Her gaze was thus subjected to a torrid test (*Nc.*,XVIII.53 ; *Ys.*, XI.45). This game of revealing and concealing on her part invoked for her a comparison with *nalini* with partly blossomed and partly contracted flowers. (*Nc.*,XVIII.52; *Ys.*, XI.46). The watershed in the affair is represented by the eventual burst of passions which hitherto had their fire smothered by the elixir of shyness (*Nc.*,XVIII.57; *Ys.*,XI.50). Hereafter, her mischevious aversion caused by an occasional desire to tantalize the over-zealous hero apart, she is not only a willing partner in the act but can gleefully muster the temerity to initiate it. With such a responsive partner, the act, when carried out, leaves the youthful husband immersed in an ocean of bliss.[56] The bride had equal, rather greater, share in what follows the act. She now had the intemperance to confront her husband with the mirror to show him the mark she had planted on his lower lip, in the course of nocturnal orgy (*Nc.*,XVIII.125; *Ys.*,XI.75).

While Padmasundara has followed, rather reproduced in disguised terms, the relevant description in the *Nc.*, sans elaboration , it would have been beyond his ethos to succumb to Śrīharṣa's vulgarity in depicting with gusto even the process of ejaculation (*Nc.*,XVIII.114-116). And herein he stands closer to Kālidāsa. To Kālidāsa again he, like Śrīharṣa, is indebted for the Rathoddhatā metre he has employed to describe the orgy.

The *Nc.* closes with a gorgeous description of evening followed by twilight and moonrise, spread over the whole of twenty-second canto. It provides an apt backdrop to the sexual sports of the youthful couple and enables the poet to finish his poem, loaded with data sufficient to frustrate even a mature scholarship, on a happy note. Determined to put to shame even the science of grammar,[57] Śrīharṣa has brought into play, as evidenced by a series of learned forms, his undisputed skill in grammar and has indulged in worst monstrosities in the form of far-fetched fancies, not precluding abstruse mythological conceits[58], in the description of a phenomenon tender enough to prompt a well-equipped author into charming poetry. Padmasundara has meticulously adhered to Śrīharṣa's scheme of things in concluding his poem with the corresponding depiction to which he has appended, as a counterpart to Canto Nineteen of the *Nc.*, a description of day-break and sunrise.

The two poets have waxed eloquent in describing the fleeting phenomenon at dusk, with a host of images. Śrīharṣa has described with a Rūpaka the splendour of evening and the stars, emerging soon thereafter. The hunter of the evening has mercilessly slain the mighty tusker, that is, day. The thick blood welling from his massive body has assumed the form of the rediant glow that adorns the western horizon. And the stars with pleasing flicker are said to be the mass of pearls, emanating from his harrowed forehead. Padmasundara has fondly transplated the Rūpaka in his description, the replacement of the hunter by a lioness notwithstanding (*Nc.*,XXII.9; *Ys.*,XII.6). Padmasundara shares with Śrīharṣa the representation of sun as a mass of gold. Śrīharṣa has depicted the sky as a simpleton, who has disposed of the well-tested gold (sun) to secure a heap of cowries (stars). With trifle modification, Padmasundara has contrasted the knave sky with the astute occidental hill. The mount has appropriated from the sky the large ball of gold, with its purity tested in the fire of evening, and has cunningly sold to it, in return, crores of useless cowries, feigning as stars (*Nc.*,XXII.13 ; *Ys.*,XII.8).

Darkness and moonrise have evoked rich imagery on the part of Śrīharṣa. And Padmasundara has expectedly been quick to share it, as it suited his purpose. He is indebted to Śrīharṣa for the strained Rūpaka which seeks to envisage the sky as an inverted earthen vase and the sun as a mighty lamp, in describing the pitch darkness that has crippled with its density the human vision. The vase was imaginatively placed over the lamp to gather soot, a basic ingredient of collyrium. However, despite its vastness and stoutness, the vase has given way under the weight of the mountain of soot, spilling darkness everywhere.[59]

The rising moon, as described by Padmasundara, amounts to be, for all purposes, a replica of the parallel description in the *Nc.* In fact, his penchant for abstruse conceits has been more pronounced here. As remarked earlier, the description of day-break, positioned towards the close of the twelfth canto of the *Ys.*, is more of an epitome than an adaptation of the corresponding description in the nineteenth canto of the *Nc*. Here Śrīharṣa has embarked upon the dubious course of still more baffing conceits.[60] The conception of rays as a broom, which, in one sweep, chases away the pearls (stars), fallen from the pleasure-beds of the divine couples, offends good taste (*Nc.*,XIX.13; *Ys.*,XII.65). One of the choicest monstrosities is committed in representing the day-break as a fowler, who has let loose in the sky, the hawk of sun. Apprehensive of its swoop, the moon has sought the safety of the ocean for its protege, the hare *(śaśa)*. The crows of darkness have fled. The swarm of pigeons, that is stars, is resorting to various acrobatic flights to escape from the deadly clutches of the hawk (*Nc.*,XIX.12; *Ys.*,XII.78).

Padmasundara has thus done a good job in preparing a full-fledged adaptation of the *Nc*. In view of his religious predilection, one may be tempted to label it as a Jaina recension of Śrīharṣa's peom. There is, however, nothing in the poem to uphold such a claim. If anything it is the Hindu religious that breathes through the *Yadusundara*.

REFERENCES

1. Ed. Śivadatta Śarmā, Nirṇaya Sāgāra Press, Bombay, 1933
2. ग्रन्थग्रन्थिरिह क्वचित्क्वचिदपि न्यासि प्रयत्नान्मया
   प्राज्ञंमन्यमना हठेन पठिती मास्मिन्खलः खेलतु ।। *NC.*,XXII.153
3. Caṇḍikāprasāda Śukla : *Naiṣadha-pariśīlana*, Allahabad, 1960, pp.110-140
4. Ed. Haragovinda Dasa, Benaras city, 1918
5. KM 67
6. For the quantum of debt Devavimala owes to the author of the *Nc.*, see the paper on "Devavimala's indebtedness to Śrīharṣa," in the subsequent pages.
7. *Yadusundara* is known through its solitary *MS*. (No.2858, *Puṇya*), deposited with the L.D. Institute of Indology, Ahmedabad. Thanks are due to Sh. Dalasukhabhai Malavaṇiyā for kindly lending me the *MS*. It has been recently edited by D.P. Raval, L.D. Series, 105
8. Nathu Ram Premi : *Jaina Sāhitya Aura Itihāsa,* Bombay, 1956, pp.396-403
9. *Nc.*, II.78-86,95 ; *Ys.*, I.6,8
10. परिखावलयच्छलेन या न परेषां ग्रहणस्य गोचरः।
    फणिभाषितभाष्यफक्किकाविषमा कुण्डलनामवापिता ।। *Nc.*,II.95

11. *Nc.*, I.57-140 ; *Ys.*, I.45-70
12. अङ्गेन केनापि विजेतुमस्या गवेष्यते किं चलपत्रपत्रम् ।। *Nc.*, VII.91
13. त्वयाद्य तस्मिन्नपि दण्डधारिणा कथं न पत्या धरणी हृणीयते । *Nc.*, I.133
श्रुतं न चातिथ्यमिदं श्रुते क्वचित्प्रियातिथिर्यत्किल चारमर्हति । *Ys.*, II.56
14. *Nc.*, I.143 ; *Ys.*, II.56
15. *Nc.*, III.23-40; नृपेण तेनैव हि वीरप्रसूः प्रसूः। (*Ys.*,II.64) ;
जनमौलिशेखरो महद्गुणारामकरामणीयकः। (*Ys.*,II.65) ;
क्रियेत चेत्साधुविभक्तिचिन्ता व्यक्तिस्तदा सा प्रथमाभिधेया । (*Nc.*, III.23)
16. अजातपाणिग्रहणासि । Nc.,III.47; भवत्यथो यौवत-मौलिमण्डनम् । *Ys.*,II.65
17. नलेन भायाः शशिना निशेव । Nc.,III.117; राकाशशिनोर्युतिः शुभा । *Ys.*, II.68
18. ममाद्य तत्प्राप्तिरसुव्ययो वा हस्ते तवास्ते द्वयमेकशेषः। *Nc.*, III.82 ;
अलं विलम्ब्य त्वरितुं हि वेला । *Nc.*, III.91 ;
धीरं चेतो विधेहि करणीयमिदं मयैव । *Ys.*, II.76
19. मया यदालेख्यपटे व्यलेखि । *Ys.*, II.67 ;
उल्लिख्य हंसेन दले नलिन्याः। *Nc.*, VI.37
20. वेगाजगाम निषधाधिपराजधानीम् । *Nc.*, III.129
खगपुरमचिरात्प्राप विद्याधरेन्द्रः। *Ys.*, II.82
21. *Nc.*, III. 110-112 ; *Ys.*, III.33
22. निविशते यदि शूकशिखा पदे सृजति सा कियतीमिव न व्यथाम् ।।
मृदुतनोर्वितनोतु कथं न तामवनिभृत्तु निविश्य हृदि स्थितः।। *Nc.*, IV.11
23. तनुतनूरुहजव्यधतो व्यथा भवति तत्र विलासवती हृदि ।
यदुजभूभृदसौ स्थितिमाश्रयद्यदुत बाधत एव किमद्भुतम् ।। *Ys.*, III.12
24. स्मरहुताशनदीपितया तया बहु मुहुः सरसं सरसीरुहम् ।
श्रयितुमर्धपथे कृतमन्तरा श्वसितनिर्मितमर्मरमुज्झितम् । *Nc.*, IV.29
विरहदाहशमाय गृहाण या निजकरेण सरोजमुरोजयोः।
द्रुतमपि श्वसितोष्मसमीरणादजनि मुर्मुर इत्यजहात्ततः।। *Ys.*, III.21
25. निष्णातस्त्वमलमलं विलम्ब्य कार्ये---मादृशेऽस्यवन्ध्यः।*Ys.*, III.56
26. भूयादन्तर्धिसिद्धेरनुविहितभवच्चित्तता यत्र तत्र । *Nc.*, V.137
प्रत्यक्षा भवतु तनुः परैरलक्ष्या । *Ys.*, III.72
27. *Ys.*, III. 74-80
28. महाजनाचारपरम्परेदृशी स्वनाम नामाददते न साधवः। *Nc.*, IX.13
नामग्रहः स्वयमहो महतां विगानम् । *Ys.*, III.146
29. ---ससारमात्मना तनोषि संसारमसंशयं यतः। *Nc.*, IX.104
---मां दांतमेव किमु दातमलङ्करोषि । *Ys.*, III.190
30. न काकुवाक्यैरतिवाममङ्गजं द्विषत्सु याचे पवनं तु दक्षिणम् ।
दिशापि मद्भस्म किरत्वयं तया प्रियो यया वैरविधिर्वधावधिः। *Nc.*, IX.93
31. प्राणा वियोगदहनज्वलदूषरेऽस्मिन्मानसे धृतिरहो प्रतिभाति किं वः।
मत्प्राणनाथदिशमप्यनिला भवन्तः संश्लिष्य तन्मम जनुः फलिनं विदध्वम् ।।
Ys., III.178

Compare - –यह तन जारौं छ्वा है, कहौं कि पवन उडाय।
मकु तेहि मारग उडि परै, कंत धरि जेहि पाय।। (Jāyasī)

32. न भूता न च भाविनी च। *Nc.*, X.71
33. अभून्महेन्द्रादिचतुष्टयी सा चतुर्नली काचिदलीकरूपा। *Nc.*,X.18
द्विमूर्त्तिर्धनदप्रथामगाद्। *Ys.*, IV.8
34. *Nc.*, X.27,28,33,35,60 ; *Ys.*, IV. 5,10,13,14,20
35. *Nc.*, XII.9 : *Ys.*, VI.38 ; *Nc.*, XII.46 : *YS.*, VI.33
36. *Nc.*, XI. 88-93 ; *Ys.*, IV. 59-64
37. *Nc.*, XI.99 ; *Ys.*, IV.69
38. *Nc.*, XI.114-116 ; *Ys.*, IV. 75-77
39. *Nc.*, XII.33 : *Ys.*, V.39 ; *Nc.*, XII.71 : *Ys.*, V.42 etc.
40. *Ys.*, VI. 3-9 ; *Meghadūta*, II.9-12
41. *Nc.*, XIV. 18-22 ; *Ys.*, VI. 45-47
42. *Nc.*, XV.19-20 ; *Ys.*, VII. 23-24
43. विभूषणैस्तत्सुषमा महार्घताम् *Nc.*, XV.54
---विरराज भूषणगणैः सधर्मिणी। *Ys.*, VII.58
44. *Nc.*, XV.57 ; *Ys.*, VII.59
45. *Nc.*, XV.60 ; *Ys.*, VII.62
46. *Nc.*, XV.70 ; *Ys.*, VII.70
47. *Nc.*, XVI.37-38 ; *Ys.*, VIII.21-22
48. *Nc.*, XVI.4 ; *Ys.*, VIII.13
49. मुखेऽमराणामनले रदावलेरभाजि लाजैरनयोज्झितैर्द्युतिः। *Nc.*, XVI-40 ;
तस्याः करादिव हुताशनदैवतास्ये शुभ्रा रदाः शुशुभिरे मुहुरापतन्तः।
Ys., VIII.24
50. तमेकमाणिक्यमयं महोन्नतं पतद्ग्रहं ग्राहितवान्नलेन सः। *Nc.*, XVI.27 ;
माणिक्यरत्नमयमुद्यदखण्डचण्डरुग्मण्डलप्रतिममुद्धपतद्ग्रह सः। *Ys.*,VIII.17
51. स्वयं कथाभिर्वरपक्षसुभ्रुवः स्थिरीकृतायाः पदयुग्ममन्तरा।
परेण पश्चान्निभृतं न्यधापयद् ददर्श चादर्शतलं हसन्खलु।। *Nc.*, XVI.54 ;
अन्यः स्फुटस्फटिकचत्वरसंस्थिताया-
स्तन्व्या वराङ्गमनुबिम्बितमीक्षमाणः।
सामाजिकेषु नयनाञ्चलसूचनेन
सांहासिनं स्फुटमचीकरदच्छहासः।। *Ys.*, VIII.37
52. *Nc.*, XVIII.2 ; *Ys.*, XI.30
53. *Nc.*, XVIII.56 ; *Ys.*, XI.40, 49
54. *Nc.*, XVIII.35 ; *Ys.*, XI.34
55. *Nc.*, XVIII.46 ; *Ys.*, XI.40
56. *Nc.*, XVIII.124 ; *Ys.*, XI.67
57. भङ्क्तुं प्रभुर्व्याकरणस्य दर्पं पदप्रयोगाध्वनि लोक एषः। *Nc.*, XXII.84.
58. *Nc.*, XXII. 5,10,15,26,50,67

59. ऊर्ध्वार्पितन्युब्जकटाहकल्पे यद्व्योम्नि दीपेन दिनाधिपेन
न्यधायि तद्धूममिलद्गुरुत्वं भूमौ तमः कज्जलमस्खलत्किम् ।। *Nc.*, XXII.31.
उपरि लसति न्युब्जे शालाजिरप्रतिमेऽम्बरे
दिनमणिदशाकर्षज्ज्वालावलिभ्रमिमिर्धृता ।
विगलति गुरुभूय ध्वान्तं तदञ्जनपुञ्जता
प्रसृमरतरा व्यालुम्पन्ती जगज्जनितार्थताम् ।। *Ys.*, XII.15
60. *Nc.*, XIX. 7,10,61,62

A NOTE ON PADMASUNDARA'S OTHER WRITTINGS

As observed earlier, Padmasundara's versatility had unfolded itself in a wide range of writings that covered such diverse disciplines as poetry, poetics, philosophy, grammar, lexicon, music and astrology. Besides the *Yadusundara-mahākāvya* (*Ys*), exhaustively evaluated in the preceding pages, Padmasundara is known to have authored at least eighteen other works of uneven girth and worth. Most of them are, however, beyond access, strewn as they are in distant *Bhaṇḍāras*, in the form of manuscripts. That makes it difficult to subject them to a full-fledged evaluation and underscore Padmasundara's contribution to the enrichment of various aspects of Jaina philosophy and literature. Our sustained endeavours, spread over several years, have happily culminated in securing the quantum of data that should serve to adequately project the varied facets of his literary achievements.

Contrary to the *Ys*, which, as noted earlier, addresses itself to churn out an admirable counterpart to Śrīharṣa's stupendous tome, the *Naiṣadhacarita*, with trappings and mannerisms not preculding even those that offend his ethical susceptibilities ; Padmasundara's *Pārśvanāthakāvya* (*PK*) purports to be a versified biography of the twenty third pontiff of the Jaina faith. In accordance with the tenor of the vast majority of writings on Pārśvanātha, the *PK* is conceived as a cohesive entity, comprising two uneven segments that finally melt into one. The antagonism that Kamaṭha and Marubhūti, the two sons of Viśvabhūti, the Brāhmaṇa minister of the ruler of Potanā, come to nurse for each other, persists doggedly down the ages. That drives the soul of Kamaṭha to torture, in multiple ways, his younger brother's *Jīva* in the course of successive births.[1] The first two cantos, which essentially form a prologue to the poem proper, are devoted to recounting eight of Pārśva's earlier births. After undergoing grave hardships in a series of births, Marubhūti was born as a son (Pārśva) to Aśvasena, the famed king of Vārāṇasī. It is Pārśva's life-account that forms the contents of the succeeding five cantos and lends relevance to the nomenclature of the poem. Based on the Jaina Purāṇas, there can hardly be any dispute about the puranic character of the *PK*. The unending accounts of the earlier births, the active participation of the divine personages in the wide spectrum of the hero's chores and the host of eulogies (*stotras*) embedded in the body of the poem combine to impart it a puranic flavour, which is addedly strengthened by the divinity of Pārśva who is deservedly viewed as the highest *Brahman*.

One wonders what prompted Padmasundara to estimate his poem as a 'Jar brimming with erotics' (*kāvye'smin madhu-mādhurīpariṇate śṛṅgārabhṛṅgārake,* I.2). Even on close perusal of the *PK*, one hardly encounters any worthwhile depiction of the erotic sentiment. Whatever *śṛṅgāra* we have in the poem (I.25-26), is confined to the advances that the elephant (Marubhūti) makes to his mate, and, as such, it would be rated not as *Rasa*, but *Rasābhāsa*.

As a poem that accords pre-eminence to renunciation in preference to worldly pleasures, as symbolised by the hero himself, quietism unquestionably emerges as its principal sentiment. And there are events galore in the poem to occasion fulfilment of the *Śānta-rasa*. Its exuberance, however, is manifestly pronounced in Pārśva's pre-initation musings.[2] Of the subordinate rasas, Wondrous (VI.20-22) and Heroic sentiments merit notice by virtue of their intensity and profundity. The *Vīrarasa* may seem to be at odd with the character of the poem, dominated by quietism, but the battle that pits Pārśva against Kālayavana is the natural climax to a series of events and does not, therefore, appear to have been forcibly flung in the narrative. The description of the combat results in forceful emergance of the Heroic sentiment.[3]

Being primarily intended as a faithful biography of the Lord, attempted in a lucidly absorbing medium to earn righteousness in the process, the *PK* is not amenable to sustained poetic flourishes and other gimmicks that abound in the *Ys*. However, certain segments of the poem provide pleasing poetic flashes, though some of them the poet might have owed to his predecessors. The description of the physical charms of Prabhāvatī attracts attention on account of its winsome similes and imagaries.[4] Padmasundara is assuredly conscious of the role the figures of speech perform in enhancing the poetic beauties. To him, the *alaṅkāras* heighten the charms of the *Kāvya* as does youth impart captivating appearances to the body.[5] Elsewhere too he has rated his poem as *sālaṅkāra* (I-2 ; VII.64-70). Padmasundara has indeed fondly used some of the figures of speech to lend clarity to his ideas. He has decided predilection for the simile. He is at his best in mustering *upamānas* from nature. Arkakīrti's discs resulted in the annihilation of the rival forces as the mass of snow melts under the scorching rays of the sun.[6] Parisaṁkhyā, Virodhābhāsa, Tadguṇa, Kāvyaliṅga, Yamaka, Utprekṣā, are some of his other favourite *alaṅkāras.*

The well-known *Āmera Śāstra Bhaṇḍāra* of Jaipur has the proud distinction of owning an excellent MS of the *Pārśvanāthakāvya.* Though exceptionally chaste and calligra phically written, a part of the *praśati* therein is unfortunately lost. Consequently the genealogy of Chaudharī Chājū, a disciple (*āmnayī*) of Bhaṭṭāraka Kumārasenadeva of *Kāsṭhā-saṅgha* has broken off midway. The prose-*praśasti* quoted by Nāthū Rāma Premī from an unspecified MS reveals it beyond doubt that Chājū was a predcessor of Rāyamalla,[7] who had been instrumental in prompting the poet into writing the present poem, besides the *Rāyamallābhyudaya,*[7a] which, in essentials, adds up as a connected account of all the twenty-four Tīrthaṅkaras.[8] Rāyamalla was so intimately involved with the *PK* that Padmasundara has warmly acknowledged it at several places in the poem.[9] The *PK* was completed in V.S. 1615 (1558 A.D.) on *Mārgaśīrṣa Kṛṣṇā Caturdaśī,* corresponding to Monday.[10] As remarked earlier, the same year had witnessed the completion of *Rāyamallābhyudaya.*[11] Written again in deference to the wishes of Rāyamalla,[12] the *Bhaviṣyadatta-caritakathā*, a story in praise of *śruta pañcamī*, was completed in V.S. 1614 on *Kārttika śuklā Pāncamī.*[13]

The *Akbarasāhiśṛṅgāradarpaṇa* (*ASŚD*)[14] serves to establish Padmasundara as a literary critic of sorts. Composed of four chapters, designated, perhaps in imitation of Mammaṭa, as *Ullāsas*, the tract owes its genesis to the request of the poet's patron, the Mughal emperor Akbar[15], who was all too keen to acquire grounding in the *Rasa*-theory, as conceived and propounded in Indian aesthetics. The title is unmistakable in its import that the *ASŚD* primarily concerns itself with the erotic sentiment, which as treated in the volume, spills over more than three of its four chapters.

The *ASŚD* begins with a startling benediction. In a daring departure from the norm, it addresses itself to reverently extol *Rahamāna*, the supreme light, much in the manner of *Brahman*, to bestow beatitude on the nonarch.[16] The brief account of the Chugtai dynasty from Babur to the ruling sovereign Akbar forms, in essentials, a prelude to the exposition of the various sentiments that constitute the quintessence of Padmasundara's dissertation, because poetry shorn of *Rasa* is, to him, as insipid as food without salt and as colourless as night without moon (I.9). Padmasundara conforms to the tradition that favours nine sentiments[17] in preference to Bharata's eight. Unlike the authors of the *Daśarūupka* who discount the development of quietism in a visual art like drama,[18] a view implicitly blessed by Mammaṭa[19] and Viśvanātha,[20] no such distinction is sought to be drawn in the *ASŚD* between the two sets of sentiments. In view of his non-committal approach to the thorny issue[21] and the absence of *Vṛtti,* it is difficult to pinpoint with certitude the process of development of sentiment (*Rasa-niṣpatti*) to which Padmasundara subscribed.

The highest rung in the author's conception of *Rasas* is doubtless occupied by *Śṛṅgāra* which is precisely defined as *ratirūpā nu yā ceṣṭā dampatyoḥ sānurāgayoḥ* (I.16). while the two well-known divisions of *Śṛṅgāra*, the love in union (*sambhoga*) and separation (*vipralambha*) have met the approbattion of the noted poeticians, down the ages, Padmasundara, obviously in emulation of Rudraṭa (*KA*.xii.6), has split up *sambhoga* in two additional varieties, namely *Prakāśa-sambhoga* and *Pracchannasambhoga*. However, the illustrations worked up for the two are patently anomalous, rather self-contradictory. Verse Eighteen, though treated as an example of the former, actually illustrates *pracchannasambhoga* in so far as the union (*sambhoga*) is not explicitly described here, but only hinted. Curiously enough, the subsequent verse that seeks to describe the feelings of the heroine undergoing pangs of separation, is also taken to exemplify *prakāśa-sambhoga*. Verse Twenty, on the other hand, in view of the overt depiction of *sambhoga* therein should form an appropriate illustration of the former type, but is inexplicably projected to exemplify the second variety.

In Padmasundara's scheme of things, *Śṛṅgāra* is not confined to its traditional divisions or the myriad concomitant situations, it admits in its purview the various types of hero and heroine, the varied psychic strains that they undergo in separation and the stratagems they employ to win over their love. It is a sad commentary on Padmasundara's sense of proportion that he has recklessly squandered away almost half of his work on *nāyaka-nāyikā-bheda*, which seems to have been core to his conception of *Rasa*, blissfully forgetting that the ponderous classification hardly accords with the slimness of the volume. The four types of *nāyaka* viz. *anukūla, dakṣiṇa, śatha* and *dhṛṣṭa*, stem from the posture he chooses to strike *vis-a-vis* the heroine in the game of love, without much regard for his inherent merits that have been instrumental in prompting a distinct set of classification, mysteriously ignored by Padmasundara. While the four-fold classification, championed by him, is banal ; he seems to be especially indebted to Rudraṭa for their definitions as they occur in the *ASŚD*. The only difference is that while Rudraṭa has only defined the *nāyakas*, Padmasundara has illustrated them, as well.[22]

The classification of the heroine, not unlike the *nāyak-bheda*, substantially follows the corresponding piece in the *Sāhityadarpaṇa*. While *svakīyā* whith her three subtypes (*mugdhā, madhyā, pragalbhā*) has been disposed of in the first chapter, with appropriate definitions and illustrations, *parakīyā* and *sāmānyā* (*paṇāṅgaṅā*) have been relegated to the subsequent *Ullāsa* which also claims the eight types based on her emotional and physical state (*avasthābheda*). *Svādhīnapatikā, vāsakasajjā, vipralabdhā, khaṇḍitā, abhisarkā* and *proṣitabhartṛkā* are common to the two lists, the *abhisandhitā* and *utkā* in the *ASŚD* correspond to Viśvanātha's *kalahāntaritā* and *virahotkaṇṭhitā* respectively.[23] With further division into *uttamā, madhyamā* and *adhamā*, the types of *nāyikā* touch the staggering 384 figure (II.64). This seems to have been the norm because Viśvanātha also admits 384 kinds of the heroine (*SD*.III.87). In imitation of Viśvanātha, the author of *ASŚD* also does not rule out further - almost infinite-classification (*ASŚD*.II.71; *SD*.III.88). Viśvanātha's classification is more scientific and precise. Padmasundara has been prolix, rather dreary, in detailing the various characteristics of the heroines, though, in essentials, the two do not differ much. The banalities might appear digressive in the midst of serious exposition of *Rasa*, but this has been the wont of some of the celebrated poeticians, as well. Padmasundara has smugly emulated them without pausing to ponder whether he could afford or not the luxury within the limitations of his work.

It is in the third chapter that Padmasundara has picked up the thread of *Śṛṅgārarasa* to detail the divisions of *Vipralambha*, the second major variety of the erotic sentiment. Its classification into *pūrvarāga, māna, pravāsa* and *karuṇātmaka* (*ASŚD*.III.1), he owes to Rudraṭa (*KA*.XIV.1) and Viśvanātha (*SD*.III.187) who have likewise favoured the four-fold division. The first three have been appropriately defined and illustrated in the chapter. While the definitions largely represent a doctored version of Rudraṭa (*KA*.XIV.2-33), it is Viśvanātha's treatment thereof that is more crisp. Against the four espoused by Rudraṭa and Viśvanātha, Mammaṭa has admitted five kinds of *vipralambha: aparastu-abhilāṣa-viraherṣyā-pravāsa-śāpa-hetukaḥ.*[24] While Mammaṭa's *abhilāṣa* is but another name of *pūrvarāga*, *īrṣyā*, is here synonymous with *māna*. Unlike Viśvanātha but in keeping with Rudraṭa, Padmasundara has sought to categorise *māna* as severe (*guru*), moderate (*madhyama*) and commonplace (*adhama*), depending on the quantum of guilt of the hero (*ASŚD*.III.47-52). He has omitted *praṇayamāna*, which according to the author of the *SD*, is one of its major divisions.[25] Of the six devices employed to drive away the heroine's wrath (*māna*),[26] which again owe themselves to Rudraṭa (*KA*.XIV.27-31), Padmasundara has *prasaṅgavibhraṁśa* in place of Viśvanātha's *rasāntara* (*SD*.III.201-203). The chapter also addresses itself to detail, with apt illustrations and definitions, the ten psychic strains (*kāmadaśā*) that the lovers supposedly suffer in separation (*ASŚD*.III.7-13). The exposition is manifestly based on the *SD* (III.190-192). Both concur in the belief that despite its inclusion in the *kāmadaśās*, the description of death (*maraṇa*), in view of the discordant note it strikes,is to be avoided. However, it causes no offence if the revival of the deceased is somehow assured or it is desired under compelling reasons (*ASŚD*.III.28-29;*SD*.III.193-194). Padmasundara's definition of *Śṛngārābhāsa* is also heavily influenced by Rudraṭa.[27] Though somewhat bland, it does not offend the norm of *Rasābhāsa* which is defined by Mammaṭa as *tadābhasā anaucitya-pravartitāḥ* (*KP*.IV.36). Advances to an indifferent person doubltless offend propriety.

The fourth *Ullāsa* is marked in its inception by the definition of *Karuṇavipralambha*, which, though based on Rudraṭa and Viśvanātha, is tarnished, unlike them, by a naggng ambiguity. By admitting *vipralambha* tampered with pathos as the fourth variety, Padmasundara and his mentors have stirred an unnecessary controversy. The wailings of the hapless lover on the death or near death of his/her spouse come within the ambit of *Karuṇavipralambha*. (*ASŚD*.IV.1;*KA*. XIV.34). Viśvanātha would have it, provided their reunion is somehow assured, even by divine intervention (*SD*.III.209). *Mahāsvetā's* wailings for Puṇḍarīka, whose revival is prognosticated by an ethereal voice is the case in point. Her lamentations prior to the assurance would naturally fall in the purview of *Karuṇa-rasa*. Thereafter they belong to *Karuṇa-vipralambha*, because now she is convinced of reunion with her lover and comes to entertain *rati* for him.[28] In view of the impossibility of such supernatural occurrences in practical life, Mammaṭa and others of his ilk do not favour the *Karuṇa-vipralambha*. If ever such reunion takes place, it, by reason of its sheer abruptness, culminates in the development of *Adbhuta-rasa*. To Padmasundara the treatment of *Śṛṅgāra* constitute the life-breath of poetry, which, if shorn of the sentiment, is lifeless like a straw-man.[29]

With *Śṛṅgāra* accorded high priority, Padmasundara was left with mere eighty verses to bundle out the other sentiments, besides the *Rītis* (*Vṛttis*) with which the work closes. Despite the constraints, the treatment of the remaining sentiments is not 'incidental and cursory'. All the *Rasas* are neatly defined and appropriately illustrated with pointed reference to their permanent and accessory feelings, besides the *anubhāvas*. Some of the examples are pleasingly lucid and forceful, much different from what we encounter in standard works with respect to certain *Rasas*. The verses that exemplify *Hāsya* and *Karuṇa* are enlivened by freshness (*ASŚD*.IV.24,30), but the illustration of the *Śānta-rasa* is marred by imprecision (*ASSD*.IV.53). Rudraṭa has shunned to exemplify the various sentiments, but his definitions form the source of Padmasundara's exposition. While he concurs with Rudraṭa (*KA*.XV.1) in classifying *Vīra-rasa* into *dayāvīra, dānavīra* and *yuddhavīra;* he has addedly categorised it as *uttama, madhyama* and *adhama* and illustrated the three types with precise examples (IV.37-39). The three types of *Hāsya* also he owes to the author of the *KA* (*ASŚD*.IV.23-28, *KA*.XV.12). The rival sentiments and the relationship that subsists between different *Rasas* has been duly noticed (*ASSD*.IV.56-57). With poetic blemishes which are only illustrated, not defined (*ASSD*.IV.93-98), preceded by an account of the four *Rītis*, neatly explained and exemplified, the work comes to a close. The way Padmasundara has sought to illustrate certain sentiments with verses addressed to his patron, Akbar, projects him in poor light. His monk-hood notwithstanding, therein he sounds to be a typical court-poet out to humour the nonarch at the slightest pretext.

While the vaunt aired in the concluding verse that the *ASŚD* forms an unfailing guide to the proper understanding of the *Rasa*-theory and gaining expertise in poetry, may appear exaggerated, the tract can safely be depended upon to acquire respectable knowledge of the concept of *Rasa*, as it has been propounded by Padmasundara.

The *Jñānacandrodaya-nāṭaka* (*JC*)[30] unfolds a different facet of Padmasundara's equipment. Though entitled *nāṭaka* and divided into five acts, the *JC* is not a drama at all. It embodies in 398 verses, in different metres, the essence of Jaina philosophy, as it is propounded by Kundakunda in his monumental works, especially the *Pravacanasāra*. Notwithstanding the sectarian disparities, Padmasundara follows the great *Ācārya* and his equally brilliant scholiast, Amṛtacandra (11th century A.D.), with zealous tenacity. While some of the verses practically add up to Sanskrit rendering of the *gāthās* of the *Pravacanasāra*, some others are but versified version of the prose passages in *Ātmakhyāti* and *Tattvadīpikā*, Amṛtacandra's commentaries on *Samayasāra* and *Pravacanasāra* respectively. Otherwise also the work abounds in verbal borrowings from Kundakunda.[31]

The sister volume *Pramāṇasundara* (*PS*)[32] is an 'important contribution to the science of *pramāṇas*'. Divided into four sections, the tract deals with the definition and classification of 'proof', much in pursunance of the Jaina tradition. While the first section concerns itself with defining and discussing *pramāṇa*, the following sections successively treat *pratyakṣa, anumāna* and *āgama*, with their divisions and subdivisions, refuting in the process, the contrary views on the respective issues. In the brilliant exposition of his definition of proof- *samyaksvaparavyavasāyātmakam jñānam pramāṇam pramāṇatvānyathānupapatteḥ*- Padmasundara has been at pains to discard the various aspects of the views favoured by earlier thinkers including the Buddhists, Naiyāyikas, Mimāṁsakas, Sāṅkhyas and the Vedāntins.[33] He takes *arthāpatti* and *abhāva* to be the different forms of *anumāna*.[34] The attempt to bring *smaraṇa, pratyabhijñā* and *tarka* under the unbrella of *anumāna*[35] is evidently at odd with the Jaina tradition. He has not been indifferent either to the types of *hetu* or to the pseudo-*hetus* (*hetvābhāsas*). The validity of *āgama* can be disputed neither by *pratyakṣa* nor by *anumāna* etc.

The *Sundaraprakāśaśabdārṇava* (*SPS*) is known through its MS (No.448), deposited with the Jaina Jñān Mandira, Chāṇī (Gujarat). The *SPS* is divided into five *taraṅgas* and consists of 2783 verses. Apparently a lexicon, it is distinquished by grammatical derivation of the words included therein, in consonance with the *Sārasvata*-school of grammar. It may thus justifiably be claimed to deal with both lexicon and grammar. It is perhaps to underline its grammatical aspect that the author has termed it as *śabdānuśāsana : yathāmati mayā proktam kiñcinchabdānuśāsanam* (V.63).[36]

Padmasundara's equipment in grammar is obvious from the *Śārasvata-rūpamālā* as well. As evidenced by its codex (No.403 Puṇya), preserved in the L.D. Institute of Indology, Ahmedabad, it treats in two cantos consisting of 153 verses, the verbal forms in accordance with the *Śarasvata*-school.[37]

The Anup Sanskrit Library, Bikaner retains MSS of some of Padmasundara's other works viz. *Hāyanasundara* (No.5272), *Paramatavyavacchedasyādvādasundaradvātriṁśikā* (No.9746), *Rājapraśnīyanāṭyapadabhañjikā* besides a defective MS of *Pramāṇasundara* (No.8432), analysed earlier. The *Hāyanasundara* is noticed without mention of its author by Aufrecht in his Catalogous Catalogorum (I.765). It seeks to describe, in eight *Prakaraṇas*, the position and conjunction of the seven auspicious planets and the influence they exercise on human destiny (I.1).

Saḍabhāṣāgarbhita-nemistavagāthā, *Varamaṅgalikāstotra*, *Jambucaritra* and *prajñāpanāsūtrāvacūri* are other known works of Padmasundara. Of these, the *Jambucaritra* purports to be a biography in Prakrit verse of Jambusvāmī, the last *Kevalī* of the Jaina tradition. While the *gāthās* are in Prakrit, the *stabaka* is couched in Gujarati. A MS (No.5116) of the poem is preserved with the L.D. Institute of Indology, Ahmedabad. It is known to have been written at Kanpur, in V.S. 1868 (1811 A.D.). The L.D. Institute is in possession of a MS (No.7400) of *Prajñāpanāsūtrāvacūri* as well. Written in V.S. 1668 (1611 A.D.) at Agra, during the regime of the Mughal emperor Jahangir,[39] it adds up to be a brief gloss (*avacūri*) on Śyāmācārya's *Prajñapanāsūtra*, a Jaina canonical work. On its own admission, it closely follows Malayagiri's commentary on the *sūtra*.[40]

The Kuśalopadeśa was published in Sambodhi (Nos.2-3) but is scarce to obtain.

Thus Padmasundara is the undisputed author of as many as nineteen works. Of these the *Akbarasāhiśṛṅgāradarpaṇa, Yadusundara, Pārśvanāthakāvya, Kuśalopadeśa, Jñānacandrdayanāṭaka* and *Pramānasundara* have been published. Others are preserved in the form of MSS. *Bhāratīstvana*[41] and *Mālavarāgajinadhruvapada*[42] are known from the auto-commentary on Devavimala's *Hīrasaubhāgya*.

NOTES AND REFERENCES

1. Hemavijaya's *Pārśvanāthacarita*, at places (I.91), makes Marubhūti (also called Amarabhūti), the elder brother of Kamaṭha.

2. सर्वे भोगास्तावदापातरम्याः पर्यन्ते ते स्वान्तसन्तापमूलम् ।
तद्धानाय ज्ञानियो द्राग्यतन्ते भोगान् रोगानेव मत्वा प्रवाचः ।। *PK*.V.74
तस्माद् ब्रह्माद्वैतमव्यक्तलिंग ज्ञानानन्तज्योतिरुद्योतमानम् ।
नित्यानन्दं चिद्गुणोज्जृम्भमाणं स्वात्मारामं शर्म्मधाम प्रपद्ये ।। *PK*.V.78
3. *PK*. IV. 182-183
4. विसारितारद्युतिहारहारिणौ स्तनौ नु तस्याः सुषमामवापतुः ।
सुरापगातीरयुगाश्रितस्य तौ रथांगकुंकुमांचितौ ।। *PK*.V.19
इयं सुकेश्याः कचपाशमंजरी विधुंतुदस्य प्रतिमामुपेयुषी ।
मुखेन्दुबिम्बग्रसनैकलिप्सया तमोऽञ्जनस्निग्धविभा विभाव्यते ।। *PK*.V.34
5. सालंकारः कवेः काव्यसन्दर्भ इव स व्याभात् । *PK*.III.156
6. चक्रैरस्य द्विषच्चक्रं क्षयमापादितं क्षणात् ।
मार्तण्डकिरणैस्तीक्ष्णैर्हिमानीपटलं यथा ।। *PK*.IV.160
7. *Jaina Sāhitya Aura Itīhāsa (JSI)*, op.cit., p.402-403
7a. काव्यं कारितवानपूर्ववद्यो रायमल्लोदयम् ।
जीयादारविचन्द्रतारकमयं श्रीरायमल्लाह्वयः ।।
Rāyamallābhudaya, Praśasti,24. Quoted in *JSI*, p.401
8. चतुर्विंशतितीर्थेशकल्याणचरिताद्भुतम् ।
प्रारम्यते महाकाव्यं महापुरुषसंश्रितम् ।
Ibid, *Praśasti,*10. Quoted in *JSI*, p.399
9. शुश्रूषुस्तदकारयत्सुकवितः श्रीपार्श्वनाथाह्वयम् ।
काव्यं नव्यमिदं श्रुतिप्रमददं श्रीरायमल्लाह्वयः । *PK*.I.3
10. अब्दे विक्रमराज्यतः शरकलाभृत्तर्कभूसंमिते ।
मार्गे मास्यसिते चतुर्दशदिने सत्सौम्यवारांकिते ।
काव्यं कारितवानतीवसरसं श्रीपार्श्वनाथायह्वयं
सोऽयं नन्दतु नन्दनैः परिवृतः श्रीरायमल्लस्तदा ।। Ibid.,VII.74
The *PK* has been recently edited by Mrs. Kṣamā Munshī, Sambodhi, Vol.X.Nos.1-4 and Vol.Xi.Nos.1-4. The edition displays substantial divergences from the MS that forms the basis of our study. It is not only shorn of Praśasti, but also makes no reference to Rāyamalla who was the driving force behind the poem.
11. वर्षे विक्रमराज्यतः शरकलाभृत्तकर्मभूसंमिते ।
ज्येष्ठे मासि सिते च पंचमदिनेऽर्हद्वृत्तसन्दर्भितम् ।।
Rāyamallābhyadaya, Praśasti, 24. Quoted in *JSI*, p.401
12. येन श्रुतपंचम्याः फलसन्दर्भेण रम्यं ।
सुभविष्यदत्तचरितं कारितमात्मश्रवणहेतोः ।।
21, Quoted in *JSI*, P.400, F.N.2
13. *JSI*, p.396
14. Ed. K. Mādhava Kṛṣṇa Sarma, The Ganga Oriential Series, No.1, Bikaner, 1940.
Thanks are due to my friend, Dr. P.D. Sharma, Ex-Professor

of Sanskrit, Dungar College, Bikaner, for the pains he took in securing for me a copy of the book which otherwise is a rarity.

15. सोऽयं काव्यं कारयामास सम्राण्नानाश्रृङ्गारादिभावै रसाढ्यम् ।। *ASŚD*, I.8.
16. यत्पारेतमसः स्थितं च रहमानित्याह्वयं तत्परं
ज्योतिः साहिशरोमणे अकबर त्वां सर्वदैवावतात् । *ASŚD*, I.1
17. The *Anuyogadvārasūtra* (Bombay, 1968) is the earliest text to explicitly enumerate the nine sentiments by name. Compare नव कव्वरसा पणत्ता, p.121-124.
18. शममपि केचित्प्राहुः पुष्टिर्नाट्येषु नैतस्य ।
Daśarūpaka, Nirṇaya sāgara Press, Bombay, 1928, IV.35.
19. ---अष्टौ नाट्ये रसाः स्मृताः। *KP*.IV.29
20. ---इत्यष्टौ रसाः शान्तस्तथा मतः। *SD*.,III.182
21. विभावैरनुभावैश्च सात्विकैर्व्यभिचारिभिः।
आरोप्यमाण उत्कर्षं स्थायी भावो भवेद्रसः।।*ASŚD*, I.13
22. Rāmadeva Śukhla (ed.), *Kāvyālaṅkāra* (KA), Chowkhamba Vidya Bhavana, Vārāṇasī, 1966, XII.9-12; *ASŚD*, II.23-31
23. *Sāhityadarpaṇa* (*SD*), Lucknow, V.S.1978, III.72-73 ; *ASŚD*, II.41-58
24. Ācārya Viśveśvara (ed.), *Kāvyaprakāśa,* Jñānamaṇḍala Limited, Vārāṇasī, 1960, p.123.
25. मान कोपः स तु द्वेधा प्रणयेर्ष्यासमुद्भवः। *SD*.,III.198
26. *ASŚD*., III.62-79
27. रक्तापरक्तौ तु श्रृङ्गाराभासता मता । *ASŚD*., III.32
cf. श्रृङ्गाराभासः स तु यत्र विरक्तेऽपि जायते रक्तः ।
एकस्मिन्नपरोऽसौ नाभाष्येषु प्रयोक्तव्यः ।। *KA*.,XIV.36
28. Compare *ASŚD* ; IV.6-8
29. एतेन हीनं किं च कवेः कवित्वं
नैरस्यमेव तृणपुरुषवद् भजेत ।। *ASŚD*., IV.20
30. Ed. Nagin J.Shah, Sambodhi, Vol.VI, Nos.1-2, 1977
31. *Jñānacandrodaya-nāṭaka* (*Jc*), op.cit., Introduction, 2-3 and footnotes to the text.
32. Nagin J.Shah (ed.), Jaina Philosophical Tracts, L.D.Series 41, p.127-160
33. *Pramāṇasundara*, op. cit., p.127
34. Ibid., p.131
35. Ibid., p.130
36.- 37. Sambodhi, Vol.XII,Nos. 1-4 (Appendix 4), p.8-11.
38. Ibid., p.13.
39. सम्वत् १६६८ वर्षे---श्री आगरामहानगरे पातिसाहि श्री जहाँगीर
विजयराज्ये--लिखापितोऽयं प्रज्ञापनाग्रन्थः ।

The scribe's insertion at the end. Quoted in Sambodhi, Vol.XII.Nos. 1-4, p.11-12.

40. श्रीमलयगिरिकृतायाः प्रज्ञापनावृत्तितोऽवचूरिरियम्।
श्रीपद्मसुन्दरेण व्यरचि यथार्था सुसंक्षिप्य।। Quoted Ibid, p.12

41. *Hīrasaubhāgya*, XIV.302. Auto-Commentary : यथा पद्म-सुन्दरकृतभारतीस्तवे वारं वारं तारतरस्वरनिर्जितगगनतरङ्गा इति

42. Ibid., XI.135. Auto-Commentary :
'जिनवचनपद्धतिरुक्तिचंगिममालिनी ' इति पद्मसुन्दरकृतमालवरागध्रुवपदे ।

ŚIṢYAHITAIṢIṆĪ

A JAINA COMMENTARY ON MEGHADŪTA

The recent edition of Lakṣmīnivāsa's *Śiṣyahitaiṣiṇī* [1] marks the latest addition to the plethora of commentaries on *Meghadūta* that attest to its wide currency and popularity, down the years. As evidenced by the pre-colophon verses, Lakṣmīnivāsa was a jaina monk of the rank of *Vācaka*. A pupil of Ratnaprabha Sūri of the *Bṛhadgaccha*, he is recorded to have completed the commentary in V.S. 1514 (1457 A.D.) at Mahimanagar. The nomenclature of the commentary would suggest that the author undertook to resolve Kālidāsa's text with a view to serve the needs of the pupils, ordianed in his monastic order. Howsoever worthy the aim, Laksmīnivāsa does not measure well up to the task and his gloss miserably fails to meet the intended purpose. In all essentials, he seems to have been an ill-equipped person who undeservedly clothed himself in the robe of a scholiast. His poor equipment is acutely evident from the fact that contrary to even the most aberratious commentator, he has neither referred to nor quoted from any work, known or unknown, on rhetorics, erotics, grammar, lexicography etc., nor has he drawn upon the vast commentatorial literature, which combine to make it rather impossible to unravel the poetic beauties of the text or to determine the relevance of a corpus of tricky phrases or to underscore the validity of defiant variants. Of the four *sūtras* he has quoted in the body of his commentary, two are mauled beyond recognition, all the four being so banal as not to have been lost to even a novice. Thus incapable of whipping to advantage the available trappings, Laksmīnivāsa has sunk into cussed isolation, much in the manner of a *kūpamaṇḍūka*. His *Tīkā* is thus reduced to a bare paraphrase of the text, with the author first dealing with the principal clause, followed by other dependent phrases, against the *anvayamukhapaddhati* of Mallinātha. It would be rather a misnomer to label the *Śiṣyahitaiṣinī* as commentary. It adds up to a brief gloss (*mitā pañjikā*), aimed at extorting something out of a text that is scarcely amenable to such a poor trickery.

The gloss on the very first verse serves to bring into relief his incompetence as a commentator. In a bid to parade his acquaintance with Indian topography, Laksmīnivāsa has landed himself into absurdity by identifying Rāmagiri with Daṇḍakāraṇya. Be that as it may, most of Kālidāsa's commentators including the famed Mallinātha have grievously fumbled in locating the hill, with some of the enlightened editors not discounting the possibility of its having been as "imaginary as the mythical Alakā".[2] Mallinātha identified it with Citrakūṭa, which, though erroneous, is not as offensive as Mālyavān that Divākara had the temerity to treat but another appellation of Rāmagiri on the specious plea that the Yakṣa took up abode there in the hope that like Rāma he too would be united with his spouse. Little did Divākara realise that his contention runs counter to the adjectival clause *Janakatanayāsnānapuṇyodakeṣu*, subsequently employed in the verse and also to the temporary nature of Yakṣa's exile. Kṛṣṇapati's defence of the identification with a jibe at Śāśvata, who disputed it, albeit weakly,[3] is misplaced. Bharatamallika's observation "*kintu tatra mālyavati sasītasya rāmasyānavasthānāt janaka-tanayāsnānapuṇyodakeṣviti viśeṣaṇam na ghaṭate*",[4] on the other hand, brings out convincingly the untenability of Divākara's identification. It is a tribute to Wilson's acumen that his conjectural identification of Rāmagiri with Rāmaṭeka, about 24 miles to the north of Nagpur, is upheld, according to V.V. Mirashi, by an inscription of Pravarasena II.[5] In view of this overwhelming evidence to the contrary, Laksmīnivāsa's equating of Rāmagiri with Daṇḍakāraṇya smacks of naivete.

Laksmīnivāsa's paraphrase of *varṣabhogyeṇa* in the same verse as *varṣam yāvad bhujyate varṣabhogyastena*, is as it should be. However, the alternative interpretation needlessly offered by him (*varṣam bhāratam kṣetram tatra bhujyate...*), is childish to the extreme. The Yakṣa could not have been imprecated to suffer exile anywhere else but *Bhāratavarṣa*. Or had the Jaina monk discovered Rāmagiri in some foreign land as well ?

Verse Five is meant to underline the wide divergence between an efficient errand-bearer and the cloud, chosen by Yakṣa for the purpose; and also the latter's predicament at the moment that led him to offer an apology for the defective nature of the device[6] which incidentally evoked only reserved acceptance from such an unsparing critic as Bhāmaha.[7] The phrase *paṭukaraṇaiḥ*, used in the verse, though unmistakable in its import, has been invested with a veneer of ambiguity by the commentator with his imprecise gloss thereon: *paṭukaraṇaiḥ sakalendriyaiḥ....na durbuddhibhiḥ.* Though Laksmīnivāsa's *sakalendriyaiḥ* may ultimately melt into Mallināthā's *samarthendriyaiḥ,*[8] it misses the fact that even an able-bodied person may make a hopeless courier. It is not the physical stoutness (*sakalendriyatā*) of the messenger but his competence (*samarthendriyatā*) that is sought to be emphasised here. Mallinātha's paraphrase is intended to focus on this aspect of the messenger's equipment. Kṛṣṇapati also interprets the clause in much the similar way.[9] If, however, *sakalendriyaiḥ* is meant to contrast with *durbuddhibhhiḥ* ,with its implication as *subuddhibhiḥ,* then no offence would possibly be taken against it.

Verse Ten underscores the efficacy of hope in sustaining a love-lorn heart that is otherwise susceptible to a variety of strains not precluding its ultimate breakdown. The commentator, as is evident from his gloss, seems to read *sadyaḥpātapraṇayi* in preference to admittedly the superior reading *sadyaḥpāti praṇayi-hṛdayam.* While Laksmīnivāsa is entitled to his judgement in opting for the variant in the text, his interpretation thereof is outrageous. Not only is it marred by wilful transposition of a word that actually belongs to the subsequent compoud, it is also an exercise in futility in as much as *sadyaḥpāti* conveys the intended sense better than the grotesque *sadyaḥpāta-praṇayi.* It addedly demonstrates the commentator's inability to discern the relevance of *praṇayi-hṛdayam,* in the context. The poet evidently means to stress the fact that the emotionally surcharged heart of a lover is more disposed to suffering, in case there is no hope to sustain it.

Laksmīnivāsa's rendering of *māla*, that occurs in Verse Sixteen, as a cluster of forests between villages (*grāmantrāṭavīnam saṁgrah*) lacks sanction and is at odd with the context. In giving a multeity of meanings,[10] Kṛṣṇapati also seems to be juggling with the word. Mallinātha treats it as a name of an elevated plateau that resembled an hillock in its shape and backs up his interpretation with the lexicon *Utpalamālā* (*mālamunnatabhūtalam*). Sir A. Stein has rendered it as "an alluvial plateau", which is not far removed from Mallinātha's paraphrase. *Māla* doubtless seems to have been a hill-like elevation. The cloud is required to mount it which by itself implies it to have been a place higher than the flat ground. In view of it, Laksmīnivāsa's rendering of the term seems to be no better than a thoughtless comment.

A simple word like *pūrṇatā* in Verse Twenty (*pūrṇatā gauravāya*) also poses difficulty to our commentator. His interpretation of the term as *dhanāḍhyatā* is shorn of aptness. He is surprisingly supported by Kṛṣṇapati who also paraphrases it as *dhanavattā*. In confining *pūrṇatā* to affluence, both the commentators miss the true significance of the Arthāntaranyāsa in the verse. Since it is projected as a counterpoise to *riktatā*, it surely denotes much more than riches. Emptiness accounts for lightness. Fullness, on the other hand, imparts heaviness. It is fullness or *sārvattā*, as Mallinatha puts it, that is the sense intended here.

Verse 22 (*ambhobindugrahaṇa-caturān* etc.), believed to be spurious but commented upon by Mallinātha, again brings out the commentator's lack of critical acumen and his garbled understanding of the text. It is patently absurd on his part to treat *āliṅgitāni* in the second hemistich as an object to *mānayiṣyanti* and tag on *tvām* to *āsādya*, while the only sensible *anvaya*, as Mallinātha does it, could have been as follows: *āliṅgitāni āsādya tvām mānayiṣyanti*. Since the cloud with its rumblings had been instrumental in locking the Siddha ladies into the embraces of their lovers, it was he who deserved their (lovers') gratitude. And as their gratefulness had emanated from the pleasure of embraces imparted by their lasses, the gerundive form *āsādya* should be taken to qualify *āliṅgitāni* and not *tvām* which undoubtedly forms an object to *mānayiṣyanti*.

Mallinātha is doubtless on sound footing in treating *tīropāntastanitasubhagam* (v.25) as an adverb. His interpretation of the clause as *tīropānte taṭaprānte yat stanitam garjitam tena subhagam yathā tathā pāsyasi*, is unblemished. The cloud would enjoy the water of the Vetravati river, while making pleasantly sweet rumblings on its bank. Laksmīnivāsa takes it to be an adjective that qualfies *payaḥ* in the last *pāda*. While it is absurd to tag it to a *viśeṣya* to which it does not legitimately belong, his breath-taking rendering of *stanitena* as *vihagakūjitena* is simply outrageous. It is difficult to comprehend how the chirpings of the birds on the bank could have added charm to the water of the river. Curiously enough, he is supported in his contention by such an enlightened commentator as Kṛṣṇapati,[11] though the latter has been chary not to fall victim to the howler involved in Laksmīnivāsa's wholly unwarranted interpretation of *stanitena*. Perhaps to obviate the anomaly inherent in such a prose-order, he alternatively takes it to be an adverb. And that is the only sensible way to deal with the phrase.

Ratnacchāyā-khacita-valibhiḥ, that forms part of the first hemistich of Verse 38, is a transparently clear phrase to admit of any equivocation. As an adjectival clause, qualifing *cāmaraiḥ*, it is liable to one and only one interpretation: "the chowries had their handles (*valis*) covered with the lustre of gems studded therein". The way Laksmīnivāsa has rendered it adds up to by far the most mindless piece in his commentary. As indicated by his gloss thereon, *ratnacchāyayā khacitāḥ prakaṭīkṛtāḥ valayaḥ udaralekhāḥ yaiḥ*, he takes the *vali* in the clause to denote *trivali*. Thus to him the chowries with their gems had been instrumental in revealing the *trivali* of the dancing girls, at the Mahākāla temple. This is abhorrent to common sense. How the *cāmaras* could have bared/revealed the *trivali*, which itself must have been visible to the naked eye, passes comprehension. Going by Laksmīnivāsa's rendering, one can scarely avoid the conclusion that the chowries served the dual function of exposing the *trivali* and thereby tiring the hands of the dancing maids. No sensible person could have indulged in such fanciful atrocities.

It is awkward to compare, as implied by Laksmīnivāsa's interpretation of the phrase *kanakanikaṣasnigdhayā* (V.40), the streak of lightning with the touchstone: *kanakanikaṣavat nikaṣapaṭṭavat snigdhā arūkṣā tayā*. The two are so distinctly opposed in colour that only a blind would have the temerity to detect similarity between them. The commentator has evidently failed to appreciate the point of comparison that a scholiast of Mallinātha's calibre could have hardly missed. He has aptly paraphrased the clause as follows: *kanakasya....upalagatarekhā tasyeva snigdham tejo yasyāstayā*. Mallinatha's gloss unravels the happy similarity that exists between the lightning in the dark clouds and the streak of gold on the touch-stone. It is not the touch-stone but the streak of gold made thereon to test its purity, that is intended as an *upamāna* here. Laksmīnivāsa's gloss is wide off the mark.

Toyotsargārtham stanitena garjitena mukharo mā bhūḥ, such an interpretation of the phrase *toyotsargastanitamukharaḥ* in the same verse stems from the lack of proper understanding of the text and the phenomenon suggested therein. It suffers from the presumption that the rain is invariably preceded by thundering. It is however a common experience that the cloud does not always thunder to shed rain. Moreover, this is not the connotation that the poet means to convey here. He rather seeks to underline the *mukharatā* of the cloud that is heightened by its twin acts of thundering and raining. Mallinātha is perfectly justified in treating the clause as a *dvandva* compound *(tyotsargastanitābhyām mukharaḥ)*. As a matter of fact, his remark *nātra toyotsargasahitam stanitamiti vigrahaḥ* aims to deter any recourse to the alternative *madhyamapadalopī* compound. That cuts at the root of Laksmīnivāsa's rendering of the phrase.

The commentator reads *puṣpamoghīkṛtātmā* for *puṣpameghīkṛtātmā* in verse 46, wherein the cloud is asked to rain flowers on Skanda to demonstrate its reverence to the deity. The reading adopted by the commentator is odd enough. He has multiplied the oddity by his foolish gloss thereon: *puṣpaiḥ moghīkṛtaḥ saphalīkrtaḥ ātmā yena saḥ*. He would have us believe that the cloud had gratified itself with the mass of flowers, on Devagiri. Besides the fact that he has left unexplained how could it have happened, the interpretation runs counter to the imperatives of the context. No one in his senses would ever paraphrase *moghīkṛtaḥ* as *saphalīkṛtaḥ*, so diametrically opposed to each other are they. The cloud had been enjoined here to express regards to Skanda, stationed on the hill, with a shower of flowers. That it could have done by turning itself into a mass of flowers. This is precisely what *puṣpameghīkṛtātmā* is intended to convey. The cloud's competence to assume the form of its choosing is inherent in its epithet, *kāmarūpam maghonaḥ* (v.6)

Verse 79 describes the multifarious objects that the Kalpavṛkṣa was wont to yield in Alakā. One of the epithets employed therein, *nayanavibhramādeśadakṣam*, has been taken by the commentator as an adjective to *puṣpodbhedam*, which he enigmatically renders as *kusumacitratām*. His *anvaya* of the text, as also the interpretation of *puṣpodbheda*, is a sad commentary on his equipment. It is surprising how a commentator could be so uncanny as not to discern the appropriateness of simple phrases and their function in the context, which even a casual reader would not miss. One fails to understand how the flowers could have lent *vibhrama* to the eyes. This is the function that wine performs with a vengeance. And this is exactly how Mallinātha has treated it. Obviously it qualifies *madhu*, not *puṣpodbhedam*. Mallinātha's additional remark: *anena vibhramadvārā madhuno maṇḍanatvamanusandheyam*, is interesting.

Laksmīnivāsa's interpretation of the first *pāda* (*gatvā sadyaḥ kalabhatanutām śīghrasampātahetoḥ*) of Verse 87, again projects him in poor shade. *Kṣipram gamanārtham kalabhatanutām gatvā*, is how he has explained the line. The cloud was asked to assume the form of a young elephant not to avoid delay in proceeding further but to facilitate his entry into the Yakṣa's house and brief sojourn on the pleasure-hill, prior to that. Mallinātha's observation *śīghrapraveśārthamityarthaḥ* tellingly drives home the point. With the paraphrase *guruśarīre vilambo jāyate*, Laksmīnivāsa, on the other hand, implies that to him the cloud had not yet reached its destination. This is contrary to the facts, unfolded in the verse. It had already arrived at Yakṣa's house and was waiting for an appropriate opportunity to make its entry therein. It is interesting to find Mallinātha introduce the verse with the comment: *nijagṛhaniścayāntaram kṛtymāha.*

Pratyādeśānna khalu bhavato dhīratām kalpayāmi (V.120) has landed the commentator into illogical exposition. He has completely failed to fathom the import of the line which admittedly is liable to varied interpretation, with the commentators and editors accepting the reading and interpreting it according to their lights and preferences. But Laksmīnivāsa has strained all imaginable bounds of probability by interpreting it as: *bhavatastava dhīratām pratyākhyātum vaktum na kalpayāmi śaknomi.* What led the commentator to explain the line thus, is not easy to determine. May be his ignorance or imperviousness to poetic nuances or irresponsible approach to a very responsible task ! This is, however, what he has sought to impose on the text that it cannot be tortured to yield at all. Laksmīnivāsa has made nonsense of the verse by his indefensible gloss, a remark that may be said to apply to most of the clauses in the text, that required discernment, critical faculty and equipment born of wide and incisive learning.

Besides these exhaustive investigations into the validity of his interpretation of the text, it should be rewarding to evaluate some of the momentous variants, favoured by him. Notwithstanding the fact that the text of the *Meghadūta* has come down to us "fairly uniformly", it is known to differ, not inconsiderably, in various traditions. Lakṣmīnivāsa has naturally followed the Jaina tradition that represents by far the most bloated version of the text in admitting as many as 127 stanzas, with the Kashmirian Vallabha symbolishing the other pole with 110 verses. Laksmīnivāsa's poor judgement, so naggingly perceptible in his interpretation of the poem, is further confirmed by some of the offensive readings adopted by him.

Verse 37 asks the cloud to perform with his thunderings the function of a tabor at the evening-worship of Śiva in the Mahākāla shrine at Ujjayinī, unmindful of the long wait it might entail. As such, the text of the second line, as read by Laksmīnivāsa,...*nayanaviṣayam yāvadabhyeti bānuḥ*, is open to question. It may be said to his credit that celebrities like Vallabha,

Sumativijaya, Mahimasiṁha, Sarasvatītīrtha[12] and Kṛṣṇapati[13] also have favoured the same reading. While not meaning discourtesy to these stalwarts, one cannot be insensible to its incongruity with the context. In view of the evening-prayers at the temple wherein the cloud was to play tabor, it is the sun-set that is expected here, not its rise, as is implied in the reading *abhyeti bhānuḥ*. As his gloss affirms, Laksmīnivāsa had been unaware of the contradiction involved in his reading. Sarasvatītīrtha, on the other hand, endeavoured to smoothen the variant with the general import of the verse by paraphrasing *abhyeti* as *atikrāmati.*[14] That, however, is utterly untenable. By no stretch of imagination can *abhyeti* be persecuted to mean *atikrāmāti*. It therefore should be rejected in favour of *atyeti*, as Mallinatha has wisely done it. He seems to have been vindicated in his judgment by De's preference for the latter.[15]

Kundakṣepānugamadhukaraśrīmukhām, read in Verse 50 is out of joint with the context. What was intended as the vernacular form of the cerebral sibillant, established itself as an independent variant, without the copyists pausing to ponder over the harm they had thereby inflicted on the sense and beauty of the verse. As a matter of fact, the phrase, in its present form, has no *locus standi* in the verse because of its failure to serve the purpose it is meant to perform as an adjective to *kautuhalānām*. It stands in splendid isolation, with no function to perform. It is also of note that this variant is not noticed in any of the known MSS. The only alternative reading, encountered therein, is *o* śrījuṣām. And still Laksmīnivāsa had the cheek to explain it in a manner that forms nothing but a jumble of meaningless vocables. One hopes, he understood the import of his own interpretation !

Verse 52 refers to the efficacy of the waters of the holy Sarasvatī that had led Balarāma to discard his coveted wine and consequently rendered him pure at heart. The term used to denote the cloud's partaking of the sacred waters varies between *abhigamam* and *adhigamam*. Laksmīnivāsa prefers to read the former. The variant doubtless has the sanction of competent commentators including Mallinātha and Bharata-mallika, as also some of the modern editors like Gildemeister and S.K. De.[16] Laksmīnivāsa's rendering of the phrase as *sevanam* is almost identical with that of Mallinātha who equates it with *sevām*. Kṛṣṇapati paraphrases it as *adhigamam*. May be, he differed from the text and retained the alternative reading in his very brief gloss on the stanza. Though *sevanam* (drinking) is what is needed here, *abhi*gam hardly admits of the sense. In view of its unmistakable clarity, the variant *adhigamam* seems to be preferable.

The text of Verse 57 in Laksmīnivāsa differs substantially from that adopted by Mallinātha, Sarasvatītīrtha and others. It, however, accords with what Vallabha and Kṛṣṇapati read. While the variants in the first hemistich have equally powerful claim to merit preference because of their acute precision in the context, the reading in the third pāda, *karakāvṛṣṭihāsāvakīrṇān*, though a wee more poetic than the bland o *vṛṣṭipātāvakīrṇān*, lacks force and seems to militate against the function it should discharge in the context. It is indeed happy to compare the hail-storm with laughter, but it unwittingly diminishes the ferocity of the cloud to scare away the aggressive *Śarabhas*, who were menacingly poised to charge at him. *Karakāvṛṣṭipātāvakīrṇān,* on the other hand, dispenses with the mildness inherent in *hāsa* and thus serves to highlight the vigour of the cloud to drive away the bellicose animals. The imperatives of the situation are met better by the latter reading.

Opinion is divided with equal sharpness on the text of the second hemistich of the succeeding stanza, which, as it is read by Laksmīnivāsa, may be reproduced here.

Yasmindṛṣṭe karaṇavigamāddūramuddhūtapāpāḥ
saṁkalpante sthiragaṇapadaprāptaye śraddadhānāḥ.

Sanātana-goswamī, Mahimasiṁha and Sāroddhāriṇī also have the same text; *saṁkalpante* being additionally shared by Sumativijaya. Mallinātha, on the other hand, rejects them in favour of *ūrdhvamūddhūtapāpāḥ* and *kalpiṣyante*. While he has Vallabha's sanction for the first, *kalpiṣyante* represents an emendation of the latter's *kalpante'sya*. It is Vallabha's text that, on critical evaluation, has been found genuine, both by Wilson and S.K.De. As regards *kalpante'sya*, Īśvaracandra Vidyāsāgara's remark *ayameva pāṭhaḥ sādhīyān, nirupasargasyaiva klṛpteh paryāptivācakatvāt samityupasargayoge tu dhāturayam-arthāntaram bodhayati,*[17] clinches the issue against *saṁkalpante* and *kalpiṣyante*. However, *dūramuddhūtapāpāḥ* does not mean what is needed in the context. The sight of Śiva's foot-prints was sufficient for the devotees to achieve the rank of his *gaṇas,* after death. Whatever the text, the second half of the verse should denote nothing else. The meaning is possible with *ūrdhvam,* not with *dūram*. Since the devotees were entitled to gaṇahood after their death, *ūrdhvam* must have been the original reading. The predilection of eminent commentators like Vallabha and Mallinātha for the variant also attests to its genuineness.

The mount Kailāsa with its snow-capped peaks has been happily conceived as a mass of Śiva's laughter (61). The reading in the last *pāda* of the stanza has been the subject of much commentatorial and editorial controversy and ingenuity. Dakṣināvartanātha, Mallinātha, Kṛṣṇapati and Jinasena,[18] among others, read *pratidinamiva trayambakasyāṭṭahāsaḥ*. The other set of commentators favours *pratidiśamiva* with equal tenacity. The question, as remarked by S.K. De, really is whether temporal or spatial accumlation is meant. The third *pāda* would suggest the accumulation to have been spatial because the mount is said to encompass the sky with its peaks, covered with snow, that would make the expanse resemble Śiva's laughter heaped in all quarters. However, even the fact of the sky having been covered with its far-extending peaks would not negate the mount's situation in the north. With the reading *pratidiśamiva*, also favoured by Laksmīnivāsa, one would be driven willy-nilly to conclude that the Kailāsa was not stationed in the northern direction alone but had embraced the whole firmament in its sweep. That is contrary to the location of the mount and the sequence of the accumulation of the snow. The snow could not have covered the mount at one stroke. It must have grown to size over a considerable period of time,leading the poet to imagine that it had gathered there day by day. That should account for the south Indian commentator's preference for *pratidinamiva*.

Verse 81, that addresses itself to detail the topography of Yakṣa's house, though seemingly indisputable, has led the commentators to group themselves in two well-defined bands to confront each other, so far as a reading in the first *pāda* is concerned. A powerful set of commentators including such luminaries as Sumativijaya, Parameśvara and Kṛṣṇapati favours the ablative form and reads: *tatrāgāram dhanapatigṛhāduttareṇāsmadīyam*. Laksmīnivāsa also has *gṛhād*. Vallabha, the earliest scholiast of *Meghadūta*, is vehemently critical of the form and denounces it as *anārya*.[19] As remarked by Mallinātha, with the variant *dhanapatigṛhād*, *uttareṇa* cannot be treated as an *enabanta* form. It would naturally have to taken as an instrumental adjective to *toraṇena*. According to Bharata-mallika *uttareṇa* here denotes direction and, as such, obviously in accordance with Pāṇini II.3.29, takes ablative.[20] The *Tattvabodhinī* on the *Siddhānta-kaumudī* (II.3.31) also takes it as an adjectival clause, qualifying *toraṇena*.

In that case, it is not possible with Laksmīnivāsa to interpret it as uttara samīpe. However, those like Mallinātha who treat *uttareṇa* as a form ending in *enap* naturally substitute the ablative with the accusative case and read *dhanapatigṛhān-uttareṇa*. The *Tattvabodhinī* also seems to favour the reading when it remarks *dhanapatigṛhānuttareṇsmadiyamiti kaiścitpaṭhyate tadā tu samygeva.*[21] S.K. De is of the opinion that conformity to grammar had led the original *gṛhāt* to be modified to *gṛhān.*[22]

This multi-focal evaluation of the commentary leaves little doubt that Laksmīnivāsa was not at all equal to the task he had undertaken rather zealously. The *Śiṣyahitaiṣiṇī* is hardly true to its name. Apart from not doing *hita* to the student, it, not unoften, misleads him into a blind alley. It is undoubtedly the "smallest" commentary on one of the "greatest" poems.

REFERENCES

1. Ed. Rohiṇī Bhatta, Sambodhi, Vol.11, Nos.1-4, p.1-48, L.D. Institute of Indology, Ahmedabad.
2. S.K. De(ed.), The *Meghadūta* of Kālidāsa, Delhi, 1957, p.113
3. G.M. Bhāttācārya (ed.), *Meghadūta-ṭīkā* of Kṛṣṇapati, Kurukṣetra, 1974, p.2.
4. Ibid, p.2, F.N.2.
5. S.K. De (ed.), The *Meghadūta* of Kālidāsa, op.cit.,p.113.
6. *Kāmārtā hi prakṛtikṛpaṇāśacetanācetaneṣu. Meghadūta,5.*
7. Devendranātha Sharmā (ed.), *Kāvyālaṅkāra*, Patna, 1985, I.42-44
8. Saṁsāracandra and Mohandev Pant (eds.), *Meghadūda* with Mallinātha's Sañjīvinī, Benares, 1951, V.5.
9. *Meghadūta-ṭīka*, op.cit., V.5.
10. *Deśabhedam kṣetrabhedam vā girisīmānam vā,* Kṛṣṇapati, op.cit., p.13.
11. Kṛṣṇapati, op.cit., p.17
12. The *Meghadūta* of Kālidāsa, op.cit., p.51, F.N.34
13. *Meghadūta-ṭīka*, op.cit., p.23, Verse 35 (Text).
14. The *Meghadūta* of Kālidāsa, op.cit., p.51. F.N.34
15. Ibid, Stanza 34 (Text).
16. Ibid, p.55, F.N.49.
17. Ibid, p.57, F.N.55.

18. Ibid, p.58, F.N.58.
19. Ibid, p.64, F.N.72
20. Ibid, p.64, F.N.72
21. *Siddhānta-Kaumudī* with *Tattvabodhinī*, Delhi, 1985, p.152, Lines 28-30
22. The *Meghadūta* of Kālidāsa, op.cit., Introduction, p.XXVII.

JAYAŚEKHARA'S INDEBTEDNESS TO KĀLIDĀSA

Kālidāsa's *Kumārasambhava* (*Ks.*)[1] does not share with *Meghadūta* the proud distinction of having stirred a whole genre of literature. Of the few writings that owe their genesis to the former, the *Jaina-Kumārasambhava* (*JKs.*)[2] of Jayaśekhara Sūri (15th Century A.D.), which purports to describe, in eleven cantos, the birth of Kumāra (Bharata), stands out prominently by virtue of its poetic excellences and faithful adherence to the Mahākāvya-tradition. Whatever its sources,[3] a comparison of the *Jaina-Kumārasambhava* with Kālidāsa's poem reveals it beyond question that in the execution of his theme Jayaśekhara was deeply influenced and inspired by Kālidāsa's 'Birth of war-god'. But while Kālidāsa applied closure to his poem with an overt hint to Pārvatī's conception in the eighth canto, Jayaśekhara has stretched, without much justification, his theme to spill over five additional cantos even after a pointed allusion to the pregnancy of Sumaṅgalā, the chief wife of Ṛṣabhadeva, the hero of the poem. Both the poems, however, tend to shun the narration of the actul birth of the child, and, as such, their titles outstep the denouement of the theme as postulated in the respective poems.

The quantum of debt Jayaśekhara owes to his distinguished predecessor is highlighted by the striking resemblances in ideas and situations the *JKs.* bears with Kālidāsa's poem besides his close adherence to the scheme of theme as it unfolds itself on the canvas of the *Kumārasambhava*. Jayaśekhara does not miss the slightest opportunity to seize upon the various incidents and situations that have been so brilliantly spun out in the body of his poem by Kālidāsa. In imitation of the gorgeous account of the scenic beauties of the Himalayas in the first canto of the *Ks.*, the *JKs.* is marked, in its inception, by a graphic description of Ayodhyā, the birth-place of Ṛṣabha.[4] Though bereft of rich imagery, life-like freshness and sweet diction of Kālidāsa's muse, it does not fail to bring out in relief the poetic talents of the author. And despite wide divergences in contents, the two descriptions converge to share the common metre, *Upajāti*. The *JKs.*, not unlike its source, deals in the first canto with the earlier part of Ṛṣabha's life, from his birth to youth, which, in the process, stretches to encompass a brilliant sketch of his physical charms.[5] The description of the youthful Pārvatī in the *Ks.* emerges as one of the most charming pieces of Sanskrit poetry by dint of sheer fertility of imagination and keenness of observation on the part of the poet. The parallel description in the *JKs.* undeniably suffers by comparison, but it is not wholly shorn of beauty. Rather, Jayaśekhara's fondness for unconventional standards of comparison (*upamānas*) has saved it from degenerating into a stale catalogue of traditional human beauties.

In the second canto of the *Ks.*, a bunch of the denizens of heaven waits upon the supreme Lord Brahmā with the request to relieve them of the miseries and insults inflicted by the irrepressible demon, Tāraka. Jayaśekhara has adapted these confabulations of the deities to suit the scheme of events in his poem. In the *JKs.*, Indra himself decends upon Ayodhyā to persuade Ṛṣabhadeva to condescend to enter into marital life. Taking cue from the eulogy of Brahmā which precedes the narration of the afflictions caused to the deities, in the second canto of the *Ks.*, Jayaśekhara has incorporated in the same canto of his poem, a *stotra* sung by the divine assembly in praise of Ṛṣabha.[6] The two eulogies, however, differ widely in their contents and effect. The undercurrent of philosophical contents in the eulogy of Brahmā marks it out, without impairing its poetic excellences, as a *stotra par excellence*. Jayaśekhara's *stotra* of Ṛṣabha, on the other hand, is confined to the bald recital of the series of his previous births and the pious deeds performed by him. Compared with Kālidāsa's eulogy, it sounds dull and dry.

The charming dialouge between Indra and Spring (Vasanta) wherein the Lord of heavens abets the latter to wreck, in collusion with his friend Cupid, Śaṅkara in his supposedly unshakable concentration, forms the core of the third canto of the *Ks.* The author of the *JKs.* has paralleled it by bringing about a conversation between Indra and Ṛṣabha, which is intended to serve as an inducement to the latter to instutionalise the conjugal life by first accepting the same himself.[7] Indra's confabulations with Ṛṣabha are not negligible as a piece of poetry though the palm, as elsewhere, lies with the master. The pre-marital adornments of Sumaṅgalā and Sunandā in the canto and that of Ṛṣabha in the next, are doubtless inspired by similar adornings of Śiva and Pārvatī in the *Ks.*[8] It is to be noted here that Kālidāsa's description of the ornamentations of the youthful couple is both factual and effective, its brevity notwithstanding. In the *JKs.*, on the other hand, it all but assumes the appearance of a *nakhaśikha* portryal of human beauties. It additionally bears the stamp of artificiality, though it shares quite a few of Kālidāsa's ideas. Like Kālidāsa, Jayaśekhara revels in describing the flowers tucked in the heroine's braid,[9] the removal with perfumed powder of the oil applied to the body[10] and the bride/bridegroom as a cynosure of the spectators' gaze with the help of a Mālopamā.[11] Pārvatī is struck with wonder on seeing her adorned form in the mirror which fires her longing for the vicinity of her spouse. The idea is found repeated, with slight modification, in the *JKs.* also. The cravings of Sumaṅgalā and Sunandā were intensfied in proportion to the sound of the band of instruments signalling the bridegroom's arrival, as it drew nearer and nearer.[12]

As Jayaśekhara would have us believe, the total concourse of deities descended on the earth to participate in Ṛṣabha's marriage. Some of them with unsheathed weapons moved ahead the marriage-party which thus created an illusion of a military expedition. Jayaśekhara had an authority for such a description in Kālidāsa's poem wherein Śaṅkara is escorted to Oṣadhiprastha, among others, by seven divine mothers (*saptamātṛkās*). The effulgence of their faces seemed to transform the sky into a lake covered with a mass of lotuses.[13] Jayaśekhara, like Kālidāsa, has made, in the context, a specific mention of the auspicious sound of the ceremonial instruments.[14] At the time of departure of Śaṅkara's marriage-party in Kālidāsa's *Ks.*, the sun holds over the bridegroom a parasol fashioned by the divine architect, the Gaṅgā and Yamunā, in human form, wave chowries, and the regents of quarters tender him homage. The marriage of Ṛṣabha with his co-uterine sisters is the handwork of Indra and his consort Śacī to the extent that it seems to be divorced from reality. The immates of heaven do their bidding. Lakṣmī, Mandākinī, Sarasvatī and the quarter-damsels present the brides with priceless cosmetics and the heavenly nymphs such as Urvaśī, Rambhā, Ghṛtācī and Tilottamā mirthfully display their coveted dances.[15] While in Śaṅkara's marriage divine musicians, Viśvāvasu and others, sing the songs of his victory over the three fortified cities (*tripuravijaya*); in the *JKs.* Tumburu and Nārada wax eloquent in describing the fame and charms of Ṛṣabha which, when partaken by the divine assembly, created aversion in it to its fond drink, nectar, also.[16]

Śaṅkara proceeds to the bride's house on his famed mount, bull. Ṛṣabha used the divine elephant Airāvata for the purpose. While Śaṅkara's bull looked like dwarfish Kaliāsa, Airāvata invited comparsion with a fleeting mansion, scoffing at the loftiness of Meru.[17] Śiva is helped on Kaliāsa, to the back of his mount by Nandī; at Oṣadhiprastha he alights from it, supported by Viṣṇu. In the *JKs.*, Indra alone performs the function of both these personages. He lent a helping hand to Ṛṣabha as he descended from the divine vehicle in the bride's house and took him in his arms before he could reach the ground, on his return home.[18] In Kālidāsa's poem Śaṅkara, on arrival, is escorted to the bride by the attendants of the harem. Jayaśekhara assigns this function to a non-descript lady. With a cloth put around his neck, he is said to have been escorted by her as Prakṛtī perforce drags the soul into worldly existence.[19] Kālidāsa has drawn pointed attention to the emergence of the *sāttvikabhāvas* in the divine couple, Śiva and Pārvatī, at the time their marriage was being solemnized. Pārvatī's person was covered with horripilation and Śaṅkara's hand with perspiration. Their order has been reversed in the *Raghuvaṁśa* (VII.22). It was simply repugnant to the puritan conception of the Jaina monk to describe the semi-divine personage, Ṛṣabha, as overwhelmed, like lesser mortals, by the onrush of such emotions. In order to highlight his aversion to carnal pleasures, it was imperative to keep him unaffected by the *sāttvikabhāvas*. Jayaśekhara has, therefore, restricted them to the brides alone.[20]

Both the poems carry a graphic account of the marriage-ceremonies as they obtained in the respective eras. Kālidāsa, in consonance with his penchant for brevity, has summed up the relevant ceremonies within the space of mere eleven verses.[21] Jayaśekhara, on the other hand, in his zeal to be meticulous, has marked out a sizeable part of two consecutive cantos (IV,V) to detail the contemporary marital rites. These disproportionate descriptions constitute prolonged digressions in the poem and threaten to push the main theme into background. Some of the ceremonies described by Jayaśekhara have been borrowed from Kālidāsa's poem. To his predecessor Jayaśekhara owes some of the ideas also. On his arrival at Oṣadhiprastha, Śaṅkara is greeted with *arghya* and curd mixed with honey besides valuable gifts of excellent robes. *Arghya* forms part of the welcome that Ṛṣabha received at the bride's house.[22] In fact, the welcome accorded to Ṛṣabha and the ceremonies observed therein do not differ substantially from Kālidāsa's account. This part of the ceremony as listed in the *JKs*. comes very close to the *dhukāva*, observed in Northern India till this day, to welcome the bridegroom.

Following in the foot-steps of Kālidāsa, Jayaśekhara has taken pains to pinpoint the minutest details connected with the ceremony of marriage. Even the flame of the sacred fire on the altar and the streaks of smoke emerging therefrom have not escaped his notice. While Kālidāsa has alluded to the blazing flame in the phrase *kṛśānorudarciṣaḥ* (VII.79), Jayaśekhara has gone a step further in underlining sacred oblations as the cause of the shooting flame *mantrapūtahaviṣaḥ pariṣekāduttarottaraśikhaḥ* (V.13). The attention of both the poets was likewise drawn to the smoke preceding the blaze of fire. To Pārvatī it had all the ingredients of the ceremonial smoke. To the poet Kālidāsa, while spreading on the cheeks of the birde, it bore appearance of an ephemeral ear-lotus. In the *JKs*., while the smoke served the most obvious function of rendering the eyes red in the case of brides, it bore resemblance to the mass of bees hovering over a *campaka* garland, when it came into contact with the resplendent body of Ṛṣabhadeva.[23] On the conclusion of the marital rites, the priest of the Himalayas spells out, im brief, the duties the newly wedded couple is to discharge towards ensuring harmonious conjugal relationship. Jayaśekhara was so fascinated by these noble sentiments that he has blown a solitary verse in the *Ks*. into a full-fledged discourse on the conjugal ties, which, notwithstanding its prolixity, makes a happy reading.[24] Śiva and Umā, in Kālidāsa's poem, are treated, soon after their marriage, to a play enacted by the heavenly nymphs. Jayaśekhara assigns this function to Indra himself who, in company with his consort, regales the divine couple with an exquisite dance-performance.[25]

The description of the onrush of city-damsels, occasioned by their eagerness to have a glimpse of Ṛṣabha on his return home with his brides, is reminiscent of similar description in Kālidāsa's *Ks*., which he has fondly reproduced verbatim in the *Raghuvaṁśa* as well.[26] Originating in the *Buddhacarita* of Aśvaghoṣa, this motif has struck deep roots as is evident from the fact that it has filtered down to the medieval poets through masters like Kālidāsa, Māgha, Śrīharṣa and others. However, despite their fondness for it, the later poets, Jayaśekhara not precluded, failed to introduce any innovation in the depicition of the motif as conceived by earlier celebrities. Jayaśekhara in consequence echoes what the ealier poets, particularly Kālidāsa, had said.

Jayaśekhara, like Kālidāsa, has presented the godly hero in human garb, though the legendary character of Ṛṣabha has been more pronounced in the *JKs*. After bidding adieu the gods, who had flocked to attend his marriage, Śaṅkara, with his charming bride, entered into the sport-hall where a suitable bed had been prepared for their enjoyments. Thereafter Kālidāsa has described with abandon the love-sports of the divine couple wherein the sequence of the act and varied postures thereof, as prescribed in *the Kāmasūtra,* are sought to be compressed to present an integrated picture of youthful gaiety (canto VIII). Ṛṣabha too steps in the diamond-mansion (*maṇiharmya*) with the two brides as an aspirant to truth dives into *Śāstra* with the two-fold equipment of intellect and memory.[27] The uninhibited description of sexual orgy was abhorrent to the puritan monk. He has made a veiled allusion to it with a hint to the conception of Sumaṅgalā. As Jayaśekhara avers, Ṛṣabha enjoyed the sexual pleasures with resignation to destiny, as ordained in the previous births (VI.26). It was perhaps unavoidable to present him in this hue in order to highlight his detachment from the worldly enjoyments, howsoever odd, it may sound in the situation.

In close adherence to Kālidāsa's poem Jayaśekhara has spun out a dialouge between the hero and heroine, though in the *Ks.* it precedes the marriage while in the *JKs.* it forms a post-marital phenomenon. The young ascetic's confabulations with Umā, in the fifth canto of the *Ks.*, are rated as the finest piece of poetry on account of their dramatic effect and lively buoyancy ; the rather prolonged conversation between Ṛṣabha and Sumaṅgalā in *the JKs.* does not rise above the level of mediocrity (canto VIII).

As required by theory, Jayaśekhara has incorporated in the body of his poem a plethora of descriptions of uneven merits. Stereotyped like many others in literature, most of them are inspired by similar pieces in Kālidāsa. The description of night and moonrise in the eight canto of the *Kumārasambhava* is unmatched for its sheer poetic beauties. It serves to heighten the charms of Gandhamādana and, thereby, provides an apt setting to the love-sports of Śiva and Pārvatī. The parallel description in the *JKs.* which is superb by all standards, is also intended to form backdrop to the post-marital dalliance of Ṛṣabha and his brides. In contrast to Kālidāsa's three, Jayaśekhara has devoted eleven verses to describe the charms of the rising moon. He shares some of Kālidāsa's relevant ideas also. The night in Kālidāsa is represented to level with its darkness all that is pure or impure, straight or bent, sentient or insentient. In partial modification of the present description, the night in Jayaśekhara is credited with supernatural powers to establish the concept of perfect non-duality by wiping out with its sweep all differences emanating from distinction in colour.[28] Jayaśekhara is again indebted to Kālidāsa for his description of the mingling of nocturnal darkness with moonshine. The darkness pierced by the rays of the moon appears to Kālidāsa like the Mānasa lake which had been rendered turbid by the elephants with their sports but is now gradually returning to perspicacity. Jayaśekhara has contrasted Kālidāsa's Upamā with Arthāntaranyāsa, which invests his picture with added exquisiteness. "The moon showers splendour on the world but the night is determined to smear it dark. Even one endowed with talent/digits seldom gets the wife of his liking."[29]

Spring, as described in the third canto of the *Ks.*, forms the basis of its portrayal in the sixth canto of the *JKs.* to which the poet has appended an account of other Indian seasons. This is one of the few descriptions of Jayaśekhara that are marked by banality. Kālidāsa's delineation of the sudden departure of the sun to the northern quarter at the untimely outbreak of spring has been transplanted by the author of the *JKs.* in his description of *Śiśira.*[30] His description of morning (X.77-84) owes itself to the brilliant picture of day-break in the fifth canto of the *Raghuvaṁśa*. This is perhaps the only description in the *JKs.* which is shorter in form than the parent description in Kālidāsa. Poetically this is the finest part of the poem. An allusion to the salubrious breeze is inherent in any account of the morning. In the *Raghuvaṁśa*, the morning breeze is represented as hovering, in its impatience, to partake of the natural fragrance of Aja's mouth ; Jayaśekhara has depicted it as a paramour hastening to slip at the advent of the rightful husband of *Kamalinī*, the Sun.[31] The description of sunrise and midday, of which the former is notable for its poetic beauties, are two other such pieces as have nothing to match in Kālidāsa's *Kumārasambhava*. Kālidāsa has closed his poem with a fascinating description of the rising moon which serves to fire the love-sports of Śiva and Pārvatī. Jayaśekhara has called it a poem with an account of the scorching midday. It is doubtless consonant with Kālidāsa's scheme but aesthetically it does not seem to be wholly in tune with the conclusion of the poem. Jayaśekhara's fascination for Kālidāsa's poem is underlined by the fact that he has followed him even in the form of benediction the *JKs.* begins with, which in both the poems, is of *vastunirdeśa* type.

Besides close communion in the scheme of theme and various situations therein, as detailed above, jayaśekhara's indebtendness to Kālidāsa is highlighted by quite a few other similarities in ideas which, however, do not admit of any sequence or systematic division. Some of these nay be listed here.

(i) While describing Ṛṣabha's steadfastness in the face of irrepressible distractions, Jayaśekhara remarks :

अपि प्रवृत्तार्घविधिर्वधूद्वयीदिदृक्षया नोदमनायत प्रभुः।
समाधिनिर्धौतधियां न तादृशां स्वभावभेदे विषयाः प्रभूष्णवः।।

(*JKs*.IV.72)

This is a distinct echo of what Kālidāsa has said to drive home Śiva's unshakable concentration in the midst of frolic stirred by Cupid and his cohort.

आत्मेश्वराणां नहि जातु विघ्नाः समाधिभेदप्रभवो भवन्ति। (Ks.III.40)

(ii) Ṛṣabha's character is as inscrutable as that of Śiva.

वेद चरितं महतां कः । (*JKs*. V.9)

न सन्ति याथार्थ्यविदः पिनाकिनः । (*Ks*. V.77)

(iii) In emulation of Kālidāsa, Jayaśekhara has sought to describe the matchless beauty of the heroine's face with the help of Vyatireka. Like that of Pārvatī, Sumaṅgalā's face surpasses both lotus and moon. The two verses are so close in spirit and contents that Jayaśekhara's description appears to be a doctored version of the delineation of Pārvatī's charms in the *Ks*.

पद्मं न चन्द्रं प्रति सप्रसादं तस्योदितः सोऽपि ददाति सादम् ।
यस्या मुखं द्वावपि तावलुप्त श्रीमान् परस्फातिसहः क्व हन्त ।। (*JKs*.VI.35)

चन्द्रं गता पद्मगुणान् न भुंक्ते पद्माश्रिता चान्द्रमसीमभिख्याम् ।
उमामुखं तु प्रतिपद्य लोला द्विसंश्रयां प्रीतिमवाप लक्ष्मीः।। (*Ks*. I.43)

(iv) With their riches drained to the market of Ayodhyā, the repositories of gems-oceans (*ratnākaras*)-are stated in the *JKs*. to have been reduced to the miserable abodes of sharks. The idea is an adaptation of the splendour of Ujjayinī as described by Kālidāsa in the *Meghadūta* wherein the oceans, shorn of their coral-wealth, are viewed as a mere mass of insipid water.

पणायितुं यत्र निरीक्ष्य रत्नराशिं प्रकाशीकृतमापणेषु ।
रत्नाकराणां मकराकरत्वमेवावशिष्टं बुबुधे बुधेन ।। (*JKs*.I.11)

दृष्ट्वा यस्या विपणिरचितान्विद्रुमाणां च भंगान्
संलक्ष्यन्ते सलिलनिधयस्तोयमात्रावशेषाः ।। (*Megh*.I.34)

These comparative investigations in the two poems bring out in bold relief the extent to which Jayaśekhara is enamoured of Kālidāsa's muse. The *Kumārasambhava* forms the major source of his poem, though the imprint of the *Raghuvaṁśa* is also perceptible at places.

REFERENCES

1. Ed. M.R. Kale, Delhi, 1967
2. Ed. With Sanskrit Commentary of Dharmaśekhara Upādhyāya, Jamnagar
3. For the sources of *JKs*. see my book, *Jaina Saṁskṛta Mahākāvya*, p.25-27
4. *KS*, I. 1-16 ; *JKs*., I. 1-16
5. *Ks*., I. 20-49 ; *JKs*., I. 17-60
6. *Ks*., II. 3-15 ; *JKs*., II. 49-73
7. *Ks*., III. 1-13 ; *JKs*., III. 1-36
8. *JKs*., III. 60-81 , IV. 14-32 ; *Ks*., VII. 7-24
9. केशान्तमन्तःकुसुमं तदीयम् । *Ks*., VII.15 ; धम्मिल्लमल्लो---अन्तरालोल्लसितप्रसूनैः। *JKs*., III.64
10. (i) तां लोध्रकल्केन हृतांगतैलम् । *Ks*., VII.9
    तनूस्तदीया पाटवासकैरभाद्विशेषतः शोषिततैलताण्डवा । *JKs*., IV.15
    (ii) सा मङ्गलस्नानविशुद्धगात्री । *Ks*., VII.11
    सुवस्त्रशान्तोदकलेपभासुरः । *JKs*., IV.17
11. सा संभवद्भिः कुसुमैर्लतेव ज्योतिर्भिरुद्यद्भिरिव त्रियामा ।
    सरिद्विहंगैरिव लीयमानैरामुच्यमानाभरणा चकासे ।। *Ks*., VII.21
    यथा भ्रमर्यः कमले विकस्वरे यथा विहंग्यः फलिते महीरुहे ।
    उपर्युपर्यात्तविभूषणे विभौ तथा निपेतुस्त्रिदशांगनादृशः ।। *JKs*., IV.31
12. हरोपयाने त्वरिता बभूव । *Ks*., VII.22 ; सुमंगलासुनन्दयोरब्दसखायितं हृदा *JKs*., IV.59
13. *JKs*., IV.51 ; *Ks*., VII.38
14. उदीरितो मङ्गलतूर्यघोषः । *Ks*., VII-40 ; स्मरध्वजव्रजस्य ध्वनिरम्बराध्वनि *JKs*., IV.45
15. *Ks*., VII. 41-45 ; *JKs*., III. 51-55, IV. 47-50
16. संगीयमानत्रिपुरावदानः । *Ks*., VII.48 ; -- सुधां प्रभो पिबन्तश्चरितामृतं *JKs*., II. 4
17. बृहत्प्रमाणमारुह्य कैलाशमिव प्रतस्थे । *Ks*., VII.37
    जगाम यो जङ्गमसौधतां श्रिया । *JKs*., IV.35
    हस्तिनो हसितमेरुमहिम्नो । *JKs*., V.49
18. नन्दिभुजावलम्बी । *Ks*., VII.37, तत्रावतीर्याच्युतदत्तहस्तः *Ks*., VII-70 ;
    प्रदत्तबाहुः पविपाणिना प्रभुः। *JKs*., IV.62
    वासवः---तं दधौ द्युगतमेव । *JKs*., V.49

19. *Ks.*, VII.73 ; *JKs.*, IV.74
20. रोमोद्गमः प्रादुरभूदुमायाः स्विन्नाङ्गुलिः पुङ्गवकेतुरासीत्। *Ks.*, VII.77
 तत्करे करशयेऽजनि जन्योः संचरे सपदि सात्विकभावैः। *JKs.*, V.5.
21. *Ks.*, VII.75-85
22. ---अर्घ्यं मधुमच्च गव्यम् नवे दुकूले च-।।*Ks.*, VII.72
 निधेहि दूर्वां दधि चात्र चित्रिणि। *JKs.*, IV.64
 जगद्गरेऽत्रार्घमुपाहरद्गरे। *JKs.*, IV.70
23. *Ks.*, VII.81-82 ; *JKs.*, V. 15-16
24. *Ks.*, VII.83 ; *JKs.*, V.58-83
25. अपश्यताप्सरसां मुहूर्तं प्रयोगमाद्यं ललितांगहारम्।। *Ks.*, VII.91
 तत्र तौ प्रमदनिर्मितनृत्यौ तं च ते च परियोषयतः स्म। *JKs.*, V.53
26. *JKs.*, V.37-45 ; *Ks.*, VII.56-62
27. ------क्षितिधरकन्यामाददानः करेण
 क्षितिविरचितशय्यं कौतुकागारमगात्। *Ks.*, VII.94
 समं वधूभ्यां मणिहर्म्यमीशः। *JKs.*, VI.23
28. शुद्धमाविलमवस्थितं चलं वक्रमाजर्वगुणान्वितं च यत्।
 सर्वमेव तमसा समीकृतं धिङ्महत्त्वमसतां हृतान्तरम्।। *Ks.*, VII.57
 किं योगिनीयं धृतनीलकन्था तमस्विनी तारकशंखभूषा।
 वर्णव्यवस्थामवधूय सर्वामभेदवादं जगतस्ततान।। *JKs.*, VI.8
29. पश्य पार्वति नवेन्दुरश्मिभिः सामिभिन्नतिमिरं नभस्तलम्।
 लक्ष्यते द्विरदभोगदूषितं संप्रसीददिव मानसं सरः।। *Ks.*, VIII.60
 तितांसति श्वैत्यमिहेन्दुरस्य जाया निशा दित्सति कालिमानम्।।
 अहो कलत्रं हृदयानुयायि कलानिधीनामपि भाग्यलभ्यम्।। *JKs.*, VI.9
30. *Ks.*, III.25 ; *JKs.*, VI.69
31. स्वाभाविकं परगुणेन विभातवायुः सौरभ्यमभीप्सुरिव ते मुखमारुतस्य।।
 Ks., V.69.

 सरिदपहृतशैत्यः किंचिदाधूय वल्ली-
 र्भ्रमति भुवि किमेष्यच्छूरभीत्याऽव्यवस्थम्।। *JKs.*, X.81

A VERSIFIED ADAPTATION OF ABHIJÑĀNAŚĀKUNTALAM (I-IV)

While the *Meghadūta* inspired a whole series of literature and some of the later poems owe themselves to his *Kumārasambhava* and *Raghuvaṁśa*, Kālidāsa's *Abhijñānaśākuntalam* (*AbŚ*), despite its acclaimed dramatic merits and poetic excellences, has not exercised on the later generations of playwrights, influence strong enough to prompt them to redact it or a part thereof into a new form. Perhaps a play, however worthy, does not hold such potentialities in a strong measure. No two plays, their identity in technique apart, are known to share more than peripheral resemblances. It was left to the polymath Hemacandra to subject the first four acts of the *AbŚ* to an adaptation, in a versified form, in his *magnum opus*, the *Triṣaṣṭiśalākāpuruṣacarita* (*TŚC*).[2] While recounting the series of previous births of Pārśvanātha, the twenty-third Jaina pontiff, he details an expedition of Suvarṇabāhu, the Cakravartī king of Surapura in eastern Videha, which leads him to an unknown jungle. It is here that the canvas of the adaptation is laid, with Hemavijaya, the author of the *Pārśvanāthacarita*[3], providing additional, though inconsequent, daubs to depict an integrated picture.

In Hemacandra's version Suvarṇabāhu is sought to represent Duṣyanta, Śakuntalā has a counterpart in Padmā, the foster-daughter of the Patriarchal sage Gālava who himself is a replica of Kaṇva, the *Kulapati*. Nandā cannot but recall Śakuntalā's friends in Kālidāsa's play. The non-descript elderly Tāpasī may be taken to be an echo of Gautamī. All these *dramatis personae* join to spin out Hemacandra's redaction, which, despite its faithful adherence to the corresponding part of the *AbŚ*, does not amount to be more than a faint shadow of the play.

The *AbŚ* has no occasion to dwell upon Duṣyanta's physical prowess or his skill in warfare, but the alacrity with which he scares away the demons who meance Kaṇva's hermitage, in his absence,[4] and his glorious triumph over the ferocious Asura-hordes[5] are unmistakably intended to spotlight his valour and agility in war. Hemacandra, likewise, has sought to stress Suvarṇabāhu's valour by invoking comparison with the mighty Indra, the wielder of the thunderbolt and by making a meaningful allusion to his impetuous command.[6] While Duṣyanta is out on a hunting orgy, Suvarṇabāhu unwittingly lands himself in the forest in a bid to test a newly broken steed, which, due to its queer training, soon passes his control.[7] The horses yoked to Duṣyanta's chariot are said to have surpassed, in their speed, the horses of both Sun and Indra, whereas Suvarṇabāhu's steed, the wind incarnate and Garuḍa treading on the earth, appears, on account of its velocity, to be an additional horse of the heavenly luminary.[8] After a long and difficult journey Duṣyanta asks the charioteer to give the weary horses a refreshing bath ; Suvarṇabāhu, bereft of retinue, himself helps his horse to quench its thirst and get a bath to allay the oppressive heat.[9] Like the hermit deer, when hotly chased by Duṣyanta, the mount of Suvarṇabāhu also moved, on account of its boundings, more in the air than on the earth.[10] While Duṣyanta enters Kaṇva's grove in response to a persistent request of the anchorites, Suvarṇabābu has nothing except perhaps his curiosity to impell him to the hermitage. The author of *the TŚC* had an authority for Suvarṇabāhu's unceremonious behaviour in the *Śakuntalopākhyāna* of the *Mahābhārata* (I.70.51). Both Duṣyanta and Suvarṇabāha, while stepping into the precincts of the hermitage, are assured of happy outcome by propitious omens. Duṣyanta undergoes the throbbing of his right arm, in case of Suvarṇabāhu it is the right eye that, through palpitation, prognosticates union with the beautiful damsel (*AbŚ*, I.15 ; *TŚC*, 9.2.221).

Hemacandra is so enthralled by the beauty of various situations in the *AbŚ* that he has incorporated them in his adaptation, even at places where they do not fully glue. When in the penance-grove, Duṣyanta hears a conversation to the south of a vista of trees whence emerge the three maidens, including Śakuntalā, to water the saplings. Hemacandra has omitted reference to the *vṛkṣavāṭikā* but could not help to indicate the southern direction wherein Suvarṇabāhu detects the ascetic girl Padmā, in the company of her friend, engaged in watering the plants. *Payaskumbhaiḥ,* in the context, cannot but recall Kālidāsa's *Secanghaṭaiḥ*. Suvarṇabāhu, like Duṣyanta, is struck with the exquisite beauty of the hermit dame. In Duṣyanta's reckoning Śakuntalā's beauty is a rarity even in a seraglio tenanted by peerless women ; to Suvarṇabāhu Padmā sets at naught the heavenly nymphs and Nāga ladies alike (*AbŚ*,I.17 ; *TŚC*, 9.2.223). The hero, in both the poems, at the first instance, scans the maiden undisturbed, perched behind the trees.[11] And both are quick to notice the wide contrast between her tender form and the arduous task she has been assigned to perform, rather indiscriminately.[12] In emulation of Kālidāsa, Hemacandra pointedly alludes to the tight bark-cloth of the hermit girl. But while in Kālidāsa it is Anasūyā, a friend, who loosens Śakuntalā's garment which Priyaṁvadā had mischievously fastened tight, in the *TŚC* Padmā herself loosens it in the supposed privacy of the mādhavī-arbour, unmindful of Suvarṇabāhu lurking there.[13] Kālidāsa has drawn an extremely charming picture of the contrast the bark-cloth presents to Śakuntalā's lovely mien, heightening, at the same time,its charms. Hemacandra, on the other hand, has restricted himself to the brusque mention of *valkala*.[14] Initial misgivings apart, Duṣyanta is convinced that Śakuntalā cannot but be a Kṣatriya girl because his noble heart covets her. Hemacandra has fondly redacted this expression in his version where Suvarṇabāhu does not harbour even preliminary doubt about her origin. He is confident that she cannot be an ascetic girl, because, as in the case of Duṣyanta, his heart is full of longings for her.[15]

The bee assails Śakuntalā in its fury, when disoldged by the current of water from her pitcher ; in Hemacandra's version it makes to Padmā's face, mistaking it for a full-blown lotus (*AbŚ*, p.24, *TŚC* 9.2.228). In her bid to save herself from the meance of the bee, Padmā seeks the aid of her friend who jokingly retorts that none but Suvarṇabāhu can bail her out of the impasse, as do Anasūyā and Priyaṁvadā counsel Śakuntalā to send for Duṣyanta, in a similar situation.[16] It is here that the hero, in both the poems, emerges from his hideout and assures the hermit-girls of their safety in a language that is marked by remarkable idenity. को नाम व उपद्रोता पात्युर्वीं वज्रबाहूजे (*TŚC*, 9.2.231) is a distinct echo of the verse that follows, from the *AbŚ* :

कः पौरवे वसुमतीं शासति शासितरि दुर्विनीतानाम् ।
अयमाचरत्यविनयं मुग्धासु तपस्विकन्यासु ।। I.22

The girls are bewildered at the sudden appearance, in their midst, of a man of his majesty. It is some time before they come to their own to apprise him, in almost identical phraseology, of the predicament in which the heroine was placed.[17] He seeks to reassure them with an intimate query about the welfare of their religious observances. निष्प्रत्यूहं तपः कच्चित् (*TŚC*, 9.2.233) and अपि तपो वर्धते ? (*AbŚ*, p.27), besides similarity of expression and contents, are aimed to set at rest the apprehensions of the girls. Nandā, like Śakuntalā's friends, greets the king to a seat under a dense tree which provides an apt backdrop to the intimacy of their confabulations that were to ensue soon (*AbŚ*,p.27 ; *TŚC*,9.2.236). And not unlike them, she is overcome by his serene bearing which leads her to request him to disclose his identity (*AbŚ*,p.28 ; *TŚC*, 9.2.237). After initial vacillation, Suvarṇabāhu, in conformity with Duṣyanta's behaviour, tells an untruth, however unworthy it might have been of his high status. Both endeavour to project themselves as ministers of their respective kings, charged to ensure that the religious practices of the ascetics are carried out unobstructed (*AbŚ*,p.29 ; *TŚC*, 9.2.239). But their replies leave both Nandā and Anasūyā unconvinced. They, in their hearts, are convinced that he was none else but the king himself (*AbŚ*, p.28; *TŚC*, 9.2.240). In response to Duṣyanta's pointed query -- वयमपि तावद् भवत्योः सखीगतं किमपि पृच्छामः (*AbŚ*,p.30) -- Anasūyā recounts, in brief, the story of Śakuntalā's birth till her arrival in the hermitage. Suvarṇabāhu also learns from Nandā that Padmā was a daughter of the Vidyādhara-chief from his queen Ratnāvalī. Following her father's death and the consequent patricidal war for the throne, she was entrusted by her mother to the loving care of her brother, the ascetic Gālava, who, on the prediction of a soothsayer, knew it for certain that Cakravartī Suvarṇabāhu was to marry her (*TŚC*, 9.2.240-245).

Kaṇva had gone to the distant Somatīrtha to appease Śakuntalā's adverse fate, his long absence from the hermitage being essential for Duṣyanta's advances to Śakuntalā to flower into wedlock. Since Padmā's marriage with Suvarṇabāhu was pre-determined and Gālava had submitted to the prophecy, he had no use to undertake a long journey. And, a female ascetic actually announces his return to the hermitage soon after seeing a visiting sage off (*TŚC*, 9.2.249). Herein he stands closer to Kaṇva, as depicted in the *Mahābhārata*, who also similarly returns without loss of much time.[18] While taking leave of the hero, Padmā is one with Śakuntalā in casting a lustful gaze on him. Śakuntalā exchanges glances with Duṣyanta, feigning that a shoot has pricked her foot and her bark has got entangled in a tree . Padmā gives expression to her longings by repeatedly turning to Suvarṇabāhu in a bid to catch a sly glance.[19]

The way the Patriarchal sage Gālava comes to know of the happenings in the hermitage differs substantially from Kālidāsa's version. An etheral voice apprises Kaṇva of all that had transpired in the grove in his absence. Padmā's friend, on the other hand, takes it upon herself to intimate the anchorite of Suvarṇabāhu's advent in the hermitage and his stay nearby.[20] As in the case of Duṣyanta, Suvarṇabāhu's army in its bid to trace him converges on the *Āśrama*. Not unlike Duṣyanta, he pledges to ensure that it caused no disturbance or harm to the inmates of the grove.[21] Śakuntalā's love for Duṣyanta itself culminates in a smooth Gāndharva marriage. Gālava, in obedience to the prediction of the sage, approached Suvarṇabāhu to give him Padmā's hand which he accepts so readily (*TŚC*, 9.2.259).

All is now set for her departure from the hermitage. Like Śakuntalā, she is overwhelmed by an onrush of emotions at the impending separation from her kinsmen. She touchingly takes leave of her foster-father, mother, friends, and the eternal denizens of the *Āśrama*, the flora and fauna (*TŚC*, 9.2.267-272). Though tender in appeal, the situation does not compare favourably with the corresponding scene in the *AbŚ* wherein Kālidāsa has depicted *Karuṇarasa* so brilliantly that it serves to be an eternal index to human emotions, on the occasion. As Śakuntalā prepares herself to depart, Kaṇva spells out the duties a young bride is supposed to perform to ensure harmonious conjugal life ; in Hemacandra's version the role has been assigned to Ratnāvalī, who, in a phraseology not much dissmilar from that of Kālidāsa, urges her daughter to be discreet in her dealings with elders, friends and others alike. (*AbŚ*, IV.18; *TŚC*, 9.2.273-77). Thereafter Padmā flies in the aerial car of her husband to his capital, stopping *en route* with her maternal uncle, Ratnāvalī's step-brother. Śakuntalā had to undergo long sufferings before she could return to Hastināpura with her husband.

In view of Hemacandra's religious affiliations, his redaction of the *AbŚ* may be rated as a Jaina recension, though there is nothing to project it in a sectarian hue. The fact that he has chosen to recast it in a situation which could have been conveniently handled otherwise with equal effect, bespeaks the measure of fancy he had taken to Kālidāsa's play.

REFERENCES

1. Ed. M.R. Kale, Bombay, 1934.
2. Jaina Ātmānanda Sabhā, Bhavnagar.
3. Ed. Vela Siṁha, Vārāṇasī, 1916.
4. का कथा बाणसन्धाने ज्याशब्देनैव दूरतः। *AbŚ*., III.1.

5. चापेन तस्य त्वं रणशिरसि स्मृतो निहन्ता । *Ibid.*, VI.30.
6. अखण्डिताज्ञो मेदिन्यां सौधर्म इव वज्रभृत् । *TŚC.*, 9.2.210
7. *TŚC.*, 9.2.212-214
8. अतीत्य हरितो हरींश्च वर्तन्ते वाजिनः । *AbŚ*, p.12 ;
अपूर्वं हयमारूढः सूर्याश्वानामिवाष्टमम् । *TŚC., 9.2.211*
गरुत्मान् पादचारीव नभस्वानिव मूर्तिमान् । *Ibid.*, 9.2.214
9. ----तावदार्द्रपृष्ठाः क्रियन्तां वाजिनः । *Abś.*, p.17 ;
-----स्नपयामास तं हयम् ।
पयश्चापाययद् भूपः स्नात्वा च स्वयमप्यपात् ।। *TŚc.*, 9.2.218
10. पश्योदग्रप्लुतत्वाद्वियति बहुतरं स्तोकमुर्व्यां प्रयाति । *Abś.*, I.7;
भूस्पृग्व्योमचरो वेति नालक्षि स हयो रयात् ।। *TŚC.*, 9.2.215
11. पादपान्तर्हित एव विश्रब्धं तावदेनां पश्यामि । *Abś.*, p.19 ;
ततश्च वृक्षान्तरितो यावत्तां स व्यचिन्तयत् ।। *TŚC*, 9.2.224
12. असाधुदर्शी तत्रभवान् काश्यपो य इमामाश्रमधर्मे नियुंक्ते। *Abś*, p.19.
क्वेदं रूपं क्व कर्मेदं प्राकृतस्त्रीजनोचितम् । *TŚC.*, 9.2.226
13. अतिपिनद्धेन वल्कलेन प्रियंवदया नियन्त्रितास्मि । शिथिलय तावदेतत् ।।
Abś., p.20 ;
दृढबद्धं श्लथीकृत्य वल्कलं तत्र बालिका । *TŚC.*, 9.2.225
14. Abś., I.18 ; TŚC., 9.2.225
15. असंशयं क्षत्रपरिग्रहक्षमा यदार्यमस्यामभिलाषि मे मनः । *Abś.*, I.20.
न च तापसकन्येयं यदस्यां रागि मे मनः । *TŚC.*, 9.2.227
16. रक्षितुं त्वां कोऽन्योऽलं स्वर्णबाहुतः । *TŚC.*, 9.2.230 ;
के आवां परित्रातुम् । दुष्यन्तमाक्रन्द । *Abś.*, p.26
17. इयं नौ प्रियसखी मधुकरेणाभिभूयमाना कातरीभूता । *Abś.*, p.27
--पद्मभ्रान्त्या मुखेऽलिना । दश्यमाना कातराक्षी । *TŚC.*, 9.2.235
18. फलाहारो गतो राजन् पिता मे इत आश्रमात् ।।
मुहूर्तं सम्प्रतीक्षस्व स मां तुभ्यं प्रदास्यति ।।
Mahābhārata, Gita Press, I.73.5.
19. अभिनवकुशसूच्या परिक्षतं मे चरणं कुरबकशाखापरिलग्नं च वल्कलम् ।
Abś., p.39
पश्यन्ती वलितग्रीवा स्वर्णबाहुमहीपतिम् *TŚC.*, 9.2.251
20. शरीरं विना छन्दोमय्या वाण्या । *Abś.*, p.94
---सा सखी। सुवर्णबाहुवृत्तान्तं कथायामास संमदात् ।। *TŚC.*, 9.2.252
21. वयमप्याश्रमपीडा यथा न भवति तथा प्रयतिष्यामहे । *Abś.*, p.39.
रक्षामि बलमाश्रमात् ।। *TŚC.*, 9.2.250.

NAYACANDRA SŪRI - A LITERARY PROFILE

Though not a challenging match to stakwarts like Māgha and Śrīharṣa, Nayacandra Sūri, the celebrated author of the *Hammīra-mahākāvya* (*HM*)[1] emerges as one of the robust and colourful personalities in the vast domain of profane literature. Best known as a poet and historiographer of considerable merit, he represents an interesting amalgam of a political scientist, poetician, grammarian, erotist and Vedist all rolled to result in an integrated entity that gives him a place of pride in the Jainistic tradition. The *HM* illustrates his multiple capabilities in ample measure and thereby serves to bring into relief the various facets of his literary achievements.

Nayacandra was well-grounded in the art and science of statecraft. However, unlike Māgha his perception of politics does not degenerate into academic pedantry. He doubtless refers to such stock teminology as three powers (*śaktis*) that form the *summum bonum* of regal glory, four expedients (*upāyas*) and six means (*guṇas*);[2] politics, as visualised and formulated by him, is intended to serve as an unfailing guide to the new ruler in the difficult task of goverance.

As a man of ethos, Nayacandra views politics as an emanation of the moral apitude of the ruler. While nobility of conduct evokes spontaneous respect, its debasement spells doom. Nayacandra cautions the young ruler against excessive addition to carnal pleasures. Woman, whether attached or detached, is invariably a serious distraction that tends to sap the reservoir of royal power. In obedience to the tradition he advocates the use of expedients but is at pains to emphasize their employment with canny circumspection. *Daṇḍa*, he wisely opines, is to be resorted to after all other expedients are successively exhausted.[3] Nayacandra appears to uphold imperialistic tendencies in projecting '*ekachatra rājya*' as his ideal. To him, a hostile chieftain, antagonistic to the royal power, is not different from a poison-tree that has to be struck down to escape its baneful consequences. Valour is the most potent weapon in the armoury of the king. But, as a practical thinker Nayacandra views discretion to be the better part of valour. If what is sought to be achieved by prowess can be had through expedience or stratagem, the former should be shunned.[4] His moral overtones are again prominent in holding the futility of *digvijaya* without subduing the inner foes that are more intractable than the most hostile enemies.[5]

Nayacandra is acutely conscious of the worth of political parleys as a means to formulate policies and resolve tricky problems. To him, prudence lies in conferring with one minister and in maintaining the secrecy of confabulations. The king should seek advice of the minister after carefully forming his views on the issue. In case of concurrence, he should act accordingly. If, however, he sees merit in the advice tendered to him, he should ungrudgingly effect changes in his views. Once the policies are adopted, it is the responsibility of the ministers and other functionaries to implement them in the best interest of the state to ensure which Nayacandra advocates the appointment of trusted and faithful persons to the various posts. Restoration of a dismissed or sentenced officer to his original post tantamounts to signing one's death warrant. He continues to nurture enmity to the king thereafter and strikes with deadly strength at the earliest available opportunity.[6]

Nayachandra is unsparing in pouring abhorrence on the state-functionaries. He advises the ruler to exercise strict control on them and to exitrpate forthwith such of them as thrive through illegal methods like bribery, to the neglect of state and its people. In his political ethos the king plays mother to the poeple while the officers compare with co-wives to her. It is suicidal to hand over the baby to the step-mother. Ambitious functionaries, unless weeded out, are a permanent hazard to the security of the state and its ruler.[7]

Taxation, in Nayacandra's view, forms the basis of enonomic stability and prosperity of the state. Taxation to be successful has to be fair and indiscriminatory. The people should be taxed in a manner that does not bruise them physically or mentally.[8] It is as heinous to swell the state's coffers with harshly extorted money as to feed oneself on one's own flesh.[9] A fair policy of taxation, on the other hand, ensures fiscal security without impairing the happiness of the subjects.[10] Hostility of one's kinsmen is as harmful as excessive oppression of the people to which unwise taxation invariably leads. To Nayacandra, the two are like the opposite grinding stones which reduce the state to dust.[11]

Politics, as envisaged and formulated by Nayacandra, is summed up in the following verse :

parābhavan dviṣaccakram prabhavan nyāyavṛddhaye /
saukhyam cānubhavan sphītam sa prajāściramanvaśāt //[12]

Besides being a political scientist, Nayacandra was a gifted historian. In obedience to the tradition, he has undoubtedly presented history with attractive poetic trappings but his narrative, for the most part, is authentic, well-connected and devoid of supernatural elements that besmirch poems of this genre and thereby serve to frustrate attempts at separating chaff from the grain. Like a true historian, Nayacandra seems to have undertaken his task after subjecting the available sources to a searching scrutiny, dropping in the process what turned out to be untrustworthy. The earlier part of the poem that serves as a prologue to the main narrative, doubtless suffers from certain egregious errors. However, Nayacandra's account of Hammīra and his encounters with the Khalji hordes including the final battle, stands on firm historical footing and is happily upheld by contemporary Muslim historians.[13]

Not a poetician, Nayacandra has *en passent* expressed his views on certain rhetorical precepts as well. He seems to have been a stout champion of the *Rasa*-school of poetry to the extent that to him *Rasa* is but another name of *Kāvya*. True poetry aims at imparting undiluted pleasure (*mud*). Only lesser poets seek to conceal their lack of feelings by having recourse to verbal jugglery.[14] Nayacandra has religiously translated the ideal in the body of his poem which, in his own estimation, is intended to lend *prīti* to the cultural reader.[15] Though somewhat ambiguous on the issue, he seems to espouse *Śṛṅgāra* as the principal sentiment in poetry which he unhesitatingly elevates to a status higher than the bliss accruing from the realisation of Brahman.[16] Alternatively, he recommends the Heroic sentiment as the dominant *Rasa*. However, whatever the main sentiment, *Śṛṅgāra* invariably lends it an added flavour as does salt to food.[17] The epithet *Śṛṅgāravīrādbhuta* applied to his poem is perhaps indicative of his perference for the erotic sentiment.

He also talks of 'experience' as not being the sole cause of poetry.[18] Casual blemishes in the language, unless they miliate against sentiment, do not detract from the worth of poetry.[19] Viśvanātha was also constrained to admit this simple truth even after subjecting the epithet *adoṣau* in Mammaṭa's definition of poetry to gruesome criticism.[20]

Like Māgha, Nayacandra was well-versed in the art of erotics-*Smarakalāvidura*. The amourettes, detailed in the middle of his poem, may be out of joint with the tragic denouement, they, however, testify to his proficiency in the Kāmaśāstra. In emulation of Māgha, Nayacandra has herein sought to illustrate different types of *nāyikā* and their varied expressions and actions like *bibboka, kuṭṭamita, kilakiñcita*. As a matter of fact, he has gone a step further in expressly describing inverted cohabitation, ejaculation and such other situations which in themselves smack of unabashed obscenities.[21] If the erotist in Māgha ever met discomfiture, it was at the hands of the Jaina monk.

As a grammarian Nayacandra may not be a comparison to Bhaṭṭi or Māgha, but his learning in grammar commands attention. According to him scholarship in grammar is achieved by close study of the *Aṣṭādhyāyī* and its *Vṛtti* (perhaps *Kāśikā*) along with its commentaries.[22] Nayacandra himself appears to have mastered both which accounts for the plethora of learned usages that abound in his poem.[23] The reference to the Vedic hymns, performance of sacrifices, recitation of the *mantras*, gifts and fasts seems to indicate that Nayacandra was no mean student of Veda and Dharmaśāstra. As a poet Nayacandra favours lucidity of meaning (*nirmalārtha*) and upholds it as the basis of fame.[24] He has adhered to the precept in composing his poem. But while espousing *artha* he has not ignored *śabda* or form. Indeed he is conscious of the poetic worth of his poem. Lucidity and ornateness (*vakrimā*) combine to accord it a high place.

REFERENCES

1. Ed. Muni Jinavijaya, Jodhpur, 1968
2. *HM*, I.103,II.1,10,IX.10
3. *Ibid.*, VIII.73-78
4. *Ibid* VIII.79-83, XI.21
5. *Ibid.*, VIII.39
6. *Ibid.*, VII.96-102
7. *Ibid.*, VIII.92-95
8. *Ibid.*, VII.87
9. *Ibid.*, IX.170
10. *Ibid.*, IV.1
11. *Ibid.*, VIII.91
12. *Ibid.*, IV.31

13. For a detailed evaluation of the historical narrative see the succeeding paper *Hammīra-mahākāvya* : A unique source of the History of Raṇathambhor.
14. *HM.*, XIV.35
15. सरसजनमनःप्रीतये काव्यमेतत् । *HM.*, XIV.34
16. रतिरसं परमात्मरसाधिकम् *HM.*, VII.104
17. *Ibid.*, XIV.36
18. *Ibid.*, XIV.29-32
19. *Ibid.*, XIV.39
20. See my article *Nayacandra Sūri ke Sāhityika Adarśa, Mahāvīra - samārikā*, Jaipur, 1974, Pt.II, p.63-66
21. *HM.*, VII.83,90,101,103,112,116,121 etc.
22. *Ibid.*, VIII.105
23. चिकिर्षयाऽऽत्मनीनस्य सस्मार परमात्मनः (IV.78)
पचेलिमफलोदया (IV.87) भिदेलिमतमायतिः (IV.87)
सौख्यनाडिंधमाः (IV.116) उरःपूरं (XIII.222)
दूर्वालावं (XIII.222) अवर्द्धिष्ट (IV.39) उपाक्रांस्त । (XIII.147), etc.
24. *HM.*, VIII.9

HAMMĪRAMAHĀKĀVYA : A UNIQUE SOURCE OF THE HISTORY OF RAṆATHAMBHOR

Contrary to the mass of the so-called historical writings in Sanskrit, the *Hammīramahākāvya* (*HM*)[1] of Nayacandra Suri, a Jain monk of the *Kṛṣṇagaccha*, is characterised, by and large, by faithful representation of the historical narrative. The first seven of the fourteen cantos of the *HM*, concerned as they are with Hammīra's ancestors (I-IV) and poetic digressions (V-VII), serve as a prelude to the main theme of Hammīra's political career, distinguished by an interplay of chivalry, idealism and cynicism. The account of the early rulers doubtless suffers from frequent lapses, but for Hammīra and his immediate predecessors the *HM* forms the most complete and coherent tome, bereft of exaggerated accretions which so often cloud the kernel of historical truth in such poems. The veracity of its version is corroborated, not infrequently, by hostile Muslim chronicles, a fact which heightens the relibaility of the *HM*.

The ignominous defeat of Pṛthvīrāja in the second battle of Tarain and his consequent assasination marked the end of the glory of the Chauhans. His son Govindarāja had purchased the throne of Ajmer from the Muslim conqueror Muhammad Ghori, at a staggering price. He carved out 'with his might' a small principality with its capital at Raṇathambhor, after he was supplanted by his uncle Harirāja who subsequently made an attempt for his ouster from the new kingdom also. Harirāja's excessive indulgence to the neglect of his kingly duties resulted in his estrangement with the nobility and people alike. With discontent brewing all round, that was too good an opportunity to be missed by his erswhile enemy, Muhammad Ghori. Harirāja seems to have met a violent end. As the *HM* puts it, when attacked by the ruler of Delhi he preferred flames of pyre to an encounter with the Muslim invader.[2] Realising the futility of putting up resistance to the superior might of Ghori's forces, compounded with the absence of an heir to the throne, Harirāja's counsellors resolved to seek refuge at Raṇathambor along with the remnants of the wealth and forces of their master.[3] They were well received and appointed[4] to appropriate offices. Ajmer fell into the hands of the Muslims.[5] In view of this sequence of the historical events, Nayacandra's description of Govindarāja as a grandson of Pṛthvirāja and of his shock at the ignoble end of his uncle, as also the account of his banishment from Ajmer,[6] lack basis. With Govindarāja commences the Raṇathambhor line of the Chauhans.

Govindarāja's son and successor Bāllana (Vālhaṇa) appears to have had an inconsequential reign. The Manglana Stone Inscription of Vikrama Saṁvat (VS) 1272 (1215 A.D.) bears testimony to the fact that, like his father, he continued to recognise the suzerainty of the Delhi Sultante.[7] The narration of his exploits, in the *HM*[8] is therefore conventional. Equally unworthy was Bāllana's son Prahlādana. Prahlādana had but a brief rule. Before he succumbed to the wounds sustained in a lion-hunt, he consecrated his minor son Vīranārāyaṇa as his successor under the regency of Vāgbhaṭa, "a veritable prop to the tottering fortunes of the Chauhanas." Convinced of Vīranārāyaṇa's waywardness, Vāgbhaṭa accepted the office with reluctance.[9] Soon afterwards, he had a taste of the prince's aberratious temperament.

While proceeding to Āmrapurī (Amer) to marry the daughter of its Kacchawaha Chief, Vīranārāyaṇa was waylaid by the Muslim ruler Jalaluddin. He had to hurry back home without marrying the Amer Princess. The Muslim hordes followed him there too. But, secure in his stronghold, he appears to have successfully stood the siege. The craftty Jalaluddin, with his design frustrated on the battle-field, resolved to entrap him by stratagem. He called off the siege and hastily fell back to his capital. Subsequently he invited Vīranārāyaṇa to come to Delhi to work out a treaty, which he offered as a token of his friendship for him. Alternatively, the wily Sultan expressed his readiness to come to Raṇathambhor to consummate the proposed alliance. In his zeal to secure aid against Vigraha of Vakṣasthalapura by such a treaty, the unsuspecting Rājputa reached Yoginīpura (Delhi), scoffing at Vāgbhaṭa's wise counsel to the contrary. The prince was appearently treated with the greatest respect but after a few day's hospitality was poisoned to death. Raṇathambhor was now easily captured by the Sultan. "Once the tree is struck down, it is easy to approriate its fruit."

Stung by the contemptuous rejection of his advice, Vāgbhaṭa had already repaired to Mālava. There he got scent of a conspiracy being hatched against him by the ruler of Mālva, at the behest of the Sultan. He acted swiftly, killed the king and captured his kingdom. And, when the Kharparas (Mongols) were up in arms against Jalaluddin, he stormed Raṇathambhor with precipitate vehemence. The Muslim garrison in the fort crumbled against the vigour of his siege. Raṇathambhor was liberated like 'a digit of the moon from the jaws of Rāhu.' During his happy regime of twelve years, he is credited to have chastened many a refractory king. It was his policy to station strong garrisons on the frontiers of his kingdom.[10]

This largely correct account of the *HM* needs to be supplemented and modified in the light of independent testimony. The Muslim ruler who had wrested Raṇathambhor from Vīranārāyaṇa was Shamsuddin Iltutmish. He represents Nayacandra's Jalaluddin. He appears to have conquered the fort through treachery rather than valour. The *Tabquat-i-Nasiri* assigns the event to 1226 A.D.[11] It is difficult to identify Vigraha of Vakṣasthalapura. The king of Mālva slain by Vagbhaṭa was perhaps Devapāla for whom we have no inscription after 1235 A.D. It is sheer exaggeration to presume that he had captured the whole of Mālva. Mālva continued to be ruled by the Paramāras, though some of its far-flung areas might have passed into the hands of the neighbouring rulers. Vāgbhaṭa's son Jaitrasiṁha himself was involved in a clash with a king of Mālava.[12]

Vāgbhaṭa must have regained Ranathambhor in the year 1236.[13] The Kharparas (Mongols) mentioned in the *HM*, seem to have had no bearing on his victory, the credit for which much rest with Vāgbhaṭa's political sagacity. By all accounts Vāgbhaṭa was a powerful ruler. According to Nayacandra he humbled large number of belligerent kings and thereby acted as a prop to the fading glory of the Chauhanas.[14] The Muslim historians call him "the greatest of the Rais and the most noble and illustrious of all the princes of Hindustan."[15] The *HM* makes no mention of the two subsequent attempts made by Nasiruddin to capture the citadel in 1248 A.D. and 1253 A.D.[15a]

The *HM* passes in silence the achievements of Jaitrasiṁha, detailed in the Balvan Inscription (dated 1288 A.D,)[16] of his son Hammīra, the hero of the *HM*. Jaitrasiṁha had, besides Hammīra, two other sons, Suratrāṇa and Vīrama. After consecrating the youngest Hammīra on the throne of Raṇathambhor on Sunday, the 15th of the bright of Māgha, V.1339 (1282 A.D.), he set out to Pattana, on the bank of Chambal, to lead an ascetic life but expired at Palli, on the way.[17]

Hammīra was undeniably the mightiest and the most illustrious ruler of Raṇathambhor. In the earlier years of his reign he embarked upon a military expedition (*digvijaya*) with a well-trained army. He first reduced to submission Arjuna, the intrasigent ruler of Bhīmarasa, thence he swooped on Dhāra, "a veritable ocean of valiant warriors." Having humbled its ruler Bhoja, a compeer of his distinguished predecessor of the same name, he closed upon Ujjayinī. On the homeward journey he subdued Citrakūṭa (Chittor) and ravaging Medapāṭa (Mewār), set up his camp on Mount Ābu. The powerful ruler of Ābu was obliged to submit to him with rich presents. Thereafter he ravaged Vardhanapur, robbed Caṅga of its glory and passed through Ajmer *en route* to Puṣkara. From Puṣkara he repaired to Śākambharī (Sāmbhar) where "a salt lake was formed by the torrential tears of the womenfolk." Harring Mahārāṣṭra (Marot), Khaṇḍilla (Khandela), Campā(?), Kakarala ((Karauli?), where the lord of Tribhuvanagiri (Thānagarh) received him with valuable gifts, he returned home. Perhaps as a consummation of his *digvijaya*, he performed a Koṭiyajña at the instance of his preceptor Viśvarūpa and made liberal gifts to the Brāhmaṇas.[18]

The contemporary political situation in the country was indubitably propitious for Hammīra to undertake such a campaign. There was no powerful ruler at Delhi for four years after Balban's death in 1286 A.D. to challenge the growing might of the Chauhanas. The neighbouring kingdom of Mālava was torn by continued insurrections. The glory of Gujrat was past. Samarasiṁha of Chittor too was not an ambitious ruler.[19] However, a reference to Hammīra's Balvan Inscription of V.S.1345 (1288 A.D.) raises doubt about the *digvijaya* to have been carried out in the systematic way, in which it has been described by the author of the *HM*. The inscription speaks of two Koṭiyajñas, but does not make the slightest allusion to Hammīra's expedition. The only military achievement of Hammīra mentioned therein is his victory over the Mālava-ruler, Arjuna,[20] which might well have been the only historical truth in the otherwise fake narrative of the *digvijaya*. Arjuna of Bhīmarasa is identical with Arjuna of Mālava, mentioned in the Balvan Inscriptian, whose elephant-force was captured by Hammīra. Nayacandra seems to have interwoven the various raids launched, from time to time, on the neighbouring kingdoms into one homogeneous expedition. If at all, such raids were under-taken they are to be referred to the post-1288 era. But, in view of Hammīra's preoccupations with the Khaljis from 1291 onwards, even such a proposition appears untenable.

The political situation, however, underwent a drastic change with the emergence of the Khaljis. Incensed by the non-payment of tribute, Allauddin, according to Nayacandra, commanded his younger brother Ullu Khan (Ulug Khan) to storm the Raṇathambhor country. The Khalji forces marched unopposed upto the river Banas. Here Hammīra's general Bhīmasiṁha attacked them with vehemence at the instance of Prime Minister Dharma Siṁha, leaving the safe positions on the passes. He seems to have gained some initial advantage. Instead of taking full advantage of the gains, Bhīmasiṁha retraced his steps under an illusion of success. His soldiers were also so anxious to carry home soon the large booty they had collected. In the flush of mistaken victory, Bhīmsiṁha caused the battle-drums, seized from the enemy, to be beaten. Taking the sound as a signal for action, the Sultan's army, that was on the chase in small detachments, fell upon Bhīmasiṁha. He withstood the unequal combat valiantly but was overpowered and killed. His mission achieved, Ulug Khan retreated to Delhi.

Hammīra apportioned the blame for Bhīmasimha's defeat and death to his Chief Counsellor Dharma Siṁha. He upbraided him severly. Charging him with 'blindness' for not making the proper assesment of the enemy's strength, and with 'impotence' for letting Bhīmasiṁha die unattended, he had him actually blinded and castrated. He was replaced by Bhojadeva as Prime minister. He was also sentenced with deportation. However, the punishment was not carried out at the intercession of Bhoja.[21]

Nayacandra is obviously wrong in assinging this raid on Raṇathambhor to Allauddin's time. It actually came off in 1291 when his predecessor Jalaluddin was on the throne of Delhi. Though a weakling, he could ill afford to ignore this stronghold of the Chauhans, flourishing so close to the capital. It was in an encounter with Jalauddin Khalji's army that Bhīmasimha perished. He appears to be Amir Khusru's Sahni, "who was not a Hindu, but a hill of iron." Though the encounter involved the death of Hammīra's competent general, the invasion otherwise "ended in a fiasco"[22] for the Sultan, who, as stated earlier, had to fall back to Delhi hurriedly.

Bhoja proved unequal to the task. His inability to raise revenues commensurate with the needs of the army in the changed situation brought about his downfall. The multilated Dharma Siṁha, thirsting for revenge, convinced Hammīra through his pupil Dhārādevī, of his capability to provide finances and horses to keep the army in fine *fettle*. With his judgement clouded by avrice, he restored Dharma Siṁha to his post and in the process "signed his death warrant." Dharma Siṁha was true to his word. He filled the royal coffers with riches and refurnished the army. Thus he regained the confidence of the king but aliented the people by his unjust exactions. He called upon Bhoja, his predecessor in the office, to render an account of his department. Bhoja's pleading with the king brought him only insults. Finding the situation unbearable, he alongwith his younger brother Pīthamasiṁha escaped from the capital. Hammīra was delighted at Bhoja's exit and installed Ratipāla on his post.[23]

There are no means to verify the correctness of Dharma Siṁha's narrative. But in view of Nayacandra's general aversion to untruth, it cannot be dismissed as fictitious. Dharma Siṁha might have been reinstated in his office somewhere between 1291 and 1298 A.D. Nor are Bhoja and Pīthama unkown to the later chronicles and bardic literature.[24]

Nayacandra attributes the oppression perpetrated on the populace to Dharma Siṁha's burning desire for revenge on Hammīra. While that might have been a contributory factor, the real cause is to be found in Hammīra's faulty fiscal policies. The first Khalji raid had highlighted the need to maintain a large and well-equipped army. His resources were meagre. Heavy taxation was the method which Hammīra exploited rather zealously. That caused resentment in the people and precipitated his fall which was hastened by his unwise ouster of Bhoja.

Thirsting for Hammīra's blood, Bhoja instigated Allauddin to invade the Raṇathambhor kingdom before the exceptionally good harvest was garnered. That, he rightly believed, was sure to alienate still further, the poeple groaning under the blind minister's tyranny. The astute Allauddin saw merit in the suggestion and forthwith bade his eminent general Ulug Khan to blitz Hammīra's country with a massive army of of one lakh horses. Bhoja was rewarded with the jagir of Jagara.

The Khalji general reached the Hinduvāṭa pass, unchecked. There, in keeping with a well-planned strategy, Vīrama and seven other generals (including Muhammad Shah) of the Chauhan ruler simultaneously swooped on the army from all the eight points of the compass. The Khaljis fought with desperate courage but fled pell-mell under repeated sorties. A large booty consisting of horses, elephants and riches fell in the hands of the Chauhans. Some of the enemy's women were also taken captive. In order to proclaim his victory in the kingdom, Ratipāla forced them to sell sour milk in the countryside. To express his delight at the success of his generals, Hammīra invested Ratipāla with a gold chain. Muhammad Shah consummated the victory with a raid on Jagara. Pīthama alongwith the members of Bhoja's family was brought back to Raṇathambhor. But Bhoja escaped the fate as he was away in Delhi, at the moment.

Ulug Khan beat a hasty retreat and apprised the Sultan of his woeful tale. Allauddin flew into rage and determined to chastise the Chauhan king. Bhoja's lamentations over the loss of Jagir and family added fuel to the fire.[25]

Keen on attacking Raṇathambhor, Allauddin requisitioned reinforcements from different parts of the country,[26] and put Nusrat Khan, besides the reputed Ulug Khan, in charge of the present invasion. He himself stayed behind to keep the Chauhans in suspense about the possible reserves held in the capital. By forced marches the Khalji concourse reached the (Hinduvāṭa) pass, "drying on the way, the rivers of their waters." Chastened by the previous discomfiture, Ulug Khan resolved to gain time under the garb of a peace-offer, to negotiate the hazardous pass. Thinking that they would be tackled more effectively in the valley, the Chauhans also allowed them enter unmolested. The Khan posted his forces on strategic points. Through an envoy he urged the Chauhan king to avoid combat with the ruthless Allauddin who had laid waste many an impregnable fortress like Devagiri, and counselled him to conclude peace with his generals, who offered him two alternatives. Hammīra could either pay them a tribute of one lakh *moharas*, present four elephants, three hundred horses and his daughter, or he could surrender the four refractory Mongol Chiefs who had defected to Raṇathambhor. Hammīra contemptuously rejected both and offered Allauddin instead an equal number of sword-cuts. The Khaljis now prepared themselves for the battle. Soon there started a terrible rain of arrows. Fiery missiles were freely hurled. The Sultan's soldiery threw spears soaked in boiling oil and resin, inflicting heavy damage on the Chauhan garrison. The latter, in turn, forked away the enemy when it attempted to lay mines in the ramparts. The war engines showered intermitent volleys of stones. In one such engagement a splinter resulting from the collission of two rival stones hit and instantly killed Nusrat Khan. Ulug Khan despatched his dead body to Delhi. After he had performed his last rites, Allauddin proceeded to Raṇathambhor to assume the charge of the operation.[27] Hammīra greeted him with two sorties which left eighty five thousand Khalji soldiers dead.[28]

Ziya-u-ddin Barani's account of Allauddin's encounter with Hammīra begins with the present combat. The outcome of the earlier foray was perhaps not palatable to him.[29] The provenance of Allauddin's military levies, as detailed by Nayacandra, is conventional. There is however no gainsaying that he collected a massive army for the campaign. According to Barani, Ulug Khan, who held the territory of Biana, was sent against the fort and Nusrat Khan, who was governor of Karra that year, was ordered to march to his assistance with the army of Karra and other provinces of Hindustan.[30] The Khaljis could cross the pass this time, asserts Nayacandra, under the pretext of treaty. But it seems that because of the vastness of the Sultan's army the Chauhans preferred to stand siege rather that fight headlong on the battle-field. The army deployed by Allauddin was a sufficient indication of Hammīra's military might.

Nayacandra's description of the despatch of an envoy to the Chauhan king and his urging him to make over the Mongol Chieftains to Allauddin is corroborated by Isami. He also bears testimony to Hammīra's scornful repudiation of the envoy's demand. "I can do no harm to those who have sought asylum with me even if the Turks surround the fort from all quarters."[31]

The version of Nusrat Khan's death, as given in the *HM*, bears striking similarly to Barani's account. He bears out Nayacandra when he says that while engaged in raising a *pashib* (a sort of machan) Nusrat Khan was struck by a stone hurled by a *magribi* (war engine) from the fort. He died two or three days later. On receiving intelligence of the event, Alauddin set out to Raṇathambhor in imperial glory.[32]

Allauddin invested the fort cosely. But Uḍḍānasiṁha's loss to the marksmanship of Muhammad Shah obliged him to withdraw to the rear of the lake. The Chauhan warriors foiled him in his repeated attempts to press to the vicinity of the fort. The Sultan's soldiery formed a sort of bridge on the moat with stones, faggots and earth, which, the Chauhans, on detection, immediately burnt with the fire-balls. When the Khaljis tried to carve underground tunnels, the garrison in the fortress threw boiling oil mixed with resin on them. The enemy was scalded to death like so many fish. Those who escaped were stoned down like street dogs. Thus the doughty Chauhans filled the tunnel with the bodies of enemy's soldiers themselves. The onset of the rainy season multiplied their difficulties. This disheartened the Sultan and he apeared to be contemplating a genuine treaty when he sent for Ratipāla. Hammīra too approved of the proposed parleys thinking that these would enable him to probe the Sultan's mind.[33]

Ratipāla was received with great honour. Allauddin cunningly impressed upon him that his object in investing the fort was to get the fame of its capture. If he were to carry the citadel, he would joyfully bestow it on him. These blandishments of the wily Sultan led Ratipāla to pledge him help. And he returned as a dangerous traitor. He misreported to the king that Allauddin, unmindful of the reverses he had suffered, was determined to capture the fort. Equally unshakable was his resolve to carry away perforce the king's wife, should he hesitate to surrender his daughter to him. By a shrewd stratagem Ratipāla turned Raṇamalla also against Hammīra, who soon escaped to the enemy's camp. Ratipāla followed him. When inquired of the state of the royal stores, the Kothārī, thinking that peace would be concluded should he misrepresent, reported them empty. Shaken by the desertion of his trusted lieutenants, Hammīra now saw a potential traitor in everybody around him. He therefore offered the Mongol Chief to codnuct them to safety. Muhammad Shah vindicated his faithfulness to the king by putting his family to sword. On a subsequent visit, the king found the stores brimming with grains.[34]

Thus deceived by all, he lost hope. He flung open the doors for the people to escape. Next, he ordered the grisly *Jauhar* to be performed. The royal ladies led by the Chief Queen Aṅgāradevī perished in the flames. Jājā performed their obsequies. He also offered his head to the king as an expression of his unflinching adherence to him in that trying hour. The king then had valuables thrown in the Padmasara. Vīrama struck down the head of the deceitful Kothāri. Now Hammīra, with his nine brave warriors including Vīrama, Siṁha, Gaṅgādhara Tāka and Kṣetrasiṁha Paramar, dashed forth for the final fight. Vīrama fell first. Muhammad Shah collapsed unconscious of the wound. Hammīra fought desperately. "So torrential was the rain of arrows hurled by him that he was mistaken for the Śrāvaṇa month." But his was an unequal fight. In a bid to avoid the ignominy of falling in the enemy's hand alive, he cut down his head with the sword.[35] The fort capitulated on the sixth day of the bright half of Śrāvaṇa.[35a] Jājā defended the fort for two days more.[36]

Ratipāla was deservedly flayed alive by the Sultan ; how else the traitors would desist from their treacherous conduct.[37] Muhammad Shah entered the Sultan's assembly showing him his foot.

When accosted with the words, "what would you do to me if I spare your life", he crisply replied : "Precisely that, what you have done to Hammīra."[38]

Nayacandra's version of the final encounter between the rival forces and also of the factors leading to the capitulation of Raṇathambhor, receives remarkable corroboration from the Muslim chornicles. The investment of Raṇathambhor had turned out to be a long-drawn affair. According to Amir Khusru the siege continued for four months, from March to July.[39] Meanwhile much had happened to reduce the Khalji army to dire straits, but not a single soldier dared to desert the camp for fear of the Sultan.[40] By all accounts the Chauhans put up a stubborn resistance. In the poetic language of Amir Khusru "even the birds did not fly because of torrents of arrows from the fort. The royal falcons too could not descend on it"[41] Isami gives a vivid account of the combat which bears a striking resemblance with the *HM*. According to him, the Rai frustrated all the attempts of the imperial army (to capture the citadel). If the Turks filled the moat with wood, the Hindus would burn it at night. No harm could be done to the fort. Then the Sultan used a stratagem to which the Rai had no answer. He had the moat levelled, this time, with sand bags. Thus a passage was formed to launch an attack on the fort.[42] A similar account is to be found in Barani's *Tarikh-i-Firozshahi.*[43]

Hammīra had put on a brave face. Had Allauddin not known the actual state of the garrison, the situation might have been saved ? But the desertion of Ratipāla and Raṇamalla sealed his fate. The story of their defection, Hammīra's offer to the Mongols to conduct them to safety and the performance of *Jauhar* are all borne out by *Hammīrāyaṇa*[44] and Vidyāpati's *Dayavīrakathā* (*DVK*), being a part of *Puruṣaparīkṣā*.[45] But while the former, like the *HM*, maintains that there was no scarcity of grains in the stores, the *DVK* explicitly states that the fort was in the grip of famine.[46] That Vidyāpati's version is correct, is proved by *Khazaini-ul-Futuh* which states "yes their provisions became finished, they ate stones. Famine prevailed to such an extent in the fort that they would have purchased a grain of rice for two grains of gold but could not get it."[47] Nor is the *Jauhar* unknown to the Muslim chornicles.[48]

Ratipāla's defection and punishment are vividly described by Firishta. "Those who have betrayed their natural sovereign will never be loyal to another," said the wise Sultan. Firishta also mentions Muhammad Shah's heroic retrot to Allaudin. The sultan had him trampled under a wild tusker, but, being pleased with his courage and fidelity, gave him a decent burial.[49]

Hammīra thus emerges as a brave and, in a restricted sense, an idealistic king but, like most of the Rajput rulers of mediaval history, he suffered from an appalling lack of political sagacity. His unwise fiscal policy coupled with the sedition of his close kinsmen and counsellors caused his downfall.

REFERENCES

1. Ed. by Muni Jinavijaya, Rajasthan Oriental Research Institute, Jodhpur, 1968.
2. *HM*, IV.13-19. The correctness of Nayacandra's version is proved by *Taju-I-Ma-asir*, a contemporary source, which also vouches for Jaitra's consigning himself (alongwith his master Harirāja) to "the flames of fire." Annual Report of the Rajputana Museum, 1911-12, p.2, as quoted in Dasharatha Sharma's *Eearly Chauhan Dynasties*, 1959 p.101, fn 11
3. *HM*. IV,21-23,25-27
4. धीसखांस्तान् यथायोग्यकार्येणायोजयन्नृपः । *op.cit.*, IV.30
5. Ibid., IV.27
6. Ibid., IV.24, 29
7. *Early Chauhan Dynasties*, op.cit., p.102
8. *HM*, IV.34-36.
9. Ibid., IV.41, 71-77.
10. Ibid., IV.82-131.
11. *Early Chauhan Dynasties*, p.103.
12. *HM men aitihya sâmagrī*, p.32.
13. *Early Chauhan Dynasties*, p.103.
14. *HM*, IV.73,128.
15. *Tabquat-i-Nasiri*, E.D.II, p.370.

15a. Early Chauhan Dynasties, p.104.

16. Verses 7-8.
17. *HM*, IV. 159; VIII.56,106-109,115.
18. Ibid., IX.15-94.
19. *Hammīrāyaṇa* (Sadul Research Institute, Bikaner), Intro. p.111.
20. यः कोटिहोमद्वितयं चकार श्रेणी गजानां पुनरानिनाय ।
    निर्जित्य येनार्जुनमाजिमूर्ध्नि श्रीमालवस्योज्जगहे हठेन ।।Verse, 11.
21. *HM*. IX.100-155.

22. K.S.Lall : *History of the Khaljis*, Asia Publishing House, 1967, p.30.
23. *HM*, IX.156-188.
24. (i) भोजदेव पिण मिलौ, मिलौ भोज रातू रंतौ । *Hammīra de kavitta*, 15
    (ii) प्रीथीराज परवाण कियो पतिसाहां भेलो ।
    Kavitta Hammīra Hathāle Ra,9.
    (iii) मिलो पीथल थिर चित्तो परतापसी पण मिलो । Ibid., 10.
25. *HM*.,X.29-78.
26. To be precise from Aṅga, Tilang, Magadha, Masura, Kaliṅga, Vaṅga, Bhata, Medapāta, Pañcā, Bengal, Thamima, Bhilla, Nepal, Dahala and hilly regions. *HM*,XI.1.
27. *HM*, XI.7-8,19-25,54-61,75-103.
28. Ibid.,Xii.88.
29. Likewise he omits reference to Allauddin's expedition to Bengal which also had ended in a disaster for him. *History of the Khaljis*, Op.cit.p.77.
30. Tarikh-i-Firozshahi, E.D.,III p.172
31. Futuh Slatin, Excerpts cited in Intro. to *Hammīrāyaṇa*, p.96.
32. Ibid., p.99.
33. *HM*, XIII.32-70.
34. Ibid., XIII.71-87,134-135,136-138,151,169.
35. Ibid., XIII. 171-226.

35a. Amir Khusru gives the date of the fall of the fort as July 10, 1301 A.D. : See *Khazain- ul-Futuh*, p.41.

36. *HM*, XIV.16.
37. Ibid., XIV.21.
38. Ibid., XIV.19-20
39. *Khazain-ul-Futuh*, Excerpts quoted in Intro. to *Hammīrāyaṇa* p.91.
40. *Tarikhī-Firozshahi,* Excerpts quoted in Intro. to *Hammīrāyaṇa*, p.100.
41. *Khazain-ul-Futuh*, Op.cit.
42. *Futuh Statin*, Excerpts quoted in Intro. to *Hammīrāyaṇa*, p.97.
43. Introduction to *Hammīrāyaṇa*, p.100.
44. Ibid., p.130.
45. *DVK*, Published as Appendix 3 to *Hammīrāyaṇa*, 52-55.
46. Ibid., दुर्गे दुर्भिक्षमापतितम् p.54.
47. Habib, *Khazin-ul-Futuh*, p.40.
48. Introduction to *Hammīrāyaṇa*, p.91,97.
49. Ibid., p.102.

DEVAVIMALA'S INDEBTEDNESS TO ŚRĪHARṢA

Māgha is the undisputed master of the post-Kālidāsa Mahākāvya. His wide erudition, laboured style and pronounced penchant for elaboration coupled with a plethora of poetic motifs, assiduously fostered by him, caught the fancy of later poets of all religious persuasions, to the extent that there emerged a formidable Māgha school in Sanskrit poetry. And in comparison to him all successive poets, not precluding celebrities like Śriharṣa, tend to pale into insignificance, so far as their impact on later generations of poets is concerned. Of the few poems that have been stirred by Śrīharṣa's *Naiṣadhacarita* [1] (*Nc.*), the gigantic tome of misplaced pedantry, the *Hīrasaubhāgya* [2] (*Hs.*) of Devavimala Sūri (16th century A.D.), which, in seventeen cantos, seeks to detail the life-account of Hīravijaya Sūri, the celebrated pontiff of *Tapāgaccha* and a spiritual friend of Akbar the Great, from his birth to death through myriad socio-religious achievements, calls attention by reason of its poetic virtues and close observance of the typical *Naiṣadha*-tradition. Despite vast divergence in contents and consequent shruken avenues of imitation, Devavimala was influenced by Śrīharṣa so powerfully that, not unoften, he is seen to tread on the footsteps of his illustrious predecessor, in the matter of the form of his poem.

The *Hs* is characterised in its inception by a graphic description of Prahlādanapura, following the narration of conventional geographical divisions of the continent, *Jambūdvīpa*. The description is evidently inspired and influenced by the corresponding portrayal of Kuṇḍinapura, in the second canto of the *Nc.* But unlike Kuṇḍinapura, Prahlādanapura, as the birthplace of the hero of Devavimala's poem, holds an important place in his scheme of things. In contrast to Śrīharṣa's thirty-two verses (II.74-105), Devavimala has dealt with the town in a sizable part of the first canto (69-127). Both the descriptions seem to be actuated by an anxiety on the part of the respective poets to illustrate the various objects, prescribed by the poeticians as inalienable characteristics of the description of a town.[3] That convincingly accounts for their unanimity in detailing garden, moat, rampart, pleasure tank, mansions, market etc. as ingredients of the description. While Śrīharṣa does not hesitate to parade his misplaced love for far-fetched fancies, abstruse conceits and philosophical subtleties even in such an innocuous context, Devavimala has spun out a brilliant description of Prahlādanapura, which, its prolixity apart, makes a delightful reading by sheer sweetness of language and a refreshing moderation of his standards of comparison (*aprastutas*).

Besides unanimity in conventional objects that mark the description, Devavimala shares with Śrīharṣa quite a few ideas, some of which tend to crystalise as mannerisms in such descriptions. Both fondly describe, in this context, the embankment which in the *Hs.* is postulated as being made of moon-stones, contrary to that of sun-stones in the *Nc.*[4] In emulation of Śrīharṣa, Devavimala represents the diamond-mansions as captivating smiles of the goddess of town (*Hs.*I.104, *Nc.*II.74), and alludes to the unassailability of Prahlādanapura, which, safeguarded by a mass of flames emanating from the sun-stones, invoked comparison with the metropolis of the legendary demon, Bāṇa, similarly secured by Śiva's boon, with a nimbus of fire.[5] Both tend to highlight the rich trade in perfumes in the respective towns (*Hs.*I.105-106; *Nc.* II.90). Devavimala's description of the moon-stones which in issuing currents of water invited resemblance with the holy Ganges (I.114), owes itself to the parallel motif in the *Nc.* (II.89). Both allude to the Śālabhañjikās sculptured in the mansions of the elite. While to Śrīharṣa they were seemingly devoured by the lions painted close by (II.83), in Devavimala's poem they are respresented as heavenly nymphs rendered still with curiosity at the fantastic charms of the palatial houses (I.113).

Description of physical charms occupies quite a sizable place in the *Nc.* Apart from her cursory description in Canto Two, Śrīharṣa has described in the seventh canto of his poem, in true Kāvya style, Damayantī's form which is intended to illustrate the *nakhaśikha* delineation of human beauties, as envisaged by him. In consonance with Śrīharṣa's technique Devavimala has assigned two cantos to the corresponding description and has thereby sought to underscore his debt to the author of the *Nc.* The description of Nāthī's charms in the *Hs.* is doubtless based on the parallel depiction of Damayantī with which it shares the locale in being positioned in the second canto. But unlike the *Nc.* (II), the description in the *Hs.* is marked by prolixity and stands out prominently because of its poetic excellences. When compared with it, Śrīharṣa's corresponding description sounds dreary and far-fetched though Devavimala borrows some of his relevant ideas.[6]

Following the scheme of the author of the *Nc.*, Devavimala has set forth, in the eighth canto of his poem, a prolonged description of the beauties of the presiding deity, *Śāsanadevatā*, which, not unlike Bhaimī's portrayal in Canto Seven, stretches to assume the form of *nakhaśikha* delineation. In his eagerness to imitate Śrīharṣa, the Jaina monk has described her in perfectly human form, blissfully forgetting her divine character. It has enabled him to deal with different parts of her body to present a parallel to Śrīharṣa's description. True to the moral degeneration that had permeated all aspects of life in his days, Śrīharṣa's description threatens, not infrequently, to transgress the bounds of decency. Devavimala's monastic inhibitions have restrained him from going amock, though he had all but come within an ace of Śrīharṣa's obscenity. Śrīharṣa's description of human beauties in the seventh canto has exercised powerful influence on both the descriptions in the *Hs*, but the two are distinguished by a marked difference in spirit. In an irrespressible zeal to air his admittedly unique Śāstric learning, Śrīharṣa is so caught in the labyrinth of wild and ethereal *aprastutas* that instead of contributing to the clarity of the subject they, almost invariably, envelop it in an impervious haze. Devavimala too is not wholly absloved of abstruse or far-fetched *aprastutas*, but he has not sought to turn his poem into a playground of his scholarship. It is precisely because of this happy moderation that he has accepted only a watered - down version of Śrīharṣa's *aprastutas*. Devavimala's portrayal of human from is more poetic and enjoyable.

The communion in the description of Nāthī with that of Damayantī is striking. Both Śrīharṣa and Devavimala concur in representing the ears of their heroines as two nooses intended to outdo Varuṇa, the god of water, who, in comparsion, wields a solitary *pāśa* (*Nc.*VII.64, *Hs*. II.24). The two are again unanimous in their perception of the five fingers of the lady as replicas of the five shafts of Cupid, stuck in the quiver of hand. To Śrīharṣa, they are fitted with lustrous heads of nails and are distinguished by smooth joints, in Devavimala's view they appear to have been fashioned with the set purpose of striking simultaneously the five faces of Śaṅkara, the established foe of Cupid.[7] Śrīharṣa has described Damayantī's breasts with a Virodhābhāsa which lends them an added charm. "Though in the vicinity of moon in the form of face, the *cakravākas* of her bosoms suprisingly do not suffer separation" (*Nc.* VII. 77). Devavimala has contrasted it with an Utprekṣā. Sharing the characteristics of the *cakravāka* birds, Nāthi's breasts with dark nipples appeared to be, as it were, two full-blown lotuses with bees, in their impatience to partake of the flowery juice, settled on them (*Hs.*II.41). Damayantī's luminous back invited comparison with a golden slab, which reflecting Malli flowers tucked in the mass of her hair, seems to have been inscribed with silver letters in eulogy of Cupid. In partial modification of the idea Devavimala compares Nāthī's back, with flowers reflected in it, with a strip of sky studded with a host of planets. *Abhravīthī* indeed serves to highlight the shean of Nāthī's back.[8] Following Śrīharṣa, Devavimala represents the hips of Nāthī as a powerful disc. Whereas Damayantī is determined to vanquish the world with that disc, Nāthī's hips are designed to wreck the young ascetics in their concentration (*Nc.*VII.87, *Hs.* II.47). The author of the *Nc.* is confident that Damayantī's thighs have set at naught the trunk of elephant (VII.94), the plantain tree would muster courage to vie with their beauty only if it sheds off its substancelessness and coolness/stupidity by persistent penance (VII.93). As Devavimala would have us believe, the thighs of Nāthī were designed with the characteristics of both the trunk of elephant and plantain tree, shorn of their harshness and substancelessness respectively (II.48).

While the similarities that Nāthī bears with Bhaimī are not prodigious, the description of the person of the presiding deity, in canto VIII of the *Hs.*, follows the seventh canto of the *Nc.* so closely and bristles with verbal reminiscences thereof to the extent that it may justifiably be rated as a free adaptation of the aforesaid depicition in the *Nc.* In close communion with Śrīharṣa, Devavimala has prefixed the *nakhaśikha* portrayal of the *Śāsanadevatā* with a general description of her physical charms wherein she is marked out as a paragon of all virtues, completely divorced from physical blemishes.[9] Hereafter he has described with gusto every conceivable part of her frame. Whereas Śrīharṣa fell prey to the moral debasement of his era in gleefully describing the female privy part of Damayantī, Devavimala preferred to be meticulous to parallel the prolonged description in the *Nc.* Difference in aesthetic taste apart, the two poets agree to be repetitive. Both have chosen the identical technique of dwelling upon each part of the body with a plurality of verses. The quantum of debt that Devavimala owes to his predecessor can be gauged from the plethora of ideas and phrases he has liberally borrowed from him. Some of these may be detailed here.

Taking cue from the *Nc.*, Devavimala has represented the toes of the presiding deity as so many lines. In respect of Bhaimī they are said to have been drawn to highlight the number of quarters wherefrom the love-lorn beings are to arrive to tender her homage (*Nc.*VII.104), to Devavimala they are eloquent testimony to her triumph over the ladies of all the ten quarters (*Hs.*VIII.24). Not unlike Śrīharṣa, the author of the *Hs* envisages the back of the *Śāsanadevatā* as a golden board intended for the schooling of the child Kāma, who has lately reincarnated at Śiva's wedding with Umā.[10] The depth of Damayantī's navel is sought to be emphasised by invoking comparison, not very happily, with a pit caused by the restive elephant in uprooting its post. Its beauty in the case of the presiding deity has been underscored by an imaginative comparison with a blooming lotus.[11] Damayantī's breasts are taken to have eclipsed in beauty the frontal globes on the forehead of the elephants. This is borne out by the incontrovertible fact that while her breasts proudly flaunt strings of pearls, the elephants, out of shame, have permanently concealed them within. Effecting trifle modification, Devavimala postulates the *ibhakumbhas* to have themselves assumed the form of breasts and to have thus been rewarded handsomely with a mass of pearls, dangling thereon.[12] In describing her tender arms and breasts Śrīharṣa visualises Damayantī as river Narmadā. Her arms are like two lotus-stalks, shooting up on both sides of the river. Her breasts appear to be like two tiny islands that have emerged as the water of her childhood has dried up under the heat of Kāma. Closely following him, Devavimala also has represented the presiding deity as a river of gold but has completed the Rūpaka to depict an integrated picture of her charming beauty.[13] Both unanimously describe the lower lip as a mass of reddish rays of the newly risen moon, which itself has assumed the shape of her face.[14] They again concur in comparing the lower lip with the *bandhūka* flower to drive home its enthralling charm. "In the company of Damayantī's face (moon) her lip, red like *bandhūka*, represented the junction of the beauty of childhood and youth." Devavimala has contrasted it with an Upamā. The pure lustre of teeth, spreading on the *bandhūka*-like lip of the *Śāsanadevatā*, bore comparsion with a streak of moonshine on the red lotus.[15] In imitation of the *Nc.*, Devavimala has described the nose of the deity as Cupid's quiver. Śrīharṣa views it to have been fashioned with *tila* flowers with two arrows, left after his victory over three worlds, stuck in it (*Nc.*VII.36). In the *Hs.*, the quiver is averred to have come handy when it was discarded by Kāma, out of disgust at the loss of his might, occasioned by Śaṅkara (VIII.124). The depiction of the leaf-design on the cheeks as a cognizance of Cupid in the *Hs.* is based on the corresponding description in Śrīharṣa.[16] Damayantī's eyes are believed to have been formed with the quintessence of all relevant *upamānas*, such as the eyes of *cakoras* and deer and the lotuses (*Nc.*VII.32). Devavimala has gone a step further. In his reckoning the deity has set at naught the lotuses, *cakoras* and *khañjarīṭs* because their eyes are said to have been fashioned with the residue of the essence employed to form her eyes (*Hs* VIII.134). Devavimala was so fascinated by Śrīharṣa's present description that like him, he did not hesitate to draw similarity between the female ears and the shape of numeral nine. In the case of Damayantī, the comparison was justified because her ears were believed to have equally shared the eighteen Vidyās, *Śāsanadevatā's* ears represent her victory over the beauties of the eighteen regions of the earth.[17] And as an apt tribute to their exquisite charms, they are said to have been fashioned by the creator after acquiring expertise in the art by first practising his hand on the lotus.[18]

Notwithstanding the diverse contents, the later half of canto V of the *Hs.*, which dilates upon the events leading to the initiation of Hīrakumāra into monkhood, is wholly based on the 15th Canto of the *Nc.* It is so strewn with Śrīharṣa's ideas and phraseology that, for all purposes, it appears to be a tailored version of the aforesaid canto. In Śrīharṣa's sequence of events, the astrologers flock to determine the appropriate time for the marriage to solemnize after the *svayaṁvara* is concluded (XV.8). Hīrakumāra too invites the sooth-sayers to ascertain the moment propitious for his initiation (V.91). The pre-initiation adornments of Hīra are indebted to the pre-marital embellishments of Nala and Damayantī to the extent that they amount to be a faithful replica of the latter. Devavimala was so enamoured of this part of Śrīharṣa's poem that he thought it fit to reproduce, in his language, what his predecessor had said in the context. Like Damayantī the Kumāra is given the ceremonial bath with scented water, seated on the diamond-slab (*Nc.*XV.19,*Hs.*V.96). With her/his body dried up, after the bath, with a soft towel, both Damayantī and Hīra looked like a glittering golden statue.[19] And with Nala he shares the distinction of being adorned by persons, expert in the art (*Nc.*XV.57, *Hs.*V.59). Both the poets have sought to highlight the charms of the bodies of their respective character, emitting sweet smell born of unguents applied thereto, by an idential Atiśayokti.[20]

The description of Hīra's embellishment that follows, is an evident echo of the corresponding depiction in the *Nc*. Some of the similarities in the two deserve to be listed here. The diadem that decked the head of Hīra was, like that of Nala, studded with priceless gems (*Nc*.XV.60,*Hs*.V.106). While the strip of gold tied to Nala's forehead had the appearance of the nimbus of the moon (*Nc*.XV.61), on Damayantī's head it bore resemblance with a flash of lighting in the clouds of her hair (*Nc*.XV.32). The gold-tablet on Hīra's brow also invited comparison with the lighting with, the difference that, unlike in Damayantī's case, it had not assumed stillness (*Hs*.V.107). The round mark, in proximity to the eyebrow, on Bhaimī's forehead, looked like a bullet added to the bow of Cupid, intent upon wrecking her fortitude. Hīrakumāra's round *tilaka* is also represented as a bullet, but it is intended to serve as a missile to subdue Kāma himself. While the ear-rings, with their reflection in Nala's cheeks, appeared to be four wheels of the chariot of Cupid, in respect of Hīra they are visulised as four discs to destroy the four *Kaṣāyas* (*Nc*.XV.65,*Hs*.V.117).[21] With his person reflected in the ornaments Hīra, like Nala, had little use for the mirror.[22] The shean emanating from the ornaments was noticed not only by the people at large, but by the ornaments themselves with their eyes of gems.[23] The total effect of their adornment is sought to be driven home by both Śrīharṣa and Devavimala with a *Mālopamā*, which undoubtedly serves to highlight their charms instantaneously.[24]

The description of the impatience of the womenfolk eager to have a glimpse of Hīrakumāra, departing to be ordained into monastic life, in the *Hs*, (V.158-179) is doubtless inspired by the parallel description in the *Nc*., wherein the ladies of Kuṇḍinapura throng to see Nala, on his way to the royal palace for the wedding (XV.74-92). More than the ideas, Devavimala has borrowed the motif from Śrīharṣa, which originating in Aśvaghoṣa has struck deep roots, as is testified by the fact that it continued to be espoused unabated by Sanskrit poets, down the ages. Some of Devavimala's ideas also have their genesis in the *Nc*. With her breasts half-bared by the breeze, one of the ladies accosted Nala, as it were, with an auspicious jar which foreboded the fulfilment of his desire (XV.74). Devavimala has reproduced the idea *in toto*, in the body of his description. In emulation of Śrīharṣa, the author of the *Hs*. views the pearls, issuing in quick succession, from the broken necklace, as a shower of fried rice, *lājā*. (*HS*.V.173).

Like Kuṇḍinapura at Damayantī's marriage, Aṇhilapattana is colourfully decorated at the time of Hīra's embarking upon monastic life and a band of instruments greets the occasion (*Nc*.XV.13-18, *Hs*.V.148-157). The confabulations of the swan with Damayantī, wherein he impresses upon her Nala's myriad virtues and thereby seeks to set her heart on the lord of Niṣadha, forms the core of the third canto of the *Nc*. Devavimala has paralleled it by a delightful conversation between Hīra and his sister Vimalā (V.39-90). Here, the two apparently represent diagonally opposite views. The Kumāra seeks her permission to accept monkhood. She opposes him tooth and nail but, convinced of his resolute determination, ultimately yields to accord him approval. Inspite of different aims, the two converge on the success achieved by both swan and Hīra by sheer force of logic.

In the first canto of the *Nc*. Nala, afflicted with *pūrvarāga* for Damayantī, departs to the garden, mounted on a horse, along with his friends, to seek diversion there (*Nc*.I. 57-73). Hīrakumāra too likewise repairs, with his friends, to a garden in the vicinity of Aṇhilapattana, for undergoing initiation (*Hs*. V.132-147). Some of the details in the two descriptions are identical. The function of bringing horse to Nala and Hīra has been assigned to their repective friends (*Nc*.I.57, *Hs*. V.132). The horse, in both the poems, is said to have surpassed in pace the divine horse Uccaiśrayāḥ (*Nc*.I. 64, *Hs*.V.140).

As required by theory, Devavimala, like Śrīharṣa, has incorporated in his poem a host of descriptions of Nature of uneven merit. The description of the moon-rise in the 22nd Canto of the *Nc*. is intended to provide an apt setting to the sexual sports of the newly wedded couple, Nala and Damayantī. The corresponding description in the *Hs*. (Canto VII) likewise forms a befitting backdrop to the emergence of the deity. Both have reprsented moon-rise as a culmination of a series of natural phenomena. Besides marginal resemblances, Devavimala is indebted to the *Nc*. for some of his ideas in the context. Following Śrīharṣa the author of the *Hs*. has given a graphic account of the reddish glow of the newly risen moon, spreading in the sky. To Śrīharṣa it appears as if the sky had been sprinkled with lac-dye or smeared with *kuṁkuma* (*Nc*.XII.3). Devavimala has invested the phenomenon with human behaviour. In her joy to greet her lord, the moon, the lady of the night seems to have painted her body with *kuṁkuma* (*Hs*.VII.38) or she has applied the *kuṁkuma* marks of her hands on the path the moon, her beloved consort, is to tread (*Hs*.VII.36).

Both concur to describe, with a Rūpaka, the stars as so many pieces of bones, falling from the *kapālamālā* of Mahādeva, engaged in his favourite dance, at the close of the day (*Nc.*XXII.8,*Hs.*VII.60). Similar unanimity marks their postulating them (stars) as drops of tears gushing from the eyes of the *cakravāka* birds, undergoing pangs of separation, on the banks of the heavely Ganges (*Nc.*XXII.19, *Hs.*VII.64).

Devavimala has sought to parallel Śrīharṣa's description of day-break and sun-rise with corresponding descriptions, in parts of cantos II and IX of his poem. While Śrīharṣa has indulged in the most heinous monstrosities here, [25] the author of the Hs. has spun out a fairly brilliant portrayal of the phenomenon. The similarities between the two, however, do not purport to be more than peripheral, though both allude to the Mandeha demons and petals of roses/floral wreaths as the cause of redness that spreads in the morning sky and speak of night shorn of her hair by the rays of the sun.[26]

For Devavimala the *Nc.* is venerable like a scripture. Apart from the exhaustive similarities, as detailed above, he has liberally borrowed from it almost an unending series of usages, fondly employed by Śrīharṣa. More than two hundred such usages he has illustrated, with reference to their source, in the auto-commentary on his poem. It is a measure of the extent to which he was enthralled by Śrīharṣa's poem that like him he has turned the closing verse of each of his cantos into a miniature autobiography, giving details of his parentage besides an allusion to his preceptor, Sīhavimala.

These comparative investgations reveal beyond cavil that despite the serious limitations imposed on him by a basically diverse theme, Devavimala, in his zeal to produce a counterpart to the *Nc.* followed it minutely, almost religiously.

REFERENCES

1. Ed. Nirṇaya Sāgara Press, Bombay, 1933.
2. Kāvyamālā, 67.
3. उद्याने सरणिः सर्वफलपुष्पलताद्रुमाः ।
   पिकालिकेलिहंसाद्याः क्रीड़ावाप्यध्वगस्थितिः ॥
   Kāvyakalapalatā-vṛttiḥ, I.5.68
4. *Hs.*, I.71; *Nc.*, II.93
5. *Hs.*, I.118 ; *Nc.*, II.87
6. *Nc.*, II.25,29,38 ; *Hs.*, II. 32,25,52

7. रज्यन्नखस्याङ्गुलिपञ्चकस्य मिषादसौ हैङ्गुलपद्मतूणे ।
हैमैकपुङ्ख्यास्ति विशुद्धपर्वा प्रियाकरे पञ्चशरी स्मरस्य । *Nc.*, VII.70
शराश्रये यत्करनाम्नि कल्पिता
अमी शराः पञ्च किमङ्गुलीमयाः । *HS.*, II.37
8. अस्या खलु ग्रन्थिनिबद्धकेशमल्लीकदम्बप्रतिबिम्बवेषात् ।।
स्मरप्रशस्ती रजताक्षरेयं पृष्ठस्थलीहाटकपट्टिकायाम् ।। *Nc.*, VII.88
यदीयपृष्ठे कनकत्विषि स्मित-
प्रसूनशून्येतरकुन्तलच्छटा ।
शिलातले स्वर्गिगिरेरिव ग्रहा-
ङ्किताभ्रवीथी प्रतिबिम्बिता व्यभात् ।। *Hs.*, II,38
9. नास्पर्शि दृष्टापि विमोहिकेयं दोषैरशेषैः स्वभियेति मन्ये ।
अन्येषु तैराकुलितस्तदस्यां वसत्यसापत्न्यसुखी गुणौघः ।। *Nc.*, VII.17
-----प्रेक्ष्य गुणांस्त्रिदश्याः ।
-----प्रणेशे किमशेषदोषैः ।। *Hs.*, VIII.15
10. *Nc.*, *op.cit.*, VII.88
उमोपयामे पुनराप्तजन्म-
शिशुस्मरस्येन्द्रगुरोरुपान्ते ।
अध्येतुकामस्य कलास्त्रिदश्याः
पृष्ठस्थली हाटकपट्टिकेव ।। *Hs.*, VIII.48
11. उन्मूलितालानविलाभनाभिः---- *Nc.*, VII.85
---यदीयनाभिर्बभौ जृम्भितपद्मिनीव । *Hs.*, VIII.51
12. *Nc.*, VII.78 ; *Hs.*, VIII.70
13. *Nc.*, VII.73 ; *Hs.*, VIII.83
14. इमां दधाराधरबिम्बलीलां तस्यैव बालं करचक्रवालम् । *Nc.*, VII.52
इदं मुखीभूतमवेत्य चन्द्रं बालं तदीयं करचक्रवालम् । *Hs.*, VIII.99
15. बन्धूकबन्धूभवदेतदस्याः । *Nc.*, VII.37
बन्धूकबन्धूभवदेतदीय-दन्तच्छदे दन्तरुचिश्चकासे । *Hs.*, VIII.101
16. कपोलपत्रान्मकरात्सकेतुर्भ्रूभ्यां --- *Nc.*, VII.60
कपोलभित्तौ मृगनाभिपङ्कैश्चित्रीकृतोऽस्या मकरध्वकासे ।। *Hs.*, VIII.130
17. *Nc.*, VII.63 ; *Hs.*, VIII.142
18. अस्यैव सर्गाय भवत्करस्य सरोजसृष्टिर्मम हस्तलेखः । *Nc.*, VII.72
सृष्टिं सिसृक्षुः किमदोऽनुरूपां
विनिर्मिमीतेऽम्बुजहस्तलेखम् । *Hs.*, VIII.157
19. अदभ्रमभ्राजत---प्रकाशरोचिःप्रतिमेव हेमजा । *Nc.*, XV.24
काञ्चनप्रतिमयेव नितान्तोत्तेजनात्- । *Hs.*, V.98
20. *Nc.*, XV.25 ; *Hs.*, V.101

21. चित्तभूरथस्फुरच्चक्रचतुष्कचारुताम् । *Nc.*, xv.65
क्रोधमुख्यचतुरात्मविपक्षान्
भेत्तुकाम इव चक्रचतुष्कः । *Hs.*, V.117
22. निष्फलीचकार सेवाचणदर्पणापर्णाम् । *Nc.*, XV.70
दर्पणार्पणविधाभिरमुष्मिन्
निष्फलाभिरजनि स्वजनानाम् । *Hs.*, V.128
23. अदर्शि विस्फारितरत्नलोचनैः परस्परेणेव विभूषणैरपि । *Nc.*, XV.71
भूषणानि मृगयन्त इतीव
स्फाररत्ननयनैरिदमङ्गम् । *Hs.*, V.129
24. *Nc.*, XV.54 ; *Hs.*, V.131
25. *Nc.*, XIX.7,13,14
26. *Nc.*, XIX. 9,41,55 ; *Hs.*, IX.57,60,49

VIVĀHAVALLABHAMAHĀKĀVYA

A LOST JAINA SANSKRIT POEM

While the Jaina church occupied itself in enriching the literature, the laity took meticulous care to preserve it through various devices such as the multiplication of MSS and the establishment of libraries in different parts of the country. It is a tribuute to their catholiocity and sagacity that some of the rarest works of different sects are found in the Jaina *Bhaṇḍāras* only. However, despite all safeguards, natural factors coupled with wanton destruction by foreign marauding hordes have resulted in the loss of a sizable mass of literature. *Vivāhavallabhamahākāvya* (*VM*) is one such work which seems to have been irretrievably lost. It is known through its seventeenth canto, the full text of which is happily preserved in a Ms in the collection of Agarchand Nāhatā, the noted Jaina savant and antiquarian of Bikaner. The Ms itself is defective. Seven of its folios are lost. The remaining seventeen (8-24) contain, besides the extant canto of the *VM*, ten shorter works or parts thereof. The MS is not dated, but, on paleographic grounds, can be assigned to the fifteenth century.

As the colophon would indicate, the *VM* had for its theme the life-account of Tīrthaṅkara Neminātha, with particular stress on his proposed marriage with Rājīmatī, the charming daughter of Ugrasena. The present canto sets forth, in charming language, Rājimatī's admonition to Nemi and her realisation of the self. In view of the sequence of events of Nemi's life, as described in the *Harivaṃśapurāṇa* of Jinasena I, the admonition could have been occasioned by her rebuttal through Nemi's sudden acceptance of monkhood in preference to the joys of marital life. The young Nemi had countenanced his marriage but was so repelled by the proposed mass animal-killings that he abandoned it right in the midst of its execution. This left poor Rājīmatī aghast. But instead of dissipating herself in mundane pursuits, she follows in the footsteps of her Lord. In this philosophical canto she makes a fervent appeal to the Lord to bless her with spiritual illumination. Following this she feels with the poet that knowledge of the self alone is real. All else is illusion. It is a gateway to salvation. (3) This is also the quintessence of the teachings of the master (30). It sets at naught the physical and mental afflictions and leads to the fulfilment of desires. Self-realisation stabilises the mind which enables the person to concentrate on deeper problems of life. (24,27). Nemi's life has been the subject of two Jaina Sanskrit Mahākāvyas. Vāgbhaṭa's *Neminirvāṇa* and Kīrtirāja's *Nemināthamahākāvya* are so well known. Considering the events as set forth therein, it can be safely assumed that the *VM* must have contained at least three more cantos, describing the Lord's penance and sermon and his attainment of knowledge (*Kaivalya*) and salvation. Thus it must have been an interesting poem of twenty cantos. As such, its loss is to be lamented.

The extant canto of the poem is written in Ādi Yamaka, the last word or a part thereof of the preceding verse forming the beginning of each following verse, interspersed with other figures of speech like Upamā, Rūpaka, Anuprāsa and Virodha which demonstrate the author's penchant for the embellishment of his poem. In consonance with the injuction of the poeticians one metre (Anuṣṭup) preponderates here, which, however, changes towards the end; the last two verses being in Śikhariṇī and Śārdūlavikrīḍita. The poet wields a facile pen. The language of the poem is chaste Sanskrit with few errors, which are obviously the result of scribal negligence.

The canto is edited here for the first time. An attempt has been made to correct the text, but gaps therein have been left to themselves.

विवाहवल्लभमहाकाव्यम्

जिनेशं जगदाधारं केवलालोकभास्वरम् ।।
भगवन् भयभीतानां सर्वज्ञ शरणं भव ।। १ ।।
भवाम्भोधौ महामोहवातविघ्नविभीषणे ।
मज्जन्तं तत्त्वपोतेन त्वं मामुद्धर्तुमर्हसि ।। २ ।।
अर्हन् यदात्मज्ञानेन मोक्षसौख्यमवाप्यते ।
आत्मज्ञानं ततस्तत्त्वं सर्वमन्यत्प्रपञ्चनम् ।। ३ ।।
प्रपञ्चात् कर्मणां प्राचां यत्तत्वविरहोऽजनि ।
तमन्तरं निराकर्तुं देहि देवेश दर्शनम् ।। ४ ।।
दर्शने देवदेवस्य देवदेवस्य दर्शने ।

अन्त[2]रायाः परं कालात् केवलं कर्म्मपुद्गलाः ।। ५ ।।
पुद्गलानां परावर्त्ताः परावर्त्ताः कृता मया ।
न मया भूयमेवायं समीपस्थो निरीक्षितः ।। ६ ।।
निरीक्षितो न केनापि न केनापि परीक्षितः ।
गुरोरयोगान्मोहात् वा गतः साक्षादलक्षताम् ।। ७ ।।
अलक्षो लक्षतां याति रूपवानप्यरूपताम् ।
आत्मज्ञानं विना नाथ तत्स्वरूपे न तिष्ठति ।। ८ ।।
तिष्ठति स्थापितो नैव प्रेषितो[3] नैव यात्यसौ ।
कर्मणां वशगा स्वामिन् दुर्लङ्घ्या हि भवस्थितिः ।। ९ ।।
स्थितिरेकैव भविनां भवाब्धौ भवितव्यता ।
शुभाशुभमनोयोगात् जिनेश सुखदुःखदा ।। १० ।।
दुःखदा[4] रिद्रयदहनं संतोषामृतभावितम् ।
आत्मज्ञानं यदा देव सर्वसिद्धिस्तदा मम ।। ११ ।।
ममतामिश्रिते चित्ते मम तापो महान् भवेत् ।
ममताविरहान् नाथ मम तावत् महासुखम् ।। १२ ।।
सुखात्संतोषकल्पद्रुछायाविश्रामितं मनः ।
मनोरथान् जिनाधीश पूरयाशु मनोहितान् ।। १३ ।।
हिताहितविचारज्ञस्तत्त्वज्ञानशलाकया ।
आत्मानं कर्म्मणो भेदात् करिष्यामि कदा पृथक् ।। १४ ।।
पृथक्भूतो भवाम्भोधे[5] र्विचरामि यदा जिन ।
तदा मां पश्यति जनो जडोन्मत्तपिशाचवत् ।। १५ ।।
पिशाचवज्जडोन्मत्तं[6] चिन्तासन्तापतापितम् ।।
संसारलहरीलीढ़ं मूढं पश्याम्यहं जगत् ।। १६ ।।
जगत्प्रचारादन्यत्तु तदेव तव लक्षणम् ।
सिद्धान्तसारमेतद्धि तत्वज्ञास्तत्र साक्षिणः ।। १७ ।।
साक्षिभूतं मनो वेत्ति...शुभे गतम् ।
यस्तत्त्ववित्स विज्ञेयः शेषः प्रावाहिको जनः ।। १८ ।।
प्रभोः प्रसादमासाद्य क्रियाकाण्डरतः सदा ।
जिन...मे कदा वैराग्यवासितम् ।। १९ ।।
वैराग्यवासितो नित्यं ब्रह्मव्रतपरायणः ।
बाह्यमाभ्यन्तरं परिग्रहत्यागं कदा श्र (ये) ।। २० ।।
कदा श्रये सुसाधूनां परिच[7]र्यापरायणः ।
मानमायाक्रोधलोभत्यागात् ध्यानं सदुत्तमम् ।। २१ ।।
उत्तमादुत्तमतरं वर्द्ध ... ... ।
कदात्मज्ञानजं ध्यानं ध्यास्याम्यात्मार्थसाधकम् ।। २२ ।।
साधकस्य न साध्यस्य भेदच्छेदपरायणः ।
अनादि (कर्म) काक्षो सं (कक्षौघं) धक्ष्यामि नितरां कदा ।।२३।।

कदा कुलालवच्चित्तं चक्रं मोहभ्रमाकुलम् ।
संकल्पभाण्डानुत्तार्य करिष्यामि स्थिरं स्थिरम् ।। २४ ।।
स्थिरासनसमासीनः स्थिरध्यानपरायणः ।
स्थिरे त्वयि स्थिरं चित्तं करिष्याम्यहं कदा ।। २५ ।।
कदा मुदा चिदानन्दकन्दांकुरु (र)महोदयम् ।
आत्मज्ञानामृरासेः (शेः) सेवयिष्ये स्वचेतसि ।। २६ ।।
चेतसा इष्यामि कोऽहं कस्मात्किमागतः ।
क्व याता किमिदं को मे कस्याहमिति तत्त्वतः ।। २७ ।।
तत्त्वतः कल्पनाजालं मूलादुन्मूल्य मानसम् ।
जाग्रन् स्वप्नभ्रमं तिष्ठन् करिष्ये (ऽ)हं स्थिरम् ।। २८ ।।
स्थिरात्स्थिरतरोऽसि त्वं चलाच्चलतरोऽस्म्यहं ।
कृपां कुरु या (यथा) नाथ त्वमात्मज्ञानदर्शनात् ।। २९ ।।
दर्शनादात्मनो मोक्षो भवो विस्मरणात्पुनः ।
इयतीयमार्हती वाणी वाग्विलासोऽपरः परः ।। ३० ।।
परोद (द्दि)ष्टं नायाति परैर्नैवापहार्यते[8] ।
कोऽहं सोऽहमिति ज्ञानं तत्त्वबुद्ध्या स्मराम्यहं ।। ३१ ।।
अहं सोऽहं सोऽहं स इति जगतां जीवनपदं
स्वपन् जाग्रन् लोक (:)स्मरति स ज्ञानविकलः ।
तदेवात्मज्ञानात्तव पदरजःकल्ककलितं ।
प्रविष्टं ध्यानाग्नौ महति मम सिद्धिं प्रकुरुते ।। ३२ ।।
इत्थं याद[9]वनन्दिनी भगवती राजीमती स्वामिनम् ।
स्तुत्वा नेमिजिनं विबुद्धहृदये स्वात्मावबोधं महः ।
पश्यन्ती[10] परमेश्वरं जिनपतिं श्रीरैवताद्रौ स्थितम्
ध्यायन्ती भवसर्वसंगविरता निन्ये निशामुत्सुका ।। ३३ ..
इति श्रीविवाहवल्लभमहाकाव्ये श्रीनेमिनाथोपालम्भने (नै)
कात्मा(त्म)ज्ञानोल्लासो नाम सप्तदशसर्ग ।।

REFERENCES

1. The MS. has प्रवञ्चनम्
2. The MS. has अन्तयाः रा
3. The MS. has प्रेषिते
4. The MS. has दुःखदारिद्रदहनं
5. The MS. has भवांभिधि
6. The MS. has जजेन्मत्तं
7. The MS. has परचर्या
8. The MS. has नौवापहार्यते
9. The MS. has या व नंदिनी
10. The MS. has पश्यी दंती

SOURCES OF PUṆYAKUŚALA'S BHARATABĀHUBALI-MAHĀKĀVYA

The *Ādipurāṇa* [1] of Jinasena and Hemacandra's *Triṣaṣṭi-śalākāpuruṣacrita* [2] (*TṢC*) may be taken to represent respectively the *Digambara* and *Śvetāmbara* versions of the fascinating story of Bharata's combat with his irrepressible brother, Bāhubali, which, with its sublime culmination and the intrepid *hauteur* breathing through it, has been a favourite theme, down the ages. Jinasena has stuffed his brief description with conventional poetic digressions, thereby giving it the form of a miniaturised Mahākāvya. Hemacandra's account, on the other hand, is judiciously balanced, its prolixity notwithstanding. In view of their unanimity on the framework of the story, Puṇyakuśala (17th century) has drawn upon both the *Ādipurāṇa* and the *TṢC* in his poem, *Bharatabāhubali - mahākāvya* [3] (*BBM*), which seeks to describe, in eighteen cantos, this enchanting theme, with usual poetic trappings. Wherever his sources differ in essentials, he has invariably followed Hemacandra's version.

In accordance with the sequence of the theme, the *BBM* is distinguished in its first canto by a happy description of the despatch of an envoy to the refractory Bāhubali to secure his submission to Bharata, the soverign of the land; besides a graphic account of scenic beauties, Bāhubali's might and unassailability of Taxila, his metropolis. While Jinasena has emphasised his political sagacity and practical wisdom [4], Puṇyakuśala, like Hemacandra [5], has sought to spotlight the envoy's skill in eloquence [6], which, as a streling virtue is intended to ensure the success of his mission. Puṇyakuśala shares with the *Ādipurāṇa* some of the features of his portrait of the journey, while for others he is distinctly indebted to Hemacandra. Taking cue from the simple Svabhāvokti in Jinasena (35.38), the author of the *BBM* has poetically represented the herds of cows, on the outskirts of Taxila, as so many masses of Bāhubali's immaculate fame, speeding to transmit it to one and all.[7] The description of the naive female guards of the paddy-fields, struck with wonder at the calm bearing of the envoy, in the *BBM*, is redolent of the corresponding depiction of the *Śāligopikās*, who, in Jinasena are described, in life-like relief, to scare away with shrill cries the swarms of parrots, menacingly descending upon their fields.[8] The *TṢC* is shorn of this happy streak of rural life. Like his sources, Puṇyakuśala is not oblivious of the affluence of Taxila's *Vaṇikpatha*.[9] Puṇyakuśala's detailed account of the lord of Taxila, which serves to underscore his heroism and regal splendour (I.71-77), owes itself to the authors of the *Ādipurāṇa* (35.45-50) and the *TṢC* (1.5.69-76), who expound in different phraseology the aforesaid virtues of Bāhubali. As in its sources, the envoy in the *BBM* is struck with amazement at Bāhubali's majesty which sends shudder down to his spine.[10]

The contents of the second canto of the *BBM* accord well with the events as they unfold themselves on the canvas of its sources. In *Ādipurāṇa* (35.57-60) and Hemacandra's poem (15.79-85) Bāhubali enquires of the envoy about the welfare of his elder brother, in general terms. Puṇyakuśala has sought to stir up fraternal affection in Bāhubali with a meaningful allusion of their childhood-sports whereby Bāhubali comes to cherish solicitude for Bharata and craves for its permanency (21-22). In response to Bāhubali's query about the purpose of his mission, the envoy in *BBM*, narrates the saga of his heroic deeds and urges him to capitulate to Bharata, shedding off his proverbial arrogance (2.37-95). All this adds up to a free redaction of the parallel pieces in the *Ādipurāṇa* (35.65-85) and the *TṢC* (1.5.87-119). As the two Purāṇas had dealt, at length, with Bharata's conquest elsewhere,[11] they have wisely skipped it over in the present context. Puṇyakuśala's account of the *digvijaya*, however, follows Hemacandra so closely that, for all purposes, it amounts to a cautious epitome of the corresponding depiction in the *TṢC* (1.4). Not unlike its sources, the *BBM* makes out seniority in age besides his *cakravartī* status as worthy of homage from Bāhubalī.[12]

Bāhubali's indignation at the insulting proposal of the envoy and his contemptuous rejection thereof, as detailed in the third canto of the *BBM*, is encountered in the *Ādipurāṇa* as well as the *TṢC*. While Jinasena has aired his equipment in Politics in stock technical phraseology, Hemacandra emerges more impressive in stoutly repudiating the envoy's overtures with robust arguments. Both concur to brand the envoy's proposal as a well-laid trap. To Jinasena it is *khalācāra* (35.94), Hemacandra ridicules it as *bakaceṣṭā* (1.5.128). In a similar vein, Puṇyakuśala has driven home the gravity of Bharata's lust for territorial aggrandisement by invoking comparison with the submarine fire which continues to rage unabated, even though it has consumed in its devasting flames ninety nine of his brothers.[13] However, Hemacandra's logic that as sons of the same father, the relationship of master and slave is incompatiable in case of Bharata and Bāhubali, has not found favour with Puṇyakuśala. So has failed to evoke acceptance from him Jinasena's argument that in his bid to usurp Bāhubali's empire, Bharata is guility of ravishing the modesty of his wife.[14] But the author of the *BBM* is in perfect agreement with the *Ādipurāṇa* (35.137) and the *TṢC* (1.5.154) in treating war as the surest means for the trial of strength.

The *Ādipurāṇa* does not have the slightest vestige of the events expounded in the concluding part of the third, and the whole of the fourth canto of the *BBM*. Bāhubali's forceful rebuttal of the envoy's porposal coupled with his out-right challenge to Bharata to try conclusions on the battle-field, serves, strangely enough, to stir fraternal feelings in Bharata and he decides, in a huff, not to strike down the creeper of conduct he had so assiduously planted in the basin of the earth.[15] In this hopeless situation, his general Suṣeṇa cheers him and impresses upon him, with well-reasoned agruments, the imperatives to humble Bāhubalī, reminding him simultaneously of his matchless prowess and the endless victories achieved by him. This part of the *BBM* follows the *TṢC* so closely that it is punctuated with a fair sprinkling of verbal borrowings therefrom and shares with it, in a garbed form, quite a few of ideas.[16] Bharata in the *TṢC* decides to suffer impudence on the part of Bāhubalī even at the cost of inviting censure for this cowardice because it is possible to secure with might all but an affectionate brother (1.5.236-237). The author of the *BBM* also has the same argument to advance against the horror of war (4.27). He has withheld allusion, in this context, to the disgust which overcomes the envoy following the failure of his mission and thereby his becoming instrumental in making war with Bāhubali a certainty (*TṢC*, 1.5.208).

The most glaring divergence in the two versions relates to the denouement of the theme, the final combat. The *Ādipurāṇa* and the *TṢC* do not contain even the slightest hint to the three-day war between the rival forces, so fondly described by Puṇyakuśala in the fifteenth canto of his poem.

As we shall see later, he is indebted for this departure to Māgha, whose description of the combat between the armies of Kṛṣṇa and Śiśupāla, as a prelude to the ultimate duel, sets a norm which the subsequent poets seek to vie with uneven success. In their treatment of the final combat and the events preceding it, Jinasena and Hemacandra reveal, between themselves, vital divergences. As the *Ādipurāṇa* would have us believe, principal ministers on both sides, anxious to avoid *pogram* which a routine war entails, urge the rival brothers to measure strength in a holy war (*dharmayuddha*). As stubborn warriors, they accept the proposal with great reluctance (36.40-44). The *BBM*, like the *TṢC*, credits the deities, who had descended on the earth to witness the unprecedented combat, with weaning them away from the prospective carnage. It certainly sounds more convincing in the situation.

In the sequence of events as detailed in the *TṢC*, it is with a plethora of arguments that the deities succeed in dissuading Bharata and Bāhubali from embarking upon destruction, inherent in a full-fledged war.[17] Puṇyakuśala has borrowed *en mass* the series of these events from the *TṢC*, though, in accordance with the form of his poem, his description thereof is invested with poetic charms. The arguments of the deities against war, as listed in the *BBM*, do not substantially differ from those in the *TṢC*, but they sound more effective in the former. "This creation emanating from Ādideva is as good as your sister. In destroying it in war, you will expose yourselves to homicide"[18] ; this is the most appropriate argument that could have been made in the situation. The phraseology in which they hold each other responsible for initiating the war, is, its sweetness apart, almost identical with that of Hemacandra.[19] Unlike the *TṢC*, Bāhubalī, in the *BBM*, first refuses to budge but ultimately accepts the suggestion of the deities to undergo trial of strength through personal combat.[20] The way Bharata demonstrates his strength in order to remove the anxiety of his soldiers, stemming from his consenting to the combat, is entirely based on Hemacandra's account (*TṢC*,1.5.553-570 ; *BBM*, 16.71-77).

The *Ādipurāṇa* records three sorties between Bharata and Bāhubali (36.45). Puṇyakuśala has followed Hemacandra in delineating this event, which forms the *summum bonum* of his poem. There is an amazing unanimity in the two works in the number, order and description of the combats. In imitation of Hemacandra, Puṇyakuśala has described four sorties, as parts of the ultimate duel. In the course of *muṣṭiyuddha*, Bāhubali, both in the *TṢC* and the *BBM*, so tosses Bharata up in the sky that he passes visibility forthwith. But, wheras in the *TṢC* he sustains him on his bed-like arms, which, his apparent hostility apart, serves to be a valid reference to his innate solicitude for his elder brother (1.5.634); their comparison with crane and fish respectively, in Puṇyakuśala's poem, highlights Bharata's helplessness in the situation (17.47).

The conclusion of the *BBM*, which compresses within its ambit many an event, including Bāhubali's resolve to shatter the disc with his fist, Bharata's return to Ayodhyā after putting Bāhubali's son on the throne, the attainment of absolute knowledge by both the brothers, is a replica of the corresponding part of the *TṢC* (1.5.730-798).

Cantos Seven and Eight of the *BBM* are replete with poetic digressions, not precluding water-sports and sexual orgy of the warriors, an inseparable part of the late Mahākāvyas. Puṇyakuśala seems to have been prompted into these digressions by Māgha, though they are found detailed in the *Ādipurāṇa*, with the difference that these concern the soldiers of Bāhubali, in the latter (35.152-236).

For the conception of his theme Puṇyakuśala is thus indebted largely to the *TṢC*, reinforced, at places, by Jinasena's version in the *Ādipurāṇa*. In its execution, however, he has been influenced by Māgha, in a strong measure. The similarities in the presentation of theme in the two poems begin with the benediction, which, in both, purports to be of the *vastunirdeśa* type. The *Śiśupālavadha* is noted for the use of Śrī in the first and last verses of its cantos. With the phrase *puṇyodaya*, in its various forms, incorporated in the last stanza of his cantos, Puṇyakuśala means to perpetuate the Māgha-tradition apart from intending it to be not-so-veiled an allusion to his name. In Canto One in Māgha, the sage Nārada descends upon Vasudeva's palace and bids Hari dispose of the Cedi king whose hostility meances men and gods alike. The *BBM*, in its inception, is marked by the despatch to Bāhubali of an envoy who is charged to pursuade him to accept Bharata's suzerainty.

In blatant depature from his major sources Puṇyakuśala, in Cantos Seven and Eight, has broken into digressions wholly unrelated to the substance of his poem, which stretch to encompass the sexual orgy of Bharata's soldiers, besides their sports in garden and water, and such other conventional descriptions. He had an authority for these diversions in Māgha. While Māgha has devoted five cantos (vii-xi) to detail them with abandon, Puṇyakuśala has wisely compressed them, sans boozing, within the space of two cantos, disposing of *Vanavīhāra* and *Jalakrīḍā* in the seventh and the rest in the eighth. Māgha has described these events systematically to accord with the injunctions of rhetorics and erotics. Puṇyakuśala's descriptions, on the other hand, are general in nature and are charactrised by lucidity and sweetness in contradistinction to Māgha's pedantry and ponderousness. Unlike Māgha, Puṇyakuśala has not sought to transform his delineation of amorous sports into a thesaurus of illustrations to different types of *Nāyikās*, though he too often tends to succumb to this temptation.[21] In fact, Puṇyakuśala was so enamoured of these discriptions in Māgha's poem that he fondly borrowed some of his ideas in the context, which, more often than not, are replete with verbal reminiscnces. Taking cue from the *Śiśupālavadha*, Puṇyakuśala presents a gallant, keen to close his lass into embrace, to lift her on to enable her to pluck flowers from the tree, she had earlier feigned to be beyond her reach, with the vital difference that in Māgha she is a *mugdhā* (timid) whereas to him she is *aśāradā* (bold).[22] In both the poems, a *prauḍhā* is represented to express her longing to hug to the *nāyaka* with a deliberate fall on him[23] and a *khaṇḍitā* punishes the offending lover by chaining him with a floral wreath.[24] These amourettes do not accord with the spirit of Māgha's theme which purports to have *Vīra* as its dominant sentiment. In the sublimity of *Śāntarasa* in the *BBM*, this orgy is wholly out of joint.

In faithful adherence to theory, Puṇyakuśala has described the six traditional seasons in attendance on the hero. While the whole of the sixth canto of Māgha, devoted to this description, is infested with Yamaka, the author of the *BBM* has taken recourse to this feat in describing the winter (5.7-25), far apart from the full-fledged treatment of the six seasons (18.1-57). Puṇyakuśala's Yamaka does not present much of difficulty in comprehending the poem. Nor is he enamoured of paranomasia, as such. Māgha, on the other hand, has purposely stretched his description by twelve more verses (6.67-78) in order to parade his undoubted skill in handling this figure of speech.

As stated earlier, neither of Puṇyakuśala's basic sources provides any clue to the war between the forces of Bharata and Bāhubali. This combat, as detailed in the *BBM*, has its genesis in the eighteenth canto of the *Śiśupālavadha* which describes in detail, the terrific battle of Kṛṣṇa's army with that of the Cedi king. Cantos Fourteen and Fifteen of the *BBM* smack of the atmosphere of the *Caritakāvyas*. While Māgha got stuck in the quagmire of literary gymnastics in the nineteenth cento, Puṇyakuśala has given an extremely readable account of the battle. This canto rather serves to highlight his poetic powers more than his skill in describing war. Puṇyakuśala seems to be keen to project this canto as a pole opposite to Māgha's *citrakāvya*. The edifice of Bharata's duel with Bāhubali is doubtless erected on the bedrock of the *TṢC*, but it has been inspired, in no small measure, by the respective combats of Śaṅkara and Kṛṣṇa with Arjuna and Śiśupāla, described in the *Kirātārjunīya* and the *Śiśupālavadha* respectively.

The description of the onrush of the city-damsels to have a glimpse of Bharata (6.15-21), on his way to Taxila, again owes itself to Māgha, who, in Canto Thirteen of his poem, has given a graphic description of the impatience of the women-folk to see Kṛṣṇa and his concourse, at the time of their entry in Indraprastha (13.30-48). Compared to Māgha, Puṇyakuśala's delineation sinks into insignificance.

Like the *Śiśupālavadha*, the *BBM* has war as its epicentre. As a consequence, the two poems seek to develop *Vīra* as their overweening sentiment, but *Śṛṅgāra* has been sketched with such zeal and tenacity that it threatens to push the *aṅgī rasa* into background. More often than not, they smack of erotic poems. Māgha's poem closes at its natural end, the assassination of Śiśupāla, in the *BBM* the war has been elevated to subline heights.

Despite his deep debt to Māgha, Puṇyakuśala has no love for his pedantic style, literary gymnastics and such other feats as serve to make his poem a *tour de force*. Here Kālidāsa is his ideal whose lucidity and sweetness of diction breathe throughout the poem.

REFERENCES

1. Ed. P.L. Jain, Bhāratīya Jñānapītha, Kāśī, 1951
2. Jaina Ātmānanda Sabhā, Bhāvanagar, 1935
3. Jaina Viśva Bhāratī, Lādnūn (Raj.), 1975
4. *Ādipurāṇa*, 35.20
5. *TŚC.*, I.35.34
6. *BBM.*, I.1
7. *Ādipurāṇa*, 35.38 ; *BBM.*, I.4
8. *BBM.*, I.38 ; *Ādipurāṇa*, 35.36
9. *BBM.*, I.56-57 ; *Ādipurāṇa*, 35.42 ; *TṢC.*, I.5.60
10. *Ādipurāṇa*, 35.55 ; *TSC.*, I.5.79 ; *BBM.*, I.78
11. *Ādipurāṇa*, 34 ; *TṢC.*, I.4
12. *Ādipurāṇa*, 35.85 ; *TṢC.*, I.5.12 ; *BBM.*, II.95
13. *BBM.*, III.14
14. *Ādipurāṇa*, 35.134
15. *BBM.*, IV.26

16. *BBM.*, III.26,104 ; *TṢC.*, I.5.221
17. *TṢC.*, I.5.478,515-516
18. *BBM.*, XVI.12
19. *Ibid.*, XVI.26-28
20. *Ibid.*, XVI.61
21. *BBM.*, VIII.30, VII.31, VIII.31, VII.59, VIII.20, VIII.40
22. *Śiśu.*, VII.49 ; *BBM.*, VII.21
23. *Śiśu.*, VII.48 ; *BBM.*, VII.38
24. *Śiśu.*, VII.52 ; *BBM.*, VII.31

SAMAYASUNDARA AND HIS CONTRIBUTION TO SANSKRIT LITERATURE

A celebrated monk of *Kharatara-gaccha*, an offshoot of the Śvetāmbara branch of the Jaina faith, Samayasundara was, by all accounts, one of the most prolific writers that the Jainistic tradition has ever known. His initiation into the monastic order by Jinacandrasūri marked the beginning of what subsequently turned out to be an extremely rewarding and chequered career, though some aspects thereof are shrouded in ambiguity, the profusion of sources notwithstanding. As affirmed by him[1] and some of his pupils,[2] he was born at Sanchor in Marwar. M.D. Desai's suggestion that he was born in V.S.1620,[3] though smugly espoused by subsequent writers, does not stand a close scrutiny. By the time he wrote his first work, the *Bhāvaśataka*, in V.S.1641, he had not only delved into the intricacies of the concept of *Dhvani*, as propounded by Mammaṭa in his *magnum opus*, the *Kāvyaprakāśa*, which he sought to present concisely therein, he had also earned by then the respectable rank of *Gaṇi*. In view of the canonical injuction [4] that the title was not to be bestowed on anyone unless he had been trained for about a decade following his initiation, and the fact that Samayasundara joined the church quite late, in the prime of his youth,[5] probably at the age of twenty; it would be sound to hold that he was ordained into monkhood some time in V.S.1630 which would convincingly push his birth back to about V.S.1610 (1553 A.D.).

Though Sakalacandra Gaṇi died soon after the young monk was assigned to him for proper training and education, it is a measure of Samayasundara's devotion to his erstwhile preceptor that he continued to honour his memory with reverential allusions to him, in almost all his writings.[6] Samayasundara had joined the church almost as an illiterate villager, but his training under the Argus eye of his new teachers, Mahimarāja and Somarāja, turned him into a versatile poet and scholar, well-versed in various branches of learning including grammar, poetics, lexicography and canonical literature besides many languages. His works on a wide variety of subjects vouch for it in an abundant measure.

Samayasundara seems to have been extraordinarily sharp and prolific in literary output. His academic equipment and meticulous adherence to religious pursuits earned him quick elevation in the heirarchy of the *gaccha*. It was nothing short of a feat that even before he came to compose his first work, he had been honoured with the cherished title of *Gaṇi*.[7] The coincidence that the rank was conferred on him alongwith his teacher, in V.S.1640, speaks volumes of Samayasundara as a monk and a potential literary prodigy. Other titles followed him in succession. The combined testimony of the *Karmacandravaṁśaprabandha* (*KVP*)[8] and the *Jainarāsasaṅgraha* [9] (*JRS*) leaves little doubt that Samayasundara graduated as a *Vācaka* not long thereafter. It happily synchronised with the conferment of rank of *Ācārya* on his teacher at Lahore in V.S.1649, on the second day of the bright half of Fālguna. While Rājasoma is unequivocal in stating that Samayasundara earned the title of *Upādhyāya* (*Pāthaka*) at Lavera (Jodhpur) from Jinasiṁhasūri,[10] one of his teachers, he is enigmatically silent on the date of the event. However, his writings reveal it beyond cavil that a long interlude of over twenty two years intervened before Samayasundara could secure the coveted title. The *Viśeṣaśataka*, written in V.S.1672, is the first work to refer to him as *Pāthaka* (*Upādhyāya*).[11] The colophon to the *Ṛṣimaṇḍalavṛtti*, assigned to the same year, also serves to uphold it. As the seniormost monk and scholar in the *gaccha*, after the death of his teacher Jinasiṁhasūri in V.S.1680, Saṃayasundara was automatically elevated to the high pedestal of *Mahopādhyāya* in accordance with the established practice. Harṣanandana has actually hailed him as *Mahopādhyāya* in his gloss on the *Uttarādhyayanasūtra* (*Śrīsamayasundaramahopādhyāyacaraṇasaroruhābhyām namaḥ*).

Samayasundara was a widely travelled person. In the absence of definite evidence, it is difficult to ascertain his itinerary prior to V.S.1644. He seems to have spent this formative period of his career in the vicinity of his teachers that served to equip him tremendously for the literary spree that followed. Thereafter his writings seem to form a reliable index to his widely diffused journeys. Their religious importance apart, these visits opened new vistas to the monk who had limited notions of the land and people. He came abreast of the rich variety that characterised the different regions of the country and, in the process, picked up quite a few of the regional languages. All this combined to make him a fuller and wiser man. By virtue of his manifold attainments he came to carry considerable weight with influential people in some of the regions and had been instrumental in securing ban on animal-slaughter and excesses on some segments of the population. Though, as stated earlier, his travels were widely dispersed, he seemed to have chiefly concentrated on his home state Rajasthan and the neighbouring Gujrat. It was there that most of his works were composed or brought to conclusion.

Samayasundara had special fascination for Ahmedabad. He spent quite a few *Caturmāsas* there, which, as borne out by his writings composed there, were literarily highly productive. He visited Ahmedabad several times between V.S.1687 and 1696. By 1696 (V.S.), being eighty-six, he had become a physical decrepit. Unfortunately, it turned out to be the most trying period of his life. His physical infirmities were exacerbated by severe mental agonies. While in V.S.1686 he had to succumb to the stubbornness of his pupil Harṣanandana which led to a schism in the church, the next year, when he was stationed at Ahmedabad, Gujrat was struck by a terrible famine. The famine broke out with such ferocity that the entire social and moral fabric was sapped dry. It took an extra-ordinarily heavy toll of life. Samayasundara himself was reduced to such dire straits that he had to sell out his books, utensils and other articles of daily use, otherwise something abhorring for a monk to do. His misery was gravely compounded by the perfidy of his pupils who, though deeply indebted to him for their manifold attainments, deserted him when he needed them most to relieve the rigours of the old age. Samayasundara has drawn a moving account of the havoc the famine spelled all around, and the ingratitude and treachery of his disciples[12] which even now sends shudder down to one's spine. The two combined to deal a deadly blow to him. He died in V.S. 1703 at the ripe age of ninety three, a broken man; indeed a painful antithesis to his otherwise smooth and respectable career.

SAMAYASUNDARA'S SANSKRIT WORKS

Samayasundara was indeed a versatile genius. He is the sole Jaina author who can be termed as the nearest approach to the legendary Hemacandra in literary output and spiritual in put. The plethora of his writings in diverse languages attests to it in an ample measure. He was equally at home in grammar, poetics, prosody, linguistics, logic, astrology and canonical and ritualistic literature. While he is credited with a large number of works in

Rājasthānī, which compel revision of some of the notions smugly clung to so far, he made substantial contributions to Sanskrit literature by his abundant and diversified writings. Some of his Sanskrit works can assuredly be claimed to be unparalleled in the domain of literature, and combine to establish him as a mighty scholar and a gifted poet. An in-depth study of his Sanskrit works could have been a rewarding exercise at any point of time. This is what is sought to be attempted here.

Samayasundara imparted a new dimension to the *Śataka* genre of literature. What was intended to enrobe the erotic or gnomic poetry, has been turned by him into an effective medium of *Śāstric* learning. His *Bhāvaśataka*, known through its solitary codex deposited with the L.D. Institute of Indology, Ahmedabad, thus seeks to detail the various divisions and sub- divisions of the *Dhvani*-form of poetry which rests on the preponderance of the suggested sense as ably propounded by Mammaṭa in his *magnum opus*.[13] What the author of *the Kāvyaprakāśa* had presented in detail, stretching it beyond imaginable bounds, Samayasundara has reduced to a tiny volume, obviously to facilitate a clearer and quicker understanding of the concept. The *Bhāvaśataka* bespeaks the zeal of the young author to delve deep into the intricacies of *Dhvani* and perpetuate its tradition, though bitterly threatened by a vast array of critics. Written in V.S. 1641 (*śaśisāgararasabhūtalasaṁvati vihitam ca Bhāvaśatakamidam*), it is believed by common consensus to be the first work of Samayasundara.

The *Samācārī-śataka*, on the other hand, is concerned with Jaina ethics. It was intended to meet the offensive viciously launched to denigrate the Jaina faith in general and the *Kharatara-gaccha* in particular. It forms part of the tradition represented by such notable writings as *Padyavyavasthā-kulaka* of Jīnacandrasūri, *Vidhiprapā* of Jinaprabhasūri and *Acāradinakara* of Vardhamānasūri. While stoutly repudiating the blashphemous charges of Dharmasāgara and others of his ilk, the author has discreetly refrained from hurling counter-accusations. The *Samācārīśataka* seeks to resolve one hundred controversial issues pertaining to ethiçs and to establish, in the process, the compatibility of the *Kharatara-gaccha* with the canon. Samayasundara has backed up his views, almost invariably, with canonical precepts, though he is not oblivious of his limitations.

The *Samācārī-śataka* is divided into five chapters (*Prakāśa*) which are further sub-divided into uneven sections (*Adhikāras*) that add up to a century to justify the title of the work. Each *adhikāra* is addressed to resolve a particular issue.

In the absence of the *Praśasti* to the work, it is difficult to ascertain the date of its composition. On the basis of a verse,[14] not found in the printed text,[15] the *Samācārī-śataka* is believed to have been concluded in V.S.1672 at Meḍatā (Jodhpur), though it was started at Siddhipuri in Sindh and a part thereof was written at Multan in V.S.1669.

Written in the same year and at the same venue,[16] the *Viśeṣa-śataka* seeks to resolve one hundred doctrinal or ritualistic problems posed by an inquisitive pupil. In consonance with his known style, the author has elucidated each issue in a lucid language, on the basis of authoritative texts. In a bid to facilitate a clearer understanding of the canonical excerpts, he has rendered in simple phraseology such of them as he deemed hard for the reader to grasp. The pieces culled from the *Sūtras*, attest to the author's unquestioned insight in those texts. Some of the quesions discussed in the *Śataka* are interesting and deserve attention. It is concluded, for instance, in the fourth *Prakaraṇa* that Jamāli would attain liberation after fifteen births. The author has upheld it on the basis of Hemacandra's *Mahāvīracarita*.

The *Vicāraśataka* also addresses itself to explain and solve a century of issues pertaining to Jaina philosophy, in a style not dissimilar from that of the preceding *Śataka*. Samayasundara meticulously adheres to the tested method of upholding the elucidation with scriptural texts. It has, however, resulted in an overabundance of doctrinal terminology creeping into the work. The *Śataka* consists of one hundred *Prakaraṇas* with each section dealing with one problem, though some of the problems spill over more than one *Prakaraṇa*. The *Praśasti* proves it beyond doubt that Meḍatā again formed the venue of its compostion, attempted two years subsequent to the *Viśeṣaśataka*, in 1674.[17]

The *Visaṁvāda-śataka* locates and enlists one hundred of such of the topics in canonical texts that are marked by bewildering inconsistency and contradiction. The author has wisely desisted from the frustrating task of explaining them away or otherwise smoothening them. The *Visaṁvāda-śataka* is known to have been composed in V.S.1685. The only known manuscript of the *Śataka*, written in V.S.1889 and preserved in the *Abhaya Jaina Granthālaya*, Bikaner, is unhappily corrupt and illegible.

Aṣṭalakṣī or *Artharatnāvalī*[18] is undoubtedly the most pedantic work of Samayasundara and has been chiefly instrumental in ensuring him abiding glory. It represents an acme to the literary feat of multiple interpretation which has a long tradition in Sanskrit. Stung by the unkind charge voiced at Akbar's court, that the jaina *Sūtras* are imprecise to the extent of being liable to manifold interpretation, Samayasundara embarked upon the frightening task of proving its veracity, in true perspective, by extorting more than ten lakh meanings from the innocuous jumble of syllables रा-जा-नो-द-द-ते-सौ-ख्य-म् (राजानो ददते सौख्यम्) However, on subsequent scrutiny, two lakh twenty thousand, four hundred and seven meanings were discarded as untenable, leaving the remaining eight lakh to impart the work the alternative appellation, it bears till date. Such literary gymnastics have doubtless fascinated the scholarly poets, but even the most erudite authors of the Sandhāna-kāvyas would pale into insignificance before Samayasundara's stupendous *tour de force*. On the author's own testimony,[19] the *Aṣṭalakṣī* was blessed by Emperor Akbar while he was camping at lahore, *en route* to Kashmir, on the thirteenth day of the bright fortnight of Śrāvaṇa in V.S.1649.

The endless interpretation of the brief sentence presupposes the author's profound equipment in Sanskrit grammar and lexicography. Samayasundara was indeed well- versed in both. He has mentioned the eight lexicons that he had mastered prior to setting himself on the prohibitive task. Queer break-up of the sentence, followed by equally startling meanings of the various units thereof has enabled the author to put incredible interpretations on it. The following renderings sufficiently reflect the poet's expertise in the art.

१. रा आजा नो अददत ईसौख्यम् ।

रा पर्यायेण श्रीः । 'अ शिवे केशवे वायौ' इति विश्वशम्भुवचनाद् अं वायुम् अजति क्षिपति धातूनामनेकार्थत्वात् भक्ष (य) तीति अचिं आजः सर्पस्तेन आ शोभा यस्य स आजाः । श्री (रा) पूर्वकः आजा श्री (रा) आजा-श्रीपार्श्वनाथः सर्पलाञ्छनात् । स नः ईसौख्यम् अददत । इति चतुर्थोऽर्थः । सर्वे ।

२. ला ज । आ नो ददते सौख्यम् ।

ला च लक्ष्मीर्लमम्बरे इति विश्वशम्भु (श्लोक १०४) वचनात् ला लक्ष्मीः । हे जा। हे जेतृपुरुष । आ इति सम्बोधने । नः अस्मभ्यं १ अस्माकं २ वा सौख्यं असौख्यं वा २ ददते । इदं भोगिनां योगिनां च वचनम् । सर्वे ।

३. ऋ-आ-अदा नो ददते असौख्यम् ।

ऋः मेषस्तम् आ सामस्त्येन अजन्ति क्षिपन्तीति रत्वे कृते राजाः सिंहादयः नः अस्माकम् असौख्यं ददते । इदं मृगाणां नचनम् ।

Some of his shorter works, especially the *stotras*, also bring out, in relief, samayasundara's equipment in literary gimmicks, not precluding Yamaka, Śleṣa and *Samasyāpūrti*. The *stotras* are mostly addressed to Pārśvanātha, though his devotion to Ṛṣabhadeva and Mahāvīra, as attested by his others writings of uneven size, is beyond dispute. Quite a few of Samayasundara's *stotras* are infested with Yamaka[20] of various hues, while some others have been pressed into service to parade his expertise in handling the Śleṣa.[21] Samayasundara could also not resist the temptation of succumbing to the various *bandhas*[22], inherent in the *Citrakāvya*, however odd they may seem in the devotional hymns. Whatever their worth as an index to the poet's pedantry, these literary gymnastics combine to turn the *stotras* into an exercise in artificiality, which otherwise are supposed to exude warmth and devotion. It, however, goes to his credit that, more often than not, he has not overstepped the bounds of moderation. Some of his *stotras* are characterised by an admixture of Sanskrit and Prākrit[23], a feat also exploited by others.

Samayasundara has tried his hand at the popular feat of *Samasyāpūrti* as well. In the *Jinasiṁhasūripadotsavakāvya,* he has sought to incorporate the last quarter of each verse of the third canto of the *Raghuvaṁśa* in the body of his poem to describe the function, arranged with fanfare, by Prime Minister Karmacanda Bacchavat, to celebrate the elevation of his teacher Jinasiṁhasūri to the rank of *Ācārya*. Even while describing an event, so distinctly apart from the original, the beauty of Kālidāsa's lines has been retained, almost intact.[24] A transcript of the poem is said to exist in the *Abhaya Jaina Granthālaya*, Bikaner.

The *Ṛṣabha-bhaktāmara-stotra* (*ṚBS*)[25], though written by way of *Samasyāpūrti* of Mānatuṅga's famed hymn, the *Bhaktāmara*, represents a pole apart from the literary trickery. Despite the constraints of *Samasyāpūrti*, the *ṚBS* is distinguished by pleasing lucidity and deep religious fervour. The similarity of theme has been instrumental in securing the warmth of devotion that pervades the *stotra*. It reads like a spontaneous outpouring of an emotionally surcharged heart. Sweet phraseology, repeatedly enlivened by Anuprāsa, serves to assure it a high place in the galaxy of devotional hymns. The verses, instanced below, would testify to its veracity.

नमेन्द्रवन्द्र कृतभद्र जिनेन्द्र चन्द्र
ज्ञानात्मदर्श- परिहृष्ट-विशिष्ट-विश्व ।
त्वन्मूर्तिरर्तिहरणी तरणी मनोज्ञे-
वावलम्बनं भवजले पततां जनानाम् ।।१।।

भास्वद्गुणाय करणाय मुदोरणाय
विद्याचणाय कमलप्रतिमेक्षणाय ।
सल्लक्षणाय जनताकृतरक्षणाय
तुभ्यं नमो जिन ! भवोदधिशोषणाय ।।२६।।

Written in V.S.1653 at Idar (Gujrat) for the author's pupil, the *Mańgalavāda* seeks to examine the objectives of the benediction (*mańgalācaraṇa*) from the standpoint of the Nyāya philosophy. The detailed evaluation led the author to conclude that the *mańgalācaraṇa* was of three types-physical, oral and mental. The absence of benediction in Keśavamiśra's *Tarkabhāṣā* is explained on the ground that it is the mental benediction that has supplanted the formal *mańgala* here. Though the work is concerned with neo-*nyāya* which is notorious for toughness, the presentation is throughout lucid and precise, shorn of unnecessary accretions or details. One of its codices forms part of the treasure of rare manuscripts in the *Abhaya Jaina Granthālaya*, Bikaner.

Samayasundara did not mean to overburden his writings with abstruse grammatical forms. However, his firm grounding in grammar is evident from his references to the *Aṣṭādhyāyī*, Hemacandra's *Lingānuśāsana*, *Kalāpavyākaraṇa* and *Viṣṇuvārtika*. *Sārasvata-vyākaraṇa-rahasya* (*SVR*) and *Sārasvata-śabda- rūpāvālī* (*SSR*), that forms a sort of supplement to the former, bear testimony to his equipment in the Sārasvata system of grammar. The initial and concluding parts of the *SVR* indicate that the author had herein dealt with the *Sārasvata- vyākaraṇa* in its entirety but the known segment is confined to the verbal forms alone, albeit in all the tenses and subdivisions. One of its MSS is known to exist in Jinaharivihāra, Palitana. The authoriship of the *SSR* has been disputed, though a verse[26] quoted by Vinayasāgara, unmistakably attributes it to Samayasundara.

The *Kālakācārya-kathā* (*KK*) forms an important contribution to the story literature. The story of Kālaka has exercised powerful influence on the Jaina society to the extent that it led to the emergence of no less than thirty works of uneven worth and girth. Samayasundara's *KK* occupies a high place in the series of similar works, attempted earlier. It is still known through its manuscripts, deposited with some of the *Bhandaras* at Bikaner, Calcutta etc. The *KK* was written in V.S.1666 while Rawal Tejsi was ruling at Vikrampur.[27] One *Kaṭhākoṣa* is also attributed to Samayasundara though it is not clear whether it was an original work or a mere collection of earlier stories. A MS of the *Kathāpatrāṇi,* written at Jalore in V.S.1695 by the author in his own hand, contains 114 stories.

The *Viśeṣa-saṅgraha*, intended to be a guide to the young students,[28] adds up, in all essentials, to a selection of excerpts from ancient texts and their commentaries, on a wide variety of subjects. The excerpts are properly referenced to facilitate quick location in the originals. The selection is a virtual boon to the researchers, the like of which is hard to come across. The *Viśeṣa-saṅgraha* was written at Lūṇakaraṇasara (Bikaner) in V.S.1685.

Some of Samayasundara's works deal with Jaina rituals and other religious observances. *Cāturmāsa-Vyākhyāna* (V.S.1665), *Śrāvakāradhanā* (V.S.1667) and *Dīkṣā-pratiṣṭhā-śuddhi* (V.S.1685) belong to this class. The last work is distinguished by a profound discussion on astrological matters. Samayasundara was brilliantly helped in its composition by his grand - pupil Jayakīrti, who was well-versed in astrology.[29]

His *Kharataragaccha-paṭṭāvalī* (*KP*) seeks to trace the genealogy of the pontiffs of the *Kharatara -gaccha*, right from Gaṇadhara Gautama, the first disciple of Lord Mahāvīra. Its value is immensely enhanced by the life-accounts of the different Ācāryas, appended to the tables. Samayasundara wrote the work at Khambat in V.S.1690.[30] The well-known *Abhaya Jaina Granthālaya* of Bikaner is said to be in possession of one of its MSS.

Tṛṇāṣṭaka, Rajo'ṣṭaka, udgacchatsūryabimbāṣṭaka and *Samasyāṣṭaka* are some of the minor works of Samayasundara that are available in print.[31]

Besides these original writings on a wide variety of subjects, Samayasundara has to his credit an equally large number of commentaries on ancient texts, both sacred and profane, that serve to establish him as a scholiast of no mean order. His commentaries concern themselves, not unlike his original works, with diverse disciplines. These seem to have been spurred by the keenness to meet the requirements of his pupils in the monastry. In view of their succinctness, most of the commentaries are appropriately called *Vṛttis*. Only a few of them are available in print, the others being scattered in various *Bhaṇḍāras* in the form of manuscripts which are hard to be secured for proper evaluation.

Of the non-Jaina works Samayasundara has chosen for elucidation, Kālidāsa's *Raghuvaṁśa* and *Kumārasambhava* deserve special attention. The two poems have indeed been worthy games for many a jaina scholiast. Samayasundara's *vṛtti* on *Raghuvaṁśa*, aptly named *Arthālāpanikā*, seeks to resolve the text in a simple language with particular stress on dissolving the compounds. At places the author has offered fresh interpretation of the well-known verses or parts thereof. The compound *pārvatīparameśvarau* in 1.1, for instance, has been interpreted as *pāravatīp'aśca rameśvaraśca iti (Śivakeśavau). Pītapratibaddhavatsām* (II.1) has likewise been given a new rendering as : *pītaḥ śankurudāhṛta ityuktatvāt pīte śankau pratibaddho vatso yasyāḥ tām.*

A copy of the *Arthālāpanikā* is preserved in the Jain Bhavan at Calcutta. It consists of sixty-seven folios. According to Vinayasāgara ji,[32] it was written at Khambat, in V.S.1692.

A similar pattern of interpretation is witnessed in the *vṛtti* on *the Kumārasambhava*. The Jinaharivihāra of Palitana (Gujrat) is in possession of a MS of the commentary which attests to its having been written in V.S.1679.

Samayasundara's gloss on the *Vṛttaratnākara* reflects his deep grasp of the science of prosody. By virtue of its merits it commands a high place in the mass of commentaries it has evoked, down the years. Composed of six chapters, the *vṛtti* is known to have been concluded in V.S.1694 on the auspicious day of the Dīpavālī.[33] Three of its manuscripts are deposited with the jain Bhavan, Calcutta.

Samayasundara is credited with the commentaries on *Meghadūta* and the third canto of *Māghakāvya* also. The latter is known through its solitary MS preserved in the Surāṇā Library at Chūru (Raj.).

His *Tīkā* on *Vāgbhaṭālankāra* of Vāgbhaṭa is intended to unravel the essence of Sanskrit Poetics, as it is propounded in the work. The commentary is marked by a pleasing clarity and performs well the purpose it is expected to discharge. While elucidating the various concepts discussed by Vāghaṭa, the commentator has not shunned to evaluate the views enunciated on them by other writers. That invests the commentary with a critical flair. It was primarily meant to serve as a guide to the author's pupil Harirāma in prosecuting his studies in Poetics. It is known for certain to have been composed in V.S.1692.[34]

It is again to his keenness to minister to the needs of the students that his gloss on the *Daśavaikālikasūtra*, one of the most sacred texts of the Jainas, owes its origin.[35] The *Daśavaikālika-sūtra* has been commented upon, down the years, by a large number of enlightened scholars including the polymoth Haribhadrasūri, whose commentary Samayasundara denounces as abstruse (*viṣama*).[36]

Samayasundara has handled the Prakrit text with assured authority. The *Dīpikā* unmistakably betrays his deep grasp of the vast mass of canonical literature. His claim that the gloss, though exhaustive, is characterised by lucidity and ease, is not unjustified. It indeed serves to project the contents of the text in bold relief. On the author's own testimony, the gloss was written at Khambat, in V.S.1691 (*śaśinidhiśṛṅgāramite varṣe*).

His commentary on Bhadrabāhu's *Kalpasūtra*, another equally sacred text, is aimed to serve a higher purpose, much beyond the academic needs of the monastic students. The *Kalpasūtra* is known to have evoked, over the ages, as many as ninety commentaries. Samayasundara seems to have gone through at least a majority of them with a good sieve. He was justiftiably convined of the merits of his *Kalapalatā*,[37] which, he asserts, with an egoistic air,was sure to surpass the earlier glosses and commentaries.[38]

Though begun at Lūṇakaraṇasara, it was completed at Riṇipura, some time between V.S.1684 and 1685, when as confirmed by the *Duriyarasamīra-vṛtti* and the *Yati-ārādhanā* respectively, Samayasundara was camping there.[39]

Written at Ahmedabad in V.S.1688, Samayasundara's gloss on the *Navatattvaprakaraṇa*, popularly known as *Navatattva-vṛtti (saṁvat-vasu-gaja-rasa-mite)*, has the undoubted merit of driving home, in lucid and simple phraseology, the essence of the nine *tatttvas*, that form the core of the Jaina doctrine, and, as such, serves as a gateway to the abstruse tenets of the Āgamas.

The *Daṇḍakaprakaraṇa* of Muni Gajasāra consisting of 42 Prakrit stanzas has also received Samayasundara's attention. The gloss seeks to explain each *gāthā* concisely in a manner that the true import thereof is brought home without any ambiguity sticking to it. It was written at Ahmedabad in V.S.1696. A MS of the gloss is preserved in the collection of the late Puran Chand Nahar of Calcutta.

Himself a noted writer of devotional hymns, Samayasundara could have hardly ignored the *Stotras*, which command as much reverence as the canonical texts, nay are more popular with the laity. He has indeed elucidated some of the more popular *Stotras* with his glosses and notes. Besides the great *Bhaktāmara* and *Kalyāṇamandira*, Samayasundara has commented upon *Ṛṣi-maṇḍala, Saptasmaraṇa, Duriyarasamīra* and *Jayatihuṇa*. While his glosses on the last three are available in print, those on *Bhaktāmara, Kalyāṇamandira* and *Ṛṣi-maṇḍala* are known to exist in the form of manuscripts only.

Samayasundara is also stated to have commented upon *Vimalastuti*, *Liṅgānuśāsana*, *Aniṭakārikā*, *Sārasvatavyākaraṇa Verayatha* and *Cattāri paramāṅgāni* which are scarce to obtain. The *vṛtti* on *Sandehadohāvali* of Jinadattasūri, a work on Jaina ethics, was written in V.S.1693.

Thus Samayasundara was a man of many parts. He embodied the tradition of sound and multi-facet scholarship that has unfortunately faded out. The mere quantum of his literary output would do credit to the greatest author. And what has been revealed here pertains to one language only. His writings in Rājasthānī form a formidable mass of literature.

REFERENCES

1. *Sītārāma-Caupāi*, 6.3.50, Bikaner, V.S.2019
2. *Naladavadantī-rāsa*, Ed. R.C. Shah, Bharata Prakāśana, Ahmedabad, Appendix III, p.137
3. *Ānandakāvya-mahaodadhi, part* 7, Jaina Pustakoddhāra Fund, *Bombay, V.S.1982*
4. *Vyavahārasūtra*, Sanderav, 1980 A.D., 3.7, 10.24-27
5. नवयौवन भर संयम संग्रह्यौ । Harṣanandana
6. *Daśavaikālika-vṛtti, Praśasti*, 2-3; *Bhāvaśataka*, 99 etc.
7. तच्छिष्यसमयसुन्दरगणिना स्वाभ्यासवृद्धिकृते । *Bhāvaśataka, 99*
8. गुणविनयसमयसुन्दरगणी कृतौ वाचनाचार्यौ । *KVP, 62*
9. वाचकपद गुणविनय नइ, समयसुन्दर नइ दीधउरे । *JRS, Part III*
10. *Naladavadantī-rāsa*, Appendix 3, Rājasoma's *Samayasundaragītam*, p.133
11. तच्छिष्य-समयसुन्दरपाठकैरकृत शतकमिदम् । *Viśeṣaśatakam, 4.*
12. (a) *Satyāsīya-duṣkāla-varṇana-Chattīsī* (Rājasthanī), *Kusumāñjali*, Ed. Agarchand Natta and Bhanwar Lal Nahta, 4, Jagmohan Mallik Lane, Calcutta-7, P.501-512.
    (b) *Guru-duḥkhita-vacanam* (Sanskrit), Ibid., p.417-419
13. काव्यप्रकाशे शास्त्रे ध्वनिरिति संज्ञा निवेदिता येषाम् ।
    वाच्यातिशायिव्यङ्ग्यान् कवित्वभेदानहं वच्मि ।। *Bhāvaśataka, 2.*
14. *Kusumāñjali*, op.cit., Vinayasāgara's introductory write-up, Mahopādhyāya Samayasundara, p. 53, F.No.14.
15. ŚrīJinadattasūri-Jñānabhaṇḍāra, Bombay, V.S.1993.
16. *Kusumāñjali,* op.cit., P.53, F.N.16

17. *Vicāraśataka, Praśasti*, 1.
18. Ed. Hira Lal R. Kapadia, D.L. Jaina Pustakoddhāra Saṁsthā, Bombay.
19. *Anekārtha-ratna-mañjūṣa*, D.L. Jaina Pustakoddhāra Fund, Bombay, V.S.1989, P.65
20. *ŚrīPārśvanātha-yamaka-baddha-laghu-stavanam, Kusumāñjali*, op.cit., P.187; *ŚrīPārśvanātha-yamaka-bandhastotram*, Ibid.,192; *Yamakamayam Pārśvanātha- laghu-stvanam*, Ibid., 621, *Yamakamayam Mahāvīra-bṛhad- stavanam*, Ibid., P.622-623.
21. *Śrī Cintāmaṇi Pārśvanātha-śleṣamaya-laghu-stavanam*, Ibid., P.188; *Nānāvidha-sleṣsmayam Śrī-Ādinātha-stotram*, Ibid., 615.
22. *ŚrīPārśvanāthasya śṛṅkhalāmaya-laghu-stavanam*, Ibid., P.189; *Śrī Pārśvanātha-śṛṅgāṭakabandha-stavaṇam*, Ibid., P.193 etc.
23. *Sanskrit-Prakrit-bhāsāmayam- SrīPārśvanāthāṣṭakam*, Ibid., P.196.
24. यदूर्ध्ववरेखाभिधमंह्रिपंकजे
    भवान् ततः पूज्यपदं प्रलब्धवान् ।
    प्रभो । महामात्यवितीर्णकोटिशः-
    सुदक्षिणाऽदो हृदः । लक्षणं दधौ ।।1।।
25. *Kusumāñjali*, op.cit., P.604-614
26. सारस्वतस्य रूपाणि पूर्ववृत्तेरलीलिखत् ।
    स्तम्भतीर्थे मधौ मासे गणिसमयसुन्दरः । *SSR, Praśasti, 1.*
27. *KK, Praśasti*, 1.
28. *Viśeṣa-saṅgraha, Praśasti*, 3-4
29. *Dīkṣā-pratiṣṭhā-śuddhi, Praśasti*, 1-2
30. *KP, Praśasti*, 1.
31. *Kusumāñjali*, op.cit., P.494-497
32. *Kusumāñjali*, op.cit., His write-up, Mahopādhyāya Samayasundara, P.51, F.N.6
33. *Vṛttaratnākara-vṛtti, Praśasti*, 2
34. *Vāgbhaṭālaṅkāra-ṭīkā, Praśasti*, 3
35. मया तु शीघ्रप्रबोधाय शिष्यार्थं सुगमा कृता ।
36. हरिभद्रकृता टीका वर्तते विषमा परम् ।

37. Śrī jinadattasūri-jñāna-bhaṇḍāra, Bombay, V.S.1996
38. वक्ष्येऽहं कल्पसूत्रस्य व्याख्यानि नव स्फुटम् ।
    सुगमानि सुबोधानि नानाग्रन्थानुसारतः ।।
    न सूत्रं नावचूरिश्च न वृत्तिर्नान्यपत्रकम् ।।
    ग्राह्यं व्याख्यानवेलायां पुस्तकेऽस्मिन् करस्थिते ।। *Kalpalatā*, 2-3
39. *Kalpalatā*, *Praśasti*, 17

A NOTE ON SĀRASVATAMAṆḌANA

The combined testimony of the *Śṛṅgāramaṇḍana* and *Campūmaṇḍana* reveals it beyond doubt that Prime Minister Maṇḍana had made substantial contribution towards enriching Sanskrit grammar, as well. While in the former he proudly projects himself as the illustrious author of the *Sārasvataa-maṇḍana* with equal fondness he terms the *Campūmaṇḍana* as a work brotherly (junior) to it.[1] As is evident from its title, especially the alternative appellation *Sārasvatasūtravṛtti*, the *Sārasvatamaṇḍana* purports to be a brief gloss *(vṛtti)* on Anubhūti-svarūpa's *Sārasvatavyākaraṇa*, which, not unlike other similar attempts, seeks to compress Sanskrit grammar, as exhaustively propounded in Pāṇini's *Aṣṭādhyāyī*, within the space of mere seven hundred aphorisms. Suchlike compendiums are a vertiable boon to the beginner, and serve as a gateway to the intricacies of Sanskrit grammar and semantics. The *Sārasvatavyākaraṇa* indeed evoked wide following in the Jainistic tradition. It was perhaps to respect the tradition and minister to the academic needs of the young student that Maṇḍana took it upon himself to resolve the text with his perceptive *vṛtti*, other glosses thereon notwithstanding.

Unlike his other writings, the *Sārasvaṭamaṇḍana* is unhappily not available in print. Of two of its manuscripts deposited with the Bhandarakar Oriental Research Institute, Poona, the one (New No.36), copied in V.S. 1632, is in a better state of preservation. Running into as many as 121 folios, the Ms is a riddle of sorts. While it is legible for the most, the text is hopelessly tarnished by tantalizing ambiguity and incoherence. The way the scribe has recklessly mutilated the simple words and known *sūtras* is an eloquent, though sad, commentary on his poor equipment in Sanskrit. He had no qualms in turning *baṁhayati* into *Caṁhayati*, *śāsa anuśiṣṭau* into *āsa anuśiṣṭau*, *rāto ñau puk* into *rāto nau puk*. The Ms is infested with such fearsome howlers, though the scribe is blissfully unaware of their gravity. With such a hopeless text, it is well-nigh impossible to decipher sizable parts of the codex or extort any connected meaning therefrom. It is thus a frustrating exercise to subject the *Sārasvatamaṇḍana* to a sustained appraisal. Nevertheless, a patient study and analysis of the text, as it exists, throw up certain features which seem to settle down as the distinguishing characteristics of the *vṛtti.*

Maṇḍana's gloss is as exhaustive and useful to unravel the mysteries of the *Sārasvatavyākaraṇa* as a *vṛtti* on a grammatical text can be. The author has indeed made a commendable attempt to elucidate the *Sārasvta* text with his lucid gloss. His simple language and down-to-earth style combine to prompt the reader to negotiate the jungle of the corrupt text with a modicum of grit. Taken together, the *vṛtti* reflects, in no small measure, the author's equipment in grammar which his biographer Maheśvara has underscored with warmth and frequency.[2]

What strikes one most is Maṇḍana's technique of resolving the text. While, in keeping with the norm, he has sought to deal with the *Sārasvatavyākaraṇa* sequentially, reproducing the *sūtras* followed by his gloss thereon; not infrequently he chooses to be casual in merely paraphrasing the apporisms in his language, without quoting them bodily. No serious offence may be taken against the method in so far as it serves to unfold the import of the relevant sūtras, but it can hardly be claimed to be scientific or adequate enough to grapple with a tough discipline like grammar.

Maṇḍana was actuated by the desire to make Anubhūtisvarūpa's text, the clearest possible. In order to realise his objective he has resorted to a variety of devices. The most fruitful has been the method to explain the more important / intricate *sūtras* by dissolving the various compounds and / or paraphrasing the various units they are composed of, much in the manner of a commentator on drama or poetry. His *vṛtti* is therefore brimming with expressions like विगृह्य व्याचष्टे, स्पष्टत्वाद् व्याचष्टे, विशेषमाह. An idea of his anxiety to ensure transparence to his elucidation can be had from the gloss on so well-knwon a *sūtra* as जनिकर्तुः प्रकृतिः. Says he : जनिर्जनिधात्वर्थो जननमिति यावत् । जनेः कर्ता जनिकर्ता तस्य प्रकृतिः मूलकारणम् । एतदेव स्पष्टत्वाद् व्याचष्टे । जायमानस्य कार्यस्य मूलकारणमपादाननसंज्ञं भवति ।[3] He has not refrained from dissolving such simple compounds as स्तोः and अभ्वोः in स्तोः श्चुभिः श्चुः and अभ्वोर्णादौ respectively. This is how he has explained the latter aphorism -- अश्च भूश्च तयोः, अभ्वो इति विगृह्य व्याचक्षाणो अभ्वोरित्यत्र उवभावदोषं शब्दनिर्देशत्वेन परिहरन् व्याचष्टे पूर्वस्याकारस्य भूशब्दस्य आकारादेशो भवति णादौ सति दीर्घकरणं पूर्वाकारविषयं न भ्वर्थु तेन ह्रस्व इति ह्रस्वः ।[4] Maṇḍana has the wont to shed light in his glosson other related issues, as well. Why *i* in the *sūtra* इ यं स्वरे stands for long *i* also, is lucidly explained in the *vṛtti*. When a short vowel is used in the *sūtra*, it denotes both of its forms; but when followed by *t* or *kāra*, it stands for itself alone: इति दीर्घमपि संगृह्णाति यतो वर्णग्रहणे सवर्णग्रहणम् । तपरकरणे कारग्रहणे च तावन्मात्रग्रहणमिति[5]

It is simply beyond the tiny frame of the *vṛtti* to sequentially dwell upon the formation of the whole gamut of words. The feat can possibly be accomplished in an exhaustive commentary (*bhāṣya*). Maṇḍana's *vṛtti* interestingly seeks to instruct, within its limits, the reader in the process of formation of words, explaining the procudure often with the *sūtras*, but mostly without them, with mere reference to the sequence involved therein. The style doubtless involves repetition but is extremely beneficial to the young reader, not well-equipped to try conclusions, on his own. This is how he explains the formation of the *yaṅanta narinṛtyate* and causative *pācayati*.

नृती गात्रविक्षेपे-यङ्, द्वित्वम्, उपधाया रीगागमः नरीनृत्यते । पच ञिप्रत्ययः ञित्वादत उपधाया इति वृद्धिः, धातुसंज्ञा, तिबादय, अप् कर्तरि गुण, अयादेशः पाचयति ।

Pada forms the life-breath of Sanskrit grammar. It is so sacrosanct to it that all else including the usage, sinks into insignificance. Maṇḍana has been happily chary of the pitfalls inherent in the system. He, therefore, set himself on illustrating, not infrequently, the use of a plethora of forms with brief but apt examples. The device serves to bring him closer to the present-day grammarian, who is so keen to acquaint the reader with usage by mustering appropriate illustrations from ancient texts or those of his own. This is how he means to exemplify the various forms, accomplished in his *vṛtti* : अभूत् वृष्टिः, जगामागत्स्यो दक्षिणां दिशम्, चखान कूपम्, जंगम्यते तुरगः, गायत्र्योपतिष्ठते, मूत्रमुच्चरति ।

With a view to ensure clarity to the subject and invest it with added interest, Maṇḍana has occasionally resorted to the style of the ancient *Bhāṣyas* in posing queries with respect to certain aspects of the issue under discussion and meeting them convincingly. That he resorted to it in the brief gloss, speaks volumes of his anxiety to dispell complexity from grammar that is otherwise inherent in it. Thus, in case of the example दधि इह intended to illustrate the *savarṇadīrgha sandhi*, he raises, by way of *pūrvapakṣa*, the pertinent question as to why the *sūtra* इ यं स्वरे that precribes the substitution of *ya* for *i* if it is followed by a vowel, does not apply here. He explains it on the ground that a special rule with its specific application takes precedence over a general rule which has indefinite sweep.[6] Likewise his *vṛtti* on the *sūtra* 'द्विश्च' which provides for doubling the root in case it is followed by the desiderative suffix स, Maṇḍana asks inquisitively why the augment *iṭ* is not added to the root *bhū* in accordance with the rule सिसतासीस्यपामिट्. It has been met with the simple aphorism 'वुः' which negates the augment *iṭ* after roots ending in *u, a* and *grah, guha* etc. The *sūtra* 'नानिट्' explains away the subsequent query that why the root *bhū* does not take *guṇa*, though it is followed by an *ārdhadhātuka* suffix (गुणः कुतो न भवति).

It is again to facilitate a clearer understanding of the text that the Prime Minister has inducted in the body of his gloss, the views of the preceding grammarians, both named and unnamed. He has referred to their observations by the stock phrase '*iti kecit*'. In the *vṛtti* on some of the *sūtras* he has quoted a multiety of alternative opinions. While explaining the aphorism 'लिङ्गार्थे प्रथमा' which prescribes the use of the nominative case, he has three views to offer, besides his own which combine to reveal the fierce controversy that has raged, down the ages, with respect to its interpretation.[7] At one place, he has quoted Pāṇini, *Kāśikā* and *Nyāsa* by name, but the text is so corrupt that it is difficult to make out what was actually intended here. The nomenclatures of the tenses in the *Sārasvatavyākaraṇa* widely differ from those in Pāṇini. They are uniformly named after the point of time they represent. Thus *laṭ* therein is *vartamāna, luṭ śvastana* and *liṭ* is *ṇabādiprakriyā*. Maṇḍana has invariably equated them with the better-known Pāṇinian appellations which go far to remove the mist of ambiguity about them.

The *Sārasvatamaṇḍana* begins with an autobiographic verse in the *Śārdūlavikrīḍita* metre, which sets forth the details of Maṇḍana's lineage and attributes his success to the lotus-like feet of Jinendra. It is followed by an exhaustive evaluation of the *maṅgalācarāṇa* of the *Sārasvatavyākaraṇa*, which runs as follows.

प्रणम्य परमात्मानं बालधीवृद्धिसिद्धये ।
सारस्वतीमृजु कुर्वे प्रक्रियां नातिविस्तराम् ।।

Maṇḍana is justified in his belief that the benediction has the sanction of the ancient masters. Thus in 'सिद्धे शब्दार्थसम्बन्धे,' Patañjali has intended the word *siddha* to perform the function of the *maṅgalācaraṇa*. The imperatives of the benediction are likewise met by the auspicious word *vṛddhi* in the first *sūtra* of the

Aṣṭādhyāyī (वृद्धिरादैच्). The author of the *Mahābhāṣya* insists on the benediction not only in the beginning of the work, but in the middle and end as well, because in his view it brings name to the work and ensures fulfilment of the readers' cherished desires.[8] Maṇḍana has sought to respect the tradition in his gloss which is distinguished by benediction at the three prescribed places.

Maṇḍana is convinced that the *lyabanta* form प्रणम्य has been accorded the first place in the benediction because of its happy connotation. Being indicative of excellence (*prakarṣa*), the author hereby means to wish the reader successive excellence in prosecuting his grammatical studies. As a matter of fact, it is the prefix *pra* that denotes excellence. *Parama* in the second phrase परमात्मानम्, he opines, denotes the infinite and inscrutable power of God, popularly known as his *māyā*, the cause of the universe.[9] The word *ātmā* is meant to underscore His omnipresence.[10] Paramātmā thus stands for Siddha Parameśvara. If dissolved as *param ātmānam*, it would be synonymous with the highest consciousness. बालधीवृद्धिसिद्धये, in his view, is intended to imply that the growth of intellect constitutes accomplishment (*siddhi*) and that adds up to one of the goals (*puruṣārtha*). The adjectival clause अनतिविस्तराम्, according to him, denies only verbosity, not the profundity of meaning. The author of the *Sārasvatavyākaraṇa* means to convey a wealth of meanings in limited words because abstruse or intricate diction tends to scare away the green horn (दुर्बोधाज्ञलस्ति बालाः).

Maṇḍana has taken the opportunity to express his views on the objects of grammar, as well. The five objectives - *Rakṣā, ūha* etc. mentioned in the *Mahābhāṣya* are so well-known.[11] But Maṇḍana soars high in holding Brahman (*Saccidānanda Paramātmā*) as the highest object of all the śāstras. That should be taken to be the objective of the prsent treatise also (*tadevātrāpi*). The fourth aphorism (*tattu samanvayāt*) of the *Brahmasūtra* describes him in detail. The author of the *vṛtti* is convinced that on closer scrutiny, *Rakṣā*, *ūha* etc. cannot be held to be the highest objectives of the study of grammar.[12]

The word सारस्वतीम् in the *maṅgala* verse, in his opinion, means सरस्वतीप्रणीताम्. The *Sārasvatavyākaraṇa* is traditionally believed to have been revealed to the author by the goddess of learning herself.

सूत्रसप्तशतीं यस्मै ददौ साक्षात् सरस्वती ।
अनुभूतिस्वरूपाय तस्मै श्रीगुरवे नमः ॥

According to Maṇḍana अनतिविस्तराम् and ऋजु reflect *laghu* and *asandeha*, admitted as two of the objectives in the *Mahābhāṣya*.

In the author's words, the present *vṛtti* is intended to dispell the haze of imprecise glosses that had enveloped Anubhūtisvarūpa's text, over the years. Besides that, the *Sārasvatamaṇḍana* is invested with historical worth in as much as it provides additional details about its author. Apart from the *Kāvyamanohara*, it is the only work to refer to him as *Saṁghapati* and *Mahāpradhāna* (Prime Minister). It is again the solitary work to highlight his manifold equipment in various disciplines with the happy phrase सर्वविद्याविशारद .[13]

REFERENCES

1. यः सारस्वतकाव्यमण्डनकविर्दारिद्र्यभूभृत्पविः । *Śṛṅgāramaṇḍana*, 107
   श्रीसारस्वतमण्डनस्य विदुषां सन्तोषदस्यानुजे । *Campūmaṇḍana*, p.35..
2. जाग्रद्व्याकरणश्च नाटकशुभालङ्कारविज्ञस्तथा । *Kāvyamanohara*, I.122
3. *Sārasvatamaṇḍana* (Ms), P. 48b, 49a.
4. *Ibid*, P.83a
5. *Ibid*, P.9a 'इ यं स्वरे' इत्यादिना यकारादयः कुतो न स्युरित्याह । सामान्यशास्त्रात् विशेषशास्त्रं बलवत् । बहुव्यापकं सामान्यम् । अल्पव्यापको विशेष । हेत्वन्तरमाह परेण पूर्वबाधो भवति । परशब्दोत्र इष्टवचनम् । तेन इष्टेन सवर्णे दीर्घत्वेन सवर्णविषये यकारादीनां बाधः ।

   Ibid, 10b, 11a
7. *Ibid*, 49b
8. मङ्गलादीनि मङ्गलमध्यानि मङ्गलान्तानि शास्त्राणि प्रथन्ते वीरपुरुषकाणि भवन्ति । आयुष्मत्पुरुषकाणि चाध्येतारश्च सिद्धार्था यथा स्युः ।

   Vyākaraṇamahābhāṣyam (Chapters 1-2), Merrut, 1977, P.33.
9. परा जगत्कारणतया उत्कृष्टा मायाशक्तिर्यस्य सः परमः ।

   Sārasvata-maṇḍana, P.1b.
10. अतति संततं गच्छति यद्वा प्राप्नोति सर्वव्यापकतया प्राप्नोति ।

    Ibid, P.1b.
11. रक्षोहागमलघ्वसन्देहाः प्रयोजनम् ।

    Mahābhāṣya, op.cit, p.5.
12. न च विचार्यमाणे रक्षोहागमादयोपि परमप्रयोजनं भवितुं शक्याः ।

    Sārasvatamaṇḍana, p.2b.

13. श्रीमन्मण्डनसंघपतिप्रणीते सारस्वतमण्डने सन्धिप्रकरणं समाप्तम् ।
Ibid, p.15a.
श्रीमण्डनः सूत्रविदल्मसाहिमहाप्रधानोप्यदधात्सुसंधीन् ।
Ibid, unnumbered verse.
इति ...श्रीमद्वाहडात्मज-सर्वविद्याविशारद-श्रीमन्मण्डन-प्रणीते सारस्वतमण्डने कृदन्तप्रकरणं समाप्तम् ।
Ibid, p.121.

INDEX